STRAIGHT FROM THE
HART

BRUCE HART

STRAIGHT FROM THE

HART

Published by ECW PRESS
2120 Queen Street East, Suite 200, Toronto, Ontario, Canada M4E 1E2

LIBRARY AND ARCHIVES OF CANADA CATALOGUING IN PUBLICATION

Hart, Bruce, 1951-
Straight From the Hart / Bruce Hart.

ISBN 978-1-55022-939-4

ALSO ISSUED AS:
978-1-77090-003-5 (PDF); 978-1-77090-004-2 (EPUB)

1. Hart, Bruce, 1951-. 2. Hart family. 3. Stampede Wrestling
(Firm)—History. 4. Wrestlers—Canada—Biography.
5. Wrestling—Alberta—History. I. Title.

GV1196.H372A3 2011   796.812092   C2010-906816-5

Editor: Michael Holmes
Cover Design: Cyanotype
Text Design: Melissa Kaita
Production and Typesetting: Troy Cunningham
All photos by Bob Leonard, unless otherwise noted
Back cover photo courtesy Alison Hart.
Printing: Webcom   1   2   3   4   5

The publication of *Straight From the Hart* has been generously supported by the Government of Ontario through Ontario Book Publishing Tax Credit, by the OMDC Book Fund, an initiative of the Ontario Media Development Corporation, and by the Government of Canada through the Canada Book Fund.

Canada

INTED AND BOUND IN CANADA

ECW PRESS
ecwpress.com

CONTENTS

RUNNING THE GAMUT

HOPES, DREAMS AND NIGHTMARES

PRAYERS AND PROMISES

HART BREAK

POST MORTEMS (OR PARTING SHOTS)

To my son Rhett,
thanks for lighting up my life

FOREWORD

Back in the day, the veil of secrecy that surrounded the wrestling business made the idea of writing a behind-the-scenes book inconceivable to me. But things began to change after Vince McMahon's curious decision to expose the business in the late '80s and early '90s. Despite what the "smart marks" were able to learn, I still had a "Las Vegas" mantra as far as my own travails were concerned — what happens in the Hart family, stays there.

The past decade, however, has seen a number of books written about the Hart family. The bio of my dad by Marsha Erb was nice — although Stu, true to his old-school roots, didn't actually divulge much about the inner workings of the business. Unfortunately, the ones written by my other family members seemed to me to have been penned either to get back at others, or to gratify their egos. Those written by outsiders, I found hard to take seriously; these people who'd never met my dad, mom or most other family members were suddenly claiming to know everything about us. Filled with conjecture, a lot of what was written was planted by people with ulterior motives.

My old friend Harley Race used to say that if you haven't walked the walk, you shouldn't be talking the talk. Having been in the eye of the hurricane for most of my life, I feel qualified to offer my perspective on the not-so-perfect storm that is wrestling. While I won't be pulling any punches (unlike the wres-tlers), I won't be taking cheap shots either.

My mission is to tell it like it is and let you, the reader, form your own opinion. It's been said that truth is stranger than fiction, and *Straight From the Hart* is testament to that.

I'd like to extend my profound gratitude to my children — Brit, Bruce Jr., Torrin, Rhett and Lara — for their unwavering love and support. As well, I'd like to thank my mom and dad; my brothers, Dean and Owen, and my sister Ellie; the Funks, Harley Race, Lou Thesz, Flyin' Brian Pillman, Gene LeBell, Peter Maivia, Bob Leonard, Ed Whalen, Pat Mitchell, my imperturbable editor, Michael Holmes, and a host of others, too numerous to acknowledge here, for having inspired and supported me along the way.

Bruce Hart, December 2010

GROWING PAINS

1
AS FAR BACK AS I CAN REMEMBER . . .

"Just when I think I'm out, they keep pulling me back in."
— Michael Corleone

Those words, from *The Godfather III*, just about say everything you need to know about my affiliation (some would say affliction) with the business of professional wrestling. Sometimes it's been an exhilarating joyride; other times it's been a daunting descent, a ride down the highway to hell. Many times I figured I'd abandoned wrestling but invariably I would find myself somehow being drawn back — like a rationalizing junkie needing just one more fix.

My earliest recollections go back to when I was a wide-eyed kid of about four or five when my dad, who was promoting shows then, would invite aspiring prospects, or "wannabes" as he called them, up to the house to test their mettle in his infamous "Dungeon." My brothers and I would sneak down the basement stairs, pry open the door and watch with morbid curiosity as the sessions unfolded.

The trainees were generally big, imposing-looking types — football players, bouncers, bodybuilders and that sort — and most of them would swagger in cockily, figuring it wouldn't take them long to master pro wrestling, which most guys thought was little more than glorified play fighting. They were in for an extremely rude awakening.

My dad — a benign version of Cerberus, the three-headed dog at the gates of hell — would usually start the proceedings by putting the neophytes over, alluding to their awe-inspiring physiques or their vaunted reputations as one-man wrecking crews, street fighters and forces to be reckoned with. At the same time, he'd further disarm them by claiming to be nursing an injury, or that he'd just eaten or some such thing, and beseech them to take it easy on him. At this juncture, the cocky, self-absorbed rookies were licking their chops and contemplating that after they'd cleaned up the mat with this phony, flaccid old pretender, they'd be able to quickly ascend to stardom in the wrestling business. By this time, the trainees were figuring this would be a cakewalk. They were chomping at the bit to chew him up and spit him out and get on to bigger and better things.

Once they did get on the mat, my dad — appearing to be powerless to repel their onslaught — would allow the overzealous trainees to push him all over, which of course served to bolster their confidence even more. All of a sudden though, my dad would turn the tables on the unsuspecting wrestlers and in a flash, they'd find themselves trapped in some excruciatingly painful submission hold. From that point on, it was all downhill, with the suddenly not-so-bombastic newcomers being put through the wringer, as my dad used to call it — enduring one torture hold after another, and wondering what this sadistic psychopath had in mind next. During the course of their introduction to wrestling, the rookies abandoned most of their dignity — as well as, I might add, assorted bodily fluids — before they were finally allowed to limp off the mat with a decidedly different perspective about what it took to make it as a pro wrestler. Some would come back, but most would never be seen or heard from again.

At the time, being a wide-eyed and impressionable little kid, I found it quite horrifying to see my father — who ordinarily seemed to be a mild-mannered, easygoing sort — transform, down in the Dungeon. It was sinister, a Jekyll and Hyde thing. I often wondered about the demons lurking within him and it wasn't until several years later that I came to understand the method to his ostensible madness.

I would discover that when Stu Hart was first introduced to the wrestling business as a teenager in the 1930s, the inner workings of the sport were a closely guarded secret — kind of like in the Mafia. It was widely thought that the best deterrent to anyone exposing them was to make them pay their dues the hard way — in the tender of blood, sweat and tears.

Although pro wrestling was a work (pre-arranged) even that far back, for public consumption, it was still perceived to be a shoot (real). Within the inner sanctum of the wrestling fraternity, it was considered the ultimate transgression to expose it, and someone who was found to have violated that sacred covenant was dealt with quite harshly — in the form of having the living shit kicked out of them by shooters and/or by being permanently blackballed.

I was later to discover that my dad's own initiation into the wrestling fraternity was, by all accounts, every bit as harsh — if not worse — as what his Dungeon victims were put through. During the Great Depression of the '30s, his family, like many others from the prairies, had been hit hard and had lost everything, including their house and all their belongings. During this stretch, his mother died and he, his father and his two older sisters, who lived in a makeshift tent on the outskirts of Edmonton, were forced to eke out a meager existence, living off the land and getting by on whatever they could beg, borrow or steal.

As most Canadians can attest, it gets bitterly cold in the prairies in the winter, so on many a cold winter's night my dad, as a means of seeking refuge from the frigid temperatures, took to hanging out at the local YMCA and in due course, a group of grizzled old pro wrestlers who worked the circuit and trained there invited him to join them on the mat. From what he told me though, they were anything but gentle with him — using him as a sparring partner or human guinea pig, applying submission holds and essentially chewing him up and spitting him out. I can still recall my dad ruefully reflecting how on some occasions he'd leave the sessions so stiff and sore he could barely limp back home. In time, the sessions toughened him, both physically and mentally, to the point that he eventually began to hold his own against the shooters. Later he came to dominate them and to give them a dose of their own bitter medicine.

While at the YMCA, my dad made the acquaintance of Jack Taylor, a vaunted old shooter who was then in the twilight of a wrestling career that had begun back in the 1890s. Taylor — a protégé of the legendary Farmer Burns, who was the founder of modern pro wrestling — gained a reputation as the toughest wrestler of his era. Many considered him to be even tougher than his stablemate and fellow Burns pupil, the iconic Iowa Assassin, Frank Gotch.

In any case, my dad would spend several years training with Taylor in the YMCA and would go on to become Canadian amateur wrestling champion. By all accounts, he was considered to have been a serious contender for Canada's first ever Olympic gold medal in wrestling at the 1940 Olympic Games, which were scheduled to take place in London.

His Olympic dreams were unfortunately derailed by a slightly deranged megalomaniac with aspirations of taking over the world — no, not Vince McMahon, but a heel named Adolf Hitler. With the onset of the Second World War, the Olympic Games were canceled and instead of shooting for glory on the mat, my dad found himself instead shooting for survival against the deadly Nazi U-boats in the North Atlantic as a member of the Canadian navy.

When the war finally ended in 1945, my dad found himself at a crossroads; he was nearly thirty and the next Olympics, which were then still up in the air, wouldn't be staged until 1948 at the earliest. Since there was no money in amateur wrestling and he'd put everything else on hold to pursue his Olympic dream, he wasn't sure if he could afford to wait that long. He asked his mentor, Taylor, for advice. Taylor told him that even if he did win the Olympics, it wouldn't necessarily translate into any monetary windfall and he advised him to turn pro. Taylor mentioned that back in 1910, when he and Frank Gotch were barnstorming on the carnival circuit with Farmer Burns, he'd been challenged by a brash young redneck from Colorado named Joe Mondt. Taylor said that he'd been able to vanquish Mondt, but that he and Burns were impressed with his cockiness and tenacity and decided to take him under their wing and have him join their touring troupe. Fast-forward a couple of decades: Mondt had gone on to become the most powerful promoter in the United States — heading up the New York–based Capital Wrestling Promotion, which would become the forerunner of the present day WWE. Taylor told my dad that if he'd like, he could arrange to get him a tryout with Mondt, and the rest, as they say, is history.

Old-school types and those who've delved into the golden age of the business are likely familiar with "Toots" Mondt — one of the most influential figures in wrestling history. Even though he'd been introduced to the business by shooters like Taylor, Burns and Gotch and later gained his reputation working with and promoting shooters like Ed "Strangler" Lewis, Stan Zbyszko and Joe Stecher, Mondt saw the potential in spicing things up a bit. He is credited with having introduced concepts such as heels (bad guys) and babyfaces (good guys), working angles and "high spots" (spectacular moves) — all of which contributed to wrestling enjoying a huge surge in popularity, and made Mondt the most powerful promoter in the business. Even though Mondt is the one credited with introducing "working" elements to the wrestling business, because of his shooter roots he was nonetheless fiercely protective of wrestling's supposed integrity. He went to inordinate lengths to maintain the notion that wrestling was real. To that end, he always had a coterie of legit tough guys on hand, just in case any of the skeptics had the audacity to suggest wrestling was "phony" or rigged.

From what my dad told me, Mondt's inner circle of shooters, or "policemen," as they were called, was also deployed, on occasion, to keep in line any of his potentially recalcitrant "stars" who had read too many of their own press clippings or had misgivings about doing a job, dropping a strap or anything like that.

Because of Mondt's affinity for shooters, my dad was welcomed with open arms and his career quickly took off. By 1946 his stock had risen to the point where he was being pushed as one of the top "faces" in the promotion, working with some of the top heels in the business at the time, including the likes of Buddy Rogers, Baron Leone, Bibber McCoy and Abe "King Kong" Kashey.

During his stay in New York, my dad made the acquaintance of Jess McMahon and his son Vince Sr. — both of whom worked in the office and lined up towns for Toots. From what my dad told me, both were nice, unassuming guys, who went out of their way to make things better for the boys.

In addition to the McMahons, my dad had a chance to rub shoulders with other notables from the New York sports and entertainment scene, including boxing legends Jack Dempsey, Joe Louis and the "Raging Bull" Jake La Motta; baseball immortals such as Joe DiMaggio, Jackie Robinson and Babe Ruth; entertainers Frank Sinatra, Jimmy Stewart and Humphrey Bogart; as well as iconic writers Ernest Hemingway and Arthur Daley — all of whom were avid wrestling fans.

Without question, though, the most noteworthy acquaintance my dad would make during his stay in the Big Apple was one Helen Smith, whom he met in the resort town of Long Beach through one of the other wrestlers, Paul Boesch, who also moonlighted as a lifeguard on the beach. They say that opposites attract and that certainly seems to have been the case here, as she was cultured and well educated — into books, the theater and art, while he was a rough-hewn country boy, mainly into sports and animals. Somehow, they hit it off and, after a whirlwind courtship, got married in 1947. This, of course, was the genesis for the so-called Hart Foundation, which would spawn not only twelve kids who were all eventually tied to the history of modern wrestling, but a myriad of bizarre and improbable story lines that no scriptwriter in his right mind could have ever dreamed up.

In 1948, my father, who was still working for Mondt, received a phone call from the mayor of Edmonton, who was a huge wrestling fan. He informed him that they'd just built a new arena and wanted to know if my dad might be interested in coming back and opening up his own wrestling promotion. Never one to turn down a challenge or an adventure, my dad decided to take him up on the offer. He and my poor mother — who probably had no idea of what she was in for — were soon heading back to the "great white North," about to launch one of the most storied and colorful promotions in the annals of wrestling.

2
BACK IN THE DAY

When my dad first opened his own promotion, the wrestling landscape was different from today's. Now, there are only two active promotions remaining — the almighty WWE and the Tennessee-based TNA. Back then there were close to thirty regional promotions or "territories" in operation across Canada and the United States, ranging from big promotions such as Toots Mondt's New York outfit, Jim Crockett's sprawling operation in the Carolinas and Aileen Eaton's Hollywood office, to smaller ones such as Mike London's Albuquerque promotion and Cowboy Len Hughes' Halifax operation, which ran only in the summertime.

Being a wrestler was different in those days as well. With over thirty promotions operating full time, there were many more wrestlers plying their trade. Wrestlers of that era rarely stayed in one place for more than a few months at a time and would travel around, like gypsies, from one territory to another — wherever their services were in demand and business was good. Because the promoters were regularly in touch with each other, it was obligatory for the wrestlers to maintain a good reputation by honoring their commitments, working hard and behaving themselves. By all accounts, however, there was no shortage of outrageous characters and behind the scenes hijinks, invariably perpetrated by pranksters and card-carrying degenerates like Ted and Vic Christy, Tommy O'Toole, Buddy Rogers, Frankie Murdoch and Paul de Galles.

While the wrestlers were obliged to keep their noses clean, so to speak, the same was true for promoters. If promoters screwed the boys on their payoffs, failed to honor their commitments or ran a sloppy operation, it didn't take long for word to spread that their territory wasn't a good place to work. Although it wasn't a perfect system by any means, it nonetheless served its purpose. The "territories" would be the mode in wrestling for the next several decades — until the scorched earth onslaught of Vincent the Conqueror in the 1980s.

When my dad was getting his own promotion off the ground in the late '40s, wrestling was in a period of flux. With the rise of television — which was just coming into vogue at the time — wrestling had enjoyed a resurgence in popularity, with acts like Gorgeous George, lady wrestlers, pseudo-Nazis and insidious Japanese villains taking center stage.

During the early stages of the television era, business was good, but many of the promoters began to take shortcuts and cut back on wrestling. They resorted, instead, to gimmicks — freaks, geeks and bullshit — and the business soon became the object of ridicule and derision, especially among traditional sports fans. Making matters worse, many of the cutthroats and shysters masquerading as promoters began stealing each other's talent, running in each other's towns and doing whatever they could to undermine each other.

As a result, the business, in general, suffered. With the future of the sport in peril, the promoters of the various territories, my dad included, convened an sos (save our sport) meeting in St. Louis. The offshoot of that meeting was the formation of a promoters' cooperative called the National Wrestling Alliance (NWA), which established territorial boundaries and interactive guidelines — not unlike a wrestling version of the United Nations. My dad later told me that the first meeting reminded him of that scene in the movie *The Godfather* where the heads of all the crime families came together to supposedly work together. While apparently there was no shortage of cutthroats, charlatans and con men among the rank and file of NWA promoters, the NWA nevertheless accomplished its goals of unifying and stabilizing the sport.

One of the things that helped accomplish that was the NWA's establishment of a universally recognized world champion who would travel to the different territories, defending his title against the top stars from each circuit. That served to give fans in each territory the perception that the local champions were world-class and, by extension, cast the whole promotion in the same light.

The NWA was fortunate to be blessed with some outstanding champions in those formative years, including the great Lou Thesz, Canada's revered "Whipper" Billy Watson, the savvy New Zealander Pat O'Connor and the swaggering "Nature Boy" Buddy Rogers.

While those guys were not only superb athletes and ambassadors who gave the belt prestige and credibility, what made them really special was their innate ability to get whomever they worked with "over," or make them look like viable contenders, which was key to making member promotions look like legitimate major league operations. In its own way, the establishment of the NWA world title served the same purpose as the Super Bowl or Stanley Cup did for the NFL or NHL in that it gave a semblance of structure and a common denomination to wrestling — something which would be instrumental in ushering in a period of prosperity and enhanced popularity for pro wrestling, during the '50s and thereafter.

3

SATURDAY MORNINGS COMING DOWN

I was born in 1951, the second of what would become a twelve-member brood. My brother Smith preceded me by two years. Keith, Wayne, Dean, Ellie, Georgia, Bret and Alison would follow in the next eight years. Ross, Diana and the youngest member of the Hart clan, Owen, were children of the '60s. Figure in the wrestlers who were always around back then and, clearly, Stu and Helen had little time for themselves.

Some of my most vivid childhood memories are of Saturday mornings, when the wrestlers would make the weekly trek up to the Hart House to pick up their paychecks. Our house, as most Calgarians can tell you, was located on an escarpment on the west end of town, overlooking the city. Although we were within the city limits, my dad, who'd grown up on a farm, seemed to think it was perfectly normal to have goats, cows, horses, chickens and turkeys (human and otherwise) wandering around the yard. Combine that with this bizarre procession of midgets, giants, wrestling bears (human and otherwise), nefarious Nazis, conniving commies, insidious Orientals and assorted other misfits and it's easy to see why most of our neighbors or anyone who happened to be driving by considered us to be some kind of cross between the Beverly Hillbillies and the

Addams Family — with just a touch of *The Twilight Zone* thrown in for good, or perhaps bad, measure.

Since my dad tended to be terminally disorganized, like I am, the pay envelopes (which were prepared by my poor, beleaguered mother) were very rarely ready on time. As a consequence, the wrestlers were forced to wait downstairs, patiently.

While the boys cooled their heels, my dad would make coffee, bacon, eggs and pancakes for them. Legend has it that one time one of the animals (I'm not sure if it was supposed to have been a dog, cat, bear or what) defecated on the floor and my dad scooped up the shit with his spatula, discarded it and then turned to whomever he was serving and inquired, "Did you want your eggs over easy?" Over the years, I swear that I must have run into dozens of wrestlers who claimed they were the recipients of said eggs. My dad, of course, used to vehemently deny that he'd ever served up any such offering — as he only served his eggs scrambled.

One of the things that really amazes me now — given today's open admission that wrestling is a work — is the lengths the wrestlers would go to, back then, to maintain the façade that wrestling was legitimate and not "phony," as they used to say.

Even though we were the promoter's kids, all the wrestlers, heels and babyfaces would arrive in separate vehicles and the heels would sequester themselves in one room, behind closed doors, while the faces would gather in another room. Although there were never staged brawls or any of that, they always maintained the pretense that they didn't like each other and would never let their guards down.

Most of the heels were pretty intimidating. I remember being uneasy around the likes of "Mad Dog" Vachon, Skull Murphy, Fritz Von Erich, Sky Hi Lee, "Iron Mike" DiBiase, the Kalmikoff Brothers and "Bulldog" Brower — all of whom bore striking resemblances to sinister villain types you'd see in the movies. Two of the most convincing bad guys were Hard Boiled Haggerty and Bob Orton Sr. — both of whom always seemed to be in a rotten mood and would scowl at us whenever they saw us. Funny enough, a few years back I was at this old-time wrestlers' reunion called Cauliflower Alley in Las Vegas and ran into them. Even though I was long since wise to the business, because of my childhood preconceptions I was still somewhat apprehensive and I mentioned that to them. They both laughed and told me that I'd just made their day.

In retrospect, I'm not sure if my dad ordered the wrestlers to kayfabe (old carny slang that roughly translates as "play the role") like that around us, or if that was just the prevailing norm. In any case, as far as we were concerned, wrestling was for real. I can still recall how, if any kids at school had the audacity — as some did — to suggest that wrestling was phony, it was a personal affront and grounds for fighting.

Many a time our school principal — this dour and austere old British fart named Mr. Broadberry — would haul our asses into the office and give us the strap for our schoolground altercations. He would then call up my dad on the phone and have him come down to reprimand us for our transgressions. My dad would make out to be displeased with us for our misbehavior, but later at home, he'd give us a pat on the back for having defended the wrestling business.

I remember one time my older brother Smith had this overbearing, big blowhard of a phys. ed. teacher named Mr. Ward, who was always making snide remarks about wrestling, claiming that it was all a sham and that he, himself, could annihilate any of those phony pretenders and that sort of thing. As a result, a lot of kids also began making fun of us and mocking the wrestling business. When my dad got wind of this, he was quite pissed off and one day, he showed up at our school, unannounced, while Ward was conducting an amateur wrestling class and making his usual disparaging remarks about the wrestling business. As Ward was babbling on, my dad casually strolled up to the mat and beckoned him to try him on for size, if wrestlers were all phonies and pushovers, as he'd been alleging.

I doubt that Ward wanted any part of my dad, but since he'd been blowing his own horn so much and was being egged on by the kids, he didn't have much choice but to accept. In a matter of seconds, my dad had him on the mat in some killer submission hold, screaming like a baby and begging for mercy. After that, we never heard Ward or any of the other kids at school cast any aspersions about wrestling being phony.

When I think back now on how guys like my dad, Haggerty, Orton and so many others used to go to such inordinate lengths to protect the business, I find it hard to fathom how Vince McMahon could have chosen to so indiscriminately expose it years later.

4
SAM THE SHAM

In the 1950s, when television was in its infancy, pro wrestling proved to be a good fit, with its good guy vs. bad guy format and its colorful cast of zany characters. Back then, there was only one television network in Canada — the government-run Canadian Broadcasting Corporation (CBC) headquartered in Toronto, Ontario.

The CBC used to broadcast Frank Tunney's Maple Leaf Wrestling show, also from Toronto, which featured guys like "Whipper" Billy Watson, Yukon Eric, Irish Pat Flanagan, Tiger Tasker, Gene Kiniski and Native American star Chief Don Eagle, among others. At the same time, my dad had some pretty decent talent himself, including the likes of Fritz Von Erich, Kinji Shibuya, the Fabulous Kangaroos, "Mad Dog" Vachon, Luther Lindsey, Johnny Valentine and Jim "Riot Call" Wright.

Because they weren't on television, our fans tended to see them as inferior to the Toronto stars, though. As a result, my dad had no choice but to import the Toronto boys to work on our shows. That posed a few problems however, as not only did the Toronto stars command hefty guarantees — considerably more than what our boys were making, which didn't sit well with our guys — but the

Toronto boys couldn't do jobs (lose) to our guys, because it wouldn't be good for the image of their promotion.

During the latter part of the decade, independent television stations began springing up across Western Canada, including ones in Calgary, Edmonton and Saskatchewan. My dad was able to start his own wrestling show, a studio program called *Mat Time*. While pretty simple and bareboned, it served its purpose as a marketing vehicle and our gates did improve as a result. In the fall of 1959, one of our heels, Iron Mike DiBiase (father of Ted "Million Dollar Man" DiBiase), who played the prototypical arrogant, swaggering American, looking down his nose at Canadians, made some insulting remark about Canadians being inbred morons. If something like that was uttered today, it wouldn't even raise an eyebrow, but in those days it was akin to treason. As a result, the TV station gave my dad a stiff reprimand and the wrestlers were forbidden from making any controversial or politically incorrect remarks.

As anyone who's ever watched wrestling can tell you, making offensive or politically inappropriate remarks is what it's all about. The toned-down, sanitized approach didn't resonate well with the fans and as a result our gates took a significant hit.

In those days, my dad used to shut down the promotion for the summer after his big Stampede Week shows in July and he'd reopen a couple of months later, in September. During our summer break, my dad was approached by the programming director of the new CTV affiliate that was opening up in the fall. He was keen on having a prime-time wrestling show and offered my dad enough incentives to make him switch stations.

Not long after he'd committed to the new station, my dad received a call from Sam Menacker, who at the time was considered the best commentator in the business — kind of like that era's Jim Ross. Menacker, with whom my dad had crossed paths back in Toots Mondt's territory, divulged that he'd just parted ways with the Indianapolis promotion and had heard, through the wrestling grapevine, that my dad might be looking for a new commentator.

Given Menacker's rep, my dad was pleased to bring him onboard, committing himself to a hefty guarantee. Business went well during the first year or so of Menacker's tenure, with gates jumping and the new, prime-time television format also being enthusiastically embraced by the viewing audience at home. Menacker, of course, was given most of the credit for the revival of the promotion, but it should be noted that my dad had provided him a stellar crew to work with, including the likes of Killer Kowalski, Nick Bockwinkel, Big Bill Miller, Bearcat Wright, Luis Hernandez, Ronnie Etchison, Czaya Nandor and Bronko Lubich, who were some of the best workers at the time. My dad also hired George Scott — who was one of the best idea men in the business and later the booker for the WWF during the glory days of Hulkamania — to help Menacker with the matchmaking.

With business really beginning to take off, my dad, at Menacker's behest, purchased a twelve-seat airplane to fly the wrestlers around the territory — which was really traveling in style for those days.

As well, my dad took some of the money he'd been making on the wrestling boom and invested in a number of other business ventures, including a Tim Hortons–style coffee/donut chain called the Sweet Shoppe and a furniture company called the Invalid Seat Company, which manufactured chairs and orthopedic devices for the handicapped. My dad also purchased a resort property west of Calgary called Clearwater Beach, which would become our family's own version of Fawlty Towers. In retrospect, my dad had uncanny business instincts but, all too often, chose to hire the wrong people for the job — a recurring pattern that would manifest itself time and again over the years.

While gates and TV ratings remained good, my dad was coming to realize why someone as highly regarded as Menacker had been available in the first place. His petulance and "my way or the highway" approach had begun to wear thin with everyone — even my mom. When he was lurking she used to sardonically claim that "there, but for the grace of God, goes God himself."

In 1963, things came to a head with Sam. During a TV taping, one of the heels — Iron Mike Sharpe — got pissed off with some snide, half-shooting putdown Menacker made about him during a promo and roughed him up, breaking his glasses and bloodying his nose. Menacker was incensed and demanded my dad fire Sharpe, but my dad calmed things down — or so he thought — by having Sharpe apologize. The next day though, Menacker flew the coop, literally — taking off in my dad's airplane, back to the United States. Making matters worse, my dad subsequently found that the plane had somehow been erroneously registered in Sam's name — apparently because he was the pilot — which meant my dad couldn't even recoup his investment.

Even so, no one was shedding any tears over Sam's departure — kind of like the old "ding, dong, the witch is dead" refrain from *The Wizard of Oz*.

5
RICHES TO RAGS

With Sam the Sham out of the picture, my dad handed the TV commentator's job to Ernie Roth, who'd recently arrived in the territory as a heel manager but had done some commentating back in his native Ohio. Roth proved to be a more than capable replacement and within a matter of weeks, our gates, which had been sluggish during the latter part of Sam's tenure, began to rebound. Heading into the peak winter season (January to April) of 1964, we were on a sustained roll, with gates the best they'd been in years.

Unfortunately, Sam Menacker would rear his ugly head one more time. When he found out that business was booming, he called the TV station manager back in Calgary and informed him that Roth was a homosexual. That probably wouldn't be of any great consequence today — in fact, it might even enhance one's ability to get hired in television, or the WWE, but in that post-McCarthy era of paranoia, it was a serious taboo.

As a result, the TV station manager — a sanctimonious Mormon — gave my dad an ultimatum: dump Roth or he'd dump the show. My dad didn't have much choice but to let Ernie go — which was pretty disheartening, as he'd been doing a hell of a job. As Roth's replacement, my dad hired a local sportscaster named Henry Viney, who specialized in curling and golf. By all accounts, Viney was a nice guy and tried hard, but he didn't seem to realize that the wrestling show was a propaganda vehicle to induce viewers to come down to the matches. Instead he treated it like golf or bowling, babbling on about all the mundane elements and going to great lengths to downplay anything controversial. It was, in fact, the exact opposite of what he should have been doing.

One time, there was a hot story line that called for our top heel — a dastardly German, by way of Ontario, named Waldo Von Erich — to ambush one of the faces, Tex McKenzie, and supposedly injure him so badly that he had to be ambulanced to the hospital. They enacted the finish so well that there was a huge outcry afterward, with concerned fans flooding the TV station switchboard, seeking to know if McKenzie was okay and protesting Von Erich's despicable tactics — all of which, of course, was the desired effect. Later on that afternoon, with the whole city still buzzing about the incident, Viney, on his evening sports broadcast, assured everyone that McKenzie was resting comfortably at home, that Von Erich really hadn't intended to hurt him and that everyone lived happily ever after — which, of course, killed all the heat.

With Viney's vapid commentating, our gates went into the toilet and by the time the promotion closed down for the summer in July of 1964, business was in the worst shape it had been since my dad had opened up back in 1948. Compounding matters, his other businesses — the donut shops and the furniture company — were also struggling. In part, this was because of a downturn in the economy, but it was also because my dad had been so preoccupied with the wrestling, he'd allowed others to run them into the ground.

As for my dad's other revenue stream, Clearwater Beach, it remained in business, but invariably seemed to lose more than it took in. That summer was a disaster, as it seemed to rain almost every weekend and holiday — which were generally the only days we made any money. That, of course, only put more pressure on the wrestling to rebound in the fall of 1964.

Unfortunately, though, the business didn't rebound, as word had spread that our promotion was on its ass. That made it tough to attract any decent talent, so we opened with an uninspiring crew of stiffs and castoffs and business continued to struggle mightily. Around that time, my dad received a call from Sandor Kovacs, the co-promoter (along with Rod Fenton) for the All-Star

Wrestling promotion in Vancouver. Kovacs said he'd heard that our promotion was struggling and proposed that his promotion and my dad's work together, with my dad replacing his TV show with the Vancouver show, flying in the Vancouver boys every few weeks, paying their salaries and splitting the gates with Kovacs and Fenton. My dad was reluctant to lose his show, but since the Vancouver office had some pretty good talent, including guys like Dean Higuchi, Dutch Savage, Karl Gotch, Jimmy Hady, Roy McClarity, Don Leo Jonathan and the Fabulous Kangaroos, and our own talent was pretty lousy at the time, he agreed to work with Kovacs and company.

Unfortunately, the cure proved worse than the disease. The Vancouver style, which was a lot slower and more conservative than our ass-kicking wrestling, never seemed to take off and gates declined even further. Making matters worse, the added expense of airfares, hotels and whatnot resulted in even more red ink for my dad, and by the end of April 1965, he had no choice but to shut down the promotion.

A week after he'd pulled the plug, on May 7, my mother gave birth to her twelfth child — my brother Owen. Ordinarily, when a new baby arrives, it's a joyous occasion, but this time around, because of all dire financial straits, it seemed to make the hard times even more pronounced.

When I look back now on that period, I kind of shudder; it reminds me of that grim John Steinbeck novel *The Grapes of Wrath* — everything bleaker than bleak. During that stretch we barely had food to put on the table and my dad — who, in days gone by, used to pull up to the local Safeway store and load up the car with groceries — now had to swallow his pride and ask the store manager if he had any black bananas, stale bread or whatever else they might give him.

Most of our clothing at the time came from the Salvation Army, which was anything but fashionable. I can recall many a time, cruel, insensitive kids at school made fun of us for our attire. My brothers and I became kind of immune to the putdowns or would, on occasion, challenge our oppressors to fights after school, but it was pretty hard on my poor sisters — who were often reduced to tears because of the insulting and derisive taunts.

When I think back now on that tough time, I find it hard to fathom why people discriminate against the poor or underprivileged. Poverty, obviously, isn't a lifestyle anyone chooses.

6
THE BIG COMEBACK

That November, with things looking increasingly bleak, my dad happened to run into Ron Chase, the new programming director of CHCT television in Calgary, which was the station my dad had been on back in the '50s. In talking, Chase mentioned that he used to be a big fan of the wrestling show and inquired as to whether my dad might be interested in coming back to his station. My dad, of course, jumped at the opportunity and they soon had agreed on bringing the show back, for the start of January 1966.

I can still recall the big smile on my dad's face when he came home that day and informed my mom that he was getting back into the wrestling business. Helen had never been a huge fan — even during the boom time — and had come to see the wrestling business as more of a curse than a cause to celebrate. She, however, seemed to realize that this was perhaps our last chance to salvage things and threw herself into the mix with as much enthusiasm and energy as she could muster.

There was only one problem though — Stu Hart didn't have two cents to rub together and the start-up costs would include refurbishing the rings, advertising and other costs, not to mention getting talent. My dad, who'd loaned thousands of dollars to friends and associates around town when business had been good, began calling around, hoping someone could oblige him, but all his supposed friends turned him down and, as the January start date loomed closer, it was beginning to look like the whole endeavor might not get off the ground — which had my mom pretty distressed.

A few weeks before Christmas, with the thermometer hovering around forty below, my dad arrived in his broken-down old Cadillac to pick us up at school and happened to run into our principal, Harold Sharlow, who, oddly enough, had at one time sold tickets for my dad, back in the '50s. As they got to chatting, my dad related how he had a chance to start up the promotion again but was strapped for cash and the whole thing appeared to be in jeopardy. Sharlow immediately offered to lend him a few thousand dollars and that would prove to save our bacon, as my dad put it.

With the money in place, my dad then embarked on trying to line up talent — which, given how tough it had been the year before, seemed a daunting task. This time around though, he had considerably better luck. One of the things that worked in our favor was the prevailing racial tension in the United States — the protest marches, Martin Luther King, the Mississippi burnings, the KKK and all of that — which made it tough for black wrestlers, especially heels, to find work.

As a result, my dad was able to secure the services of some terrific African American talent, including a colorful, outspoken black heel named Sweet Daddy Siki, who, I'm told, was the main inspiration for another black athlete making a name for himself at the time: Cassius Clay, who would later change his name to Muhammad Ali. Siki — who had bleached blond hair long before Dennis Rodman ever dreamed of it and who did cutting-edge promos — referred to himself as "Mr. Irresistible" and claimed that he was "the women's pet and the men's regret." He would prove to be an instant box office smash for our promotion. He also recommended a young black babyface he'd been tutoring — Rocky Johnson — who would similarly become a mainstay of the promotion. Years later, I would work with Rocky in Hawaii, where I made the acquaintance of his son Dwayne, who went on to star in the WWF as the Rock and has subsequently become an ever bigger star in the movies.

Not to digress, but one of the things I don't think my dad was ever really given much credit for were his efforts in breaking down the color barrier in wrestling. Back then, very few of the mainstream promoters in the States — several of whom I heard were thinly veiled racists — would use black wrestlers. Even if they did, all too often they tended to place them in demeaning, stereotypical, Amos and Andy type roles. My dad, however, for want of a better term, tended to be "color blind." If a guy was a decent performer and capable of drawing, his color, race or creed was never an impediment to getting pushed in Calgary.

When my dad had opened the promotion in 1948, one of his top babyfaces was Woody Strode — then a star with the Calgary Stampeders. Strode and Kenny Washington had been the first black players in the NFL in 1945, two years before Jackie Robinson's celebrated entrance into major league baseball. Over the years, my dad was responsible for launching the careers of countless awesome black workers, including Siki, Johnson, Luther Lindsey, Abdullah the Butcher, Junkyard Dog, George Wells, Sailor Art Thomas, "Bad News" Allen and Lethal Larry Cameron — all of whom would become major attractions in the United States, Japan and elsewhere.

If you do a little further research, you'll also find that my dad was one of the first promoters in North America to employ Japanese wrestlers. I'm not sure why they weren't welcomed in the United States — perhaps due to some lingering animosity after the Second World War — but for some reason, back in the day, very few promoters in the States seemed to want anything to do with them. My dad, however, saw the potential in using them and, over the years, helped launch a myriad of great Japanese stars, including the likes of Kinji Shibuya, Mitsu Arakawa, Mr. Hito, Kim Sakurada, Chatti Yokouchi, Junji Hirata, George Takano, Hiroshi Hase and Jushin Liger.

He also would break in several of the biggest Samoan stars, including Neff Maiava, Afa and Sika Anoia, Reno Tuufuli, Siva Afi and Alo Leilani — none of whom seemed to be able to find work before he gave them their proverbial break.

As far as the launch of the promotion goes, in addition to Siki and Johnson, my dad was able to secure the services of a few other decent hands for the January start, among them Alexander the Great (Al Ward), Stan Stasiak, Gil

Hayes, Leo Burke, his brother Yvon (the Beast), Newton Tattrie, Joe Peruzovic (later Nikolai Volkoff) and Johnny Kostas — all of whom were instrumental in helping to get the new promotion off the ground.

Necessity, as they say, is the mother of invention and that proved to be the case for us that January. Because money was so tight, my dad decided that rather than shooting a studio TV show, which was the norm back then, he'd shoot his show live at the house show in the Stampede Pavilion instead. Most other promoters of the day figured he was out of his mind, giving fans something they were accustomed to paying for for free. His peers predicted he'd be out of business in no time. That didn't prove to be the case; the show became one of the highest-rated shows in Western Canada. Nearly thirty years later, when Vince McMahon opted to do the same with *Monday Night RAW*, people in the United States hailed him as an innovative visionary — and conveniently forgot my dad had come up with the concept decades before.

For the commentator for the new show, my dad turned to a guy named Ed Whalen, who was the news director of the TV station but had done ring announcing for my dad in his native Saskatoon several years before, while he was attending university. Whalen, as anyone who ever caught our show can attest, proved to be an excellent fit; in fact, for my money, he was the best wrestling commentator ever — better, even, than Jim Ross, Gordon Solie and Lance Russell, which is saying a lot, because all of those guys were incredible.

Aside from impeccable timing, a succinct sense of humor and this innate ability to know when to let the action speak for itself, what made Whalen really exceptional was that unlike most other wrestling commentators he wasn't on the promotion's payroll and therefore refused to shill or put over anything that didn't warrant it. That proved to be of great benefit to the promotion because, if something stunk or was lousy, he refused to put it over, and since my dad backed him, implicitly, it forced the wrestlers to shape up, or they'd be shipped out.

By the same token, if something was done exceptionally well, Whalen could put it over like nobody else. He had a collection of signature sayings, like "malfunction at the junction" when referring to a mistake or screwup, and "ring-a-ding-dong-dandy" when referring to an exceptionally good match. His sayings would become part of the vernacular in Western Canada, and helped make the show an enormous hit.

Although our promotion, which was still in the trial and error process, didn't break box office records or set the wrestling world on its proverbial cauliflower ear that winter, it did well enough to break even, occasionally even turning a modest profit. This enabled my dad to stave off the creditors and financially get back on his feet.

7

A WHOLE NEW OUTLOOK

When the territory reopened I began to see the wrestling business in a totally different light. As I mentioned, when I was a kid I thought it was real and took everything at face value. Later on, in my adolescence — like a kid who outgrew Santa Claus and the Easter Bunny — I came to realize that wrestling wasn't exactly as I'd perceived. But I still allowed myself to indulge in the ostensible realism of the story lines, because, quite simply, wrestling was more fun that way.

Now, with so much now riding on the success or failure of those story lines, I was far more acutely aware of what worked and what didn't, and so took a far keener interest in the whys and wherefores of the business. Although wrestling tends to come across as individualistic, I came to realize that it's really more of a team endeavor — kind of like football — with everyone having defined roles, all of which are integral parts of the ultimate success or failure of the whole group. In football, the head coach devises the game plans, gives them to the team and endeavors to inspire or motivate them to rise to the occasion — which is the equivalent, in wrestling, to the booker.

Beyond that, in most promotions back then, the pivotal figure, or "go-to guy" — the equivalent of the quarterback on a football team — was always the top heel. Almost any territory that enjoyed any kind of success back then invariably had a dominant ass-kicker of a heel on top, usually wearing the belt or "strap," as they used to call it, in the territory. In that respect, they were much the same as any great football team, none of which attained a level of success if they didn't have some dynamic performer such as Joe Montana, Tom Brady, Peyton Manning or John Elway leading the charge.

The main role of the lead heel, of course, was to get heat or make the fans want to see him get his arrogant ass kicked by some hot babyface. The babyfaces, or "faces," as they're called these days, would line up to challenge the lead heel — much like challengers used to get in line to face boxing champions like Muhammad Ali or Joe Louis. Quite often, the match was cast as a David and Goliath showdown, with the face invariably being the game but overmatched underdog — which made him more appealing, since the average wrestling fan tends to be an underdog type himself. In most cases, the face would eventually be overcome by the big, bad wolf — usually after having worked a "program" (wrestling parlance for a series of matches), which would culminate in some kind of big blowoff like a cage match, or loser-leave-town stipulation.

At that point the vanquished babyface would typically leave the territory and head for another port of call, while the lead heel would remain on hand, like the mythical Minotaur, to take the next sacrificial offering thrown on his plate — and so on and so forth. If the top heel was drawing and able to sustain his heat, he'd remain on top for months, sometimes years, until he finally did the honors (lost) — usually to some hot, new face, or on occasion some even more dastardly new heel who was deemed worthy of ascending to the top.

Slightly below the top heels and faces on the depth chart in most territories were tag teams — faces, heels and often brother tandems, such as the Scott, Tolos or Vachon brothers. The tag teams were usually capable of putting in quality time and also served to warm up the crowd for the main events that followed.

Just below the tags were the "carpenters" — no, not the anorexic singer and her less talented, tagging along for the ride brother — but guys whose role was to put over or build up (hence the handle, carpenter) the guys who were being projected to work in main events. Over the years I've seen some awesome workers who were carpenters, including Gil Hayes, the Cuban Assassin, Dennis Stamp, Duke Myers, Arn Anderson and Eric Froelich, as well as modern day performers, such as William Regal and Chavo Guerrero Jr. — any of whom had more talent than most of the guys they were putting over but instead sacrificed themselves for the cause.

At the bottom of the wrestling pecking order were the lowly jobbers. Unlike the carpenters — who won some and lost some — the jobbers tended to be the hapless whipping boys. They were kind of like wrestling's equivalent of pawns on a chessboard. In many cases, jobbers were old-timers on the downhill slide, or unproven rookies just trying to gain some experience. It's worth noting that in the old days of the territories many a "jabroney" — as the Rock used to not so fondly refer to them — including the likes of Harley Race, Ric Flair, the Iron Sheik, Sgt. Slaughter, the Iron Sheik and even at one time the immortal Gorgeous George, began their careers getting endlessly squashed (annihilated) in one territory, only to become stars somewhere else.

Although that overview might seem a trifle simplistic, it pretty much sums up the pecking order in a typical territory back in the day. Even though the stars often used to take all the bows for the success of any given territory, in actuality, the chain — as my dad used to point out — was only as strong as its weakest link.

8
THE STOMPER

In those days, every successful promotion had some dynamic ass-kicking alpha heel as their meal ticket. In the past, our territory had had its share of awesome lead heels, many of whom I've already alluded to, but, in 1969, a new villain would emerge, superseding all who'd gone before — a one-man wrecking crew by the name of Archie "The Stomper" Gouldie.

Any heel worth his salt, of course, has the ability to get heat and make the fans' blood boil, but one of the things that really sets the great ones apart is their innate ability to make anyone they're working with look like a world beater. The Stomper was one of the best I've ever seen at this. On many an occasion, he would be matched up with run-of-the-mill faces. They hadn't set the world on fire up until that time, but when they worked with Gouldie they'd suddenly be seen as balls to the wall firebrands. The other thing that really set Archie apart as far as I was concerned was his intensity. Everything about him — from his fierce promos, to his basic black trunks and boots, and brushcut (much like modern day contemporaries Randy Orton and Stone Cold Steve Austin) — was compelling and eminently believable.

My dad had a long-running "feud" with Stomper — not unlike the storyline rivalry between Vince McMahon and Stone Cold Steve Austin in the '90s.

Like some wrestling personification of the big, bad wolf, Archie was always threatening my dad and the rest of our clan, vowing he was going to come over to our house and run roughshod. Even though I was long since "smart" to the business, his promos sounded so sinister that sometimes my brothers, sisters and I uneasily wondered if he might be serious.

With Archie ruling the roost in the spring of 1969, our business, which hadn't been drawing bad since we'd reopened but hadn't really taken off yet either, finally exploded. We would go on to have our big breakout season — by far the best since the great run Killer Kowalski, Nick Bockwinkel and company had authored back in 1960–1961.

With business doing well, my dad was finally able to breathe easier. It was nice to see him be able to indulge in getting the house — which had fallen into disrepair — fixed and to buy a new Cadillac and several pairs of Tony Lama ostrich and alligator cowboy boots. Cadillacs and cowboy boots were probably my dad's only two indulgences.

9
THE SUMMER OF '69

While our promotion was enjoying breakout success heading into the summer of 1969, a similar phenomenon was also taking place all over North America, with the emergence of a dynamic new NWA world champion, Dory Funk Jr., who had defeated Gene Kiniski for the strap that January.

I'm not sure why, but whenever Kiniski had worked our territory, the matches were always flat, so much so that when we announced that the NWA champion was coming in to defend his belt, on most occasions our gates tended to go down. People almost came to expect an uninspiring match that would invariably be decided by some lame finish, like a count out or disqualification.

Funk, though, would prove to be like a breath of fresh air to the wrestling business — kind of like when Larry Bird, Magic Johnson and Michael Jordan revitalized the NBA in the early '80s after it had been in a prolonged swoon.

In early May, my dad got a call from da new champeen, Funk, who related that he had a weekend off in early June and wanted to know if my dad would like him to come up, to help boost the gates for Stampede Week, a month hence, in July. Seeing as Funk was, at that time, the hottest thing in the business, my dad was delighted to take him up on his offer and booked him against the Stomper.

They ended up having a hell of a match, which would set things up perfectly for their Stampede Week rematch a month later — or so it appeared at the time.

That same night, a new babyface from England named Billy Robinson made his North American debut in our territory and his repertoire of quasi-amateur moves, such as suplexes and saltows, combined with the high-tech Euro style, made for a compelling hybrid — the likes of which fans in our neck of the woods had never been exposed to before and were captivated by. Since there was a three-week interlude leading up to Stampede Week and because Robinson had gotten over so well, my dad decided to throw Robinson and Stomper together for a few weeks, with the plan being for Robinson to put Stomper over to prime him for his big world title return against Funk. On paper, it looked like a good idea, and most of the fans seemed to think the same, because the following week, the Pavilion was packed, with people clamoring to see the new English sensation tackle the indomitable Stomper.

The celebrated Scottish poet Robert Burns once despaired that the best-laid plans of mice and men often go awry. To that hypothesis, he probably could have added, the best laid plans of wrestling promoters as well.

Although Stomper and Robinson appeared to be a surefire combination, for some reason their eagerly anticipated showdown didn't seem to get off the ground. Neither one appeared to be comfortable with the other's style. It went downhill from there and eventually degenerated into a half-assed shoot. As anyone who's been in our business can attest, shoot matches, under the guise of working, tend to be unadulterated abortions. It certainly proved to be the case with Billy and Archie. After about twenty minutes of clutching, grabbing and blocking, with the fans all chanting "borrrrring," Stomper, who was pretty high-strung, abruptly stormed out of the ring and was counted out — leaving Robinson as the winner of the so-called match. Stomper then informed my dad he was through and squealed out of the parking lot, which left us with no choice but to then put Robinson into the Stomper's slot against Funk for the world title the next week.

Stomper's departure was a big loss, but once in a while, out of the ashes of adversity, another star emerges — much like when Steve Young replaced Joe Montana as the quarterback of the Super Bowl champion 49ers. That's pretty much what happened this time around. Robinson's match with Funk remains one of the most awe-inspiring performances I've ever seen. An edge of your seat, nail-biting thriller, it ran the gamut of breathtaking highs and lows and, even as you were watching it, you already knew that you were watching a classic that you'd be extolling the virtues of years later — which is exactly what I'm doing now. I've seen a lot of other incredible matches since then, but for some reason that one still remains indelibly etched in my mind. It was one of the things that inspired me to become a wrestler myself.

When we shut down the territory that year for our annual summer break, there was a groundswell of optimism that we could pick up where we left off in the fall. There was just one slight problem, however. None of the key cogs from our glorious run the previous season were around. Robinson was now in Australia and Funk was, of course, back in the States defending the world title.

Beyond that, the Stomper, who'd been our other mainstay, was nowhere to be found. As a result, instead of opening with all the firepower we'd had back in July, we were forced to open instead with a motley crew of uninspiring lesser lights, including such non–household names as Bull Johnson, Steven Little Bear, Danny Lynch, Hans Streiger and Paul Hebert, as well as rookies Dan Kroffat and Gilles Poisson who would later emerge as decent hands but were then in the embryonic stages of their careers.

The consequence was that our business fell to its lowest level since the dog days of 1964. Business would continue to struggle heading into the winter, traditionally our strongest time of the year, which gave everyone, particularly my mom, increased cause for concern. Things began to take on a different complexion early in December, however.

First, the general manager of the Calgary Stampeders football team, Rogers Lehew, called my dad and said he had a big defensive tackle named Wayne Coleman, who was looking to break into the wrestling business. My dad had broken in a number of other football players who'd gone on to stardom in the ring, including Woody Strode, Wilbur Snyder, Angelo Mosca and Joe Blanchard, so he was happy to give Coleman an audition in his infamous Dungeon. Coleman was an impressive specimen, standing six-foot-five and weighing 295, with 23-inch arms and the ability to bench press over 500 pounds — which was close to the world record at that time. Beyond that, he seemed to have a natural gift of gab and exuded charisma.

While he was getting his feet wet in our territory, Coleman would make the acquaintance of this washed-up old alcoholic named Dr. Jerry Graham, who at one time had been a pretty decent heel. Graham — on the down side of his career at that time, but still a pretty fair bullshit artist — somehow seemed to make a favorable impression on Coleman, because the next thing my dad knew Coleman insisted on changing his name — to Billy Graham.

After his run in Calgary, shortly thereafter, Coleman would explode onto the scene in the States as Superstar Billy Graham — where he would become a huge star, both in the AWA and later the WWF. He would reportedly be the inspiration for a whole generation of bombastic, musclemen types, including the likes of Jesse Ventura, Hulk Hogan, the Ultimate Warrior and the Road Warriors, among others.

Not long after Coleman had hit the scene, my dad received another call — this time from Jack Britton, who was one of the promoters in Montreal. Britton (whose son Gino Brito later became a star of note) told my dad that he had a prospect named Larry Shreeve he'd been training and asked if my dad could do him a favor by booking him — to give him some seasoning. In the past, my dad had helped launch the careers of a number of guys from Montreal, including Maurice Vachon, Tarzan Tyler, Gilles Poisson, Stan Stasiak and Joe Le Duc. He told Britton to send Shreeve down.

By the time he arrived in our territory, Shreeve had changed his name to Abdullah the Butcher and had his deranged lunatic persona down pat. Much like a wrestling version of the shark in *Jaws*, he systematically destroyed anything in his path and struck fear into the hearts of wrestling fans with his relentless, bloodthirsty quest for mayhem. That movie would go on to break all existing box office records, and the same was the case for Abby: he would go on to become the hottest drawing heel in the history of our promotion — surpassing even the Stomper and Killer Kowalski.

With Abby and Coleman (Graham) more than fitting the bill as our lead heels, all we needed now were some good faces for them to work with. Shortly after the new year, my dad's wish, in that regard, would come true as Billy

Robinson — who'd been working in Australia and Japan since he left Calgary back in July — returned. Robinson would pick right up where he left off as one of the hottest faces we'd ever had.

Combining Robinson with Abby and Superstar, or "Supe" as he came to be known, we had an awesome trifecta and they would be the spearhead for our best season. Even better, they would set the stage for a period of prosperity that would extend for the next several years.

I might add that after they left our promotion, Abby, Coleman and Robinson would go on to have an even more pronounced impact on the wrestling business in the States, Japan and around the world, not only drawing huge crowds, but inspiring a host of other wrestlers to endeavor to emulate them — much like a myriad of clones sought to copy Elvis or the Beatles after they made their big splashes. Unfortunately, Abby, Coleman and Robinson are all remembered more now in a negative context than for the positives that they brought into our business.

Abby's propensity for bloodbaths, gaffing (blading oneself) and gratuitous violence inspired countless others to follow suit — to the point where it became overkill and it disgusted and turned off thousands of fans. The saturation of bloodshed and extremism replaced wrestling as the main objective and significantly compromised the work rate in the entire industry — something, I'd venture to say, that hasn't recovered to this day.

Much of Coleman's success was attributed to his awe-inspiring physique, rather than his wrestling ability. He would inspire a host of other bodybuilder types (and misguided promoters) to follow suit, with the end result being a proliferation of anabolically enhanced cohorts. That set the stage for athleticism and wrestling acumen taking a back seat to aesthetics — something that seemed to peak during the days of Hulkamania where looks definitely took precedence over substance. The offshoot has been nothing short of tragic, as a whole generation of younger wrestlers came into the business in the '80s and '90s and, having seen the success of anabolic warriors like Coleman, Hogan and countless others, decided to go that direction rather than "saying their prayers, eating their vitamins" or learning how to work. We all know how many guys have paid the price for having taken that unfortunate shortcut.

And then there's Billy Robinson. By any yardstick, he belongs in wrestling's hall of fame for having been one of the best workers of his era and a cutting-edge trendsetter. Instead though, he's been more likely a candidate for wrestling's hall of shame because of his reputation for having been a cheap shot artist and bully. Here's not to you, Mr. Robinson; heaven doesn't hold a place for those who prey — if you catch my drift.

LEARNING THE ROPES

10

"A SKINNY, WET BEHIND THE EARS PUNK"

Even though Abdullah, Coleman and Robinson all moved on after 1970, our business remained strong for the next several years, with other dynamic and talented wrestlers rising to the fore: Tor Kamata, John Quinn, Kurt Von Hess, Don Fargo, Greg Valentine, Carlos Belafonte (father of WWE star Carlito), Gil Hayes, Dan Kroffat, Tor Kamata, Bob Sweetan, Bob Lueck and Dan Kroffat, as well as British stars like Les Thornton, Angus Campbell, Geoff Portz and Kendo Nagasaki.

Because our promotion was on such a roll and wrestling seemed like it might be a lot more fun than a conventional nine-to-five endeavor, I began thinking I might like to give it a whirl. There were a couple of obstacles though. My dad was pretty savvy and well aware that wrestling was something of a perilous career choice. He therefore decreed that before any of his kids were allowed to get involved in it, we had to first get our university degrees.

Beyond that obstacle, my dad had always had a thing about size; he liked big cars (Cadillacs, in particular), big houses, big dogs and big wrestlers. In fact, if you weighed under 220, he wouldn't even consider you. I was a couple of years away from getting my university degree at that time, but, more distressingly, I was kind of a runt. Even though I'd been drinking protein shakes and eating 'til

I felt like puking, I couldn't seem to put on any weight. I was stuck around 170. As a result, it didn't look like I'd be living out my dream of being a wrestler anytime soon. Even so, as Rod Stewart once rasped, "Never give up on a dream."

Although my dad wouldn't let me wrestle, I was able to persuade him into letting me referee in some of the small towns, like Red Deer and Lethbridge, as a means of earning some walking around money. The refereeing gig actually proved to be a great learning experience, as I had a chance to see firsthand what was getting over and what wasn't — how and why. As well, it gave me insight into the interactive elements and would also alleviate most of the stage fright rookies tend to have, because I'd already been in front of an audience many times as a ref.

Aside from gleaning bits and pieces from being in the ring, I probably learned even more about the wrestling business from riding around with the wrestlers and "picking their brains" on the way to and from towns. Unfortunately, road trips are pretty much a thing of the past and one reason, I'd venture to say, why the quality of work has deteriorated so much.

Even though it didn't appear I'd be getting in the ring anytime soon, I used to eat, drink and sleep wrestling and was able to get this old Mexican heel named Frank Butcher to start training me down in my dad's Dungeon. In time, a few other young guys also joined us for our workouts, including Rick Martel, Kim Klokeid and, later on, guys like Afa and Sika Anoia. Initially, all Butcher had us doing was taking bumps, bumps and more bumps, which is wrestling parlance for break falls — body slams, hip tosses, head mares, arm drags, tackles, suplexes, you name it. He stressed that before you do anything else in wrestling, you need to know how to fall properly, otherwise you'll just get injured and if you're on the shelf or in constant pain, what's the point?

At the time, I figured he might be half-sadistic or just want to see what my pain threshold was, but, in retrospect, his emphasis on bump taking and learning how to land properly and avoid injury, while looking like you were endeavoring to inflict it, was great advice. Later on, when I was training other guys myself down in the Dungeon, bump taking was one of the first things I taught them.

Once in a while, my dad would drop down to the Dungeon when Butcher was conducting his training sessions and Martel and I would put on these pseudo-matches, implementing all the fancy moves and high spots that we'd learned — eager to impress him. Most times, he would grunt, kind of dubiously, that we should be focused more on amateur wrestling than on trying to do high spots — making some analogy about eating meat and potatoes rather than our dessert first. All things considered, I don't think he really took us all that seriously and probably perceived us a bit like little kids putting on our uniforms and trying to play baseball, hockey or whatever, like our major league heroes.

My wrestling aspirations would take an unexpected turn for the better in the summer of '72 with some help from an unlikely source — reigning world heavyweight champion Dory Funk Jr. Funk used to come up to defend the world title every Stampede Week for my dad and since my dad was usually busy as hell during that time — lining up guest appearances, working on publicity, getting his float ready for the Stampede parade and all of that — he'd have my brother Dean and me pick Dory up at the airport. We'd chauffeur him around and look after him.

Funk, whose father Dory Sr. had a promotion down in west Texas, seemed to be able to relate to us. Both second generation, we became pretty good friends, so much so that he invited Dean and me to come and visit him and his family down in Amarillo. I'm still not sure if he was kidding or not, but we took him up on his offer and set off that August, along with my brother Bret, for what would turn out to be one of those coming-of-age type adventures — kind of like *Stand by Me*.

That was the first time any of us had truly ventured beyond our home turf. In retrospect, we were naive as hell. As Dean, Bret and I — all of whom had long hair and tended to be unabashed mark types — made our way through these redneck states like Montana, Wyoming, Oklahoma and Texas, we ran into all kinds of hassles and near calamities with anally retentive truckers and narrow minded misfits, who seemed to think we were draft dodgers or hippie radicals from up North, seeking to cause problems in the land of the free and the home of the brave. Even though we endeavored to be as unobtrusive as possible, because of the prevailing norms at the time, we were routinely refused service at truck stops and restaurants along the way and on a few occasions found ourselves having to hightail it out of town with vigilantes and rednecks hot on our tails.

After having experienced, on our way down to the Lone Star State, more high spots than a Rey Mysterio/Jeff Hardy pay-per-view match, we finally arrived on Dory Jr.'s doorstep, wide-eyed and eager to hook up with "da champeen." We were chagrined when his wife, Jimi, informed us that he was still on the road — defending his strap in Florida. She said that his younger brother Terry would entertain us in the meantime.

That was the first time I met Terry Funk, who was one of wrestling's legendary characters, even back then. He came out to the house and invited us to tag along with him for a show they were having that night in Lubbock — the hometown of Buddy Holly and the Crickets, for all of you rock music trivia types. Given Terry's superstar status at the time, that would be about like Tom Brady or Peyton Manning asking some wet behind the ears young fans if they'd like to tag along for some big game. We eagerly jumped in Terry's big Buick Riviera, the kind with the boat-tail back end. We were about to embark on what would prove to be a memorable adventure — or should I say, misadventure.

Shortly after we set out, Terry pulled out a pouch of Red Man Chewing Tobacco and offered me a chaw. Back in Canada, I'd never seen chewing tobacco before, much less used it, but since I didn't want to appear to be a prude or a wimp, I took a big wad of it and stuffed it in my cheek. Not long after that, Terry began cussing that his electrical system was malfunctioning and that, as a result, his air conditioning and electric windows weren't working. Since it was well over ninety degrees out, it soon became quite stifling in the car. In the meantime, I was still chewing my big wad of tobacco and being the naive mark that I was back then, I had no idea that you were supposed to spit out the juice, rather than swallow it.

My head soon began to swim and my guts began to churn and I finally had to ask Terry to pull over, so I could puke my guts out. Terry, I noticed, seemed to be having trouble keeping a straight face and once I'd finished my upchucking on the side of the road, the air conditioning and power windows, somewhat miraculously, seemed to start working again. Just before we pulled into Lubbock,

Terry said he had an angle in mind, which entailed me pretending to be a mark in the crowd and running into the ring on the finish to save local hero Dick Murdoch. Murdoch would be caught in the Russian sleeper hold, being applied by the dastardly Boris Malenko — their top heel.

I told Terry I'd be happy to give it a shot. Since I was supposed to appear to be a "mark," Terry didn't want us to be seen getting out of his car or walking in with him, so he dropped us off what he said was a block or so from the building — which proved to be a mile or two. When we finally made it to the arena and sat down ringside and proceeded to play our roles — hardcore mark types — booing, cheering and whatnot, our actions seemed to rub some of the rednecks we were sitting near the wrong way and we almost got into a fight or two with them.

During the main event, when Malenko got his dreaded Russian sleeper hold on Murdoch, I slid under the bottom rope and jumped on Malenko's back, piggyback style.

I should note that I'd never met either Malenko or Murdoch before this and I sensed something was wrong, as Malenko tensed up and I heard him telling Murdoch "some fucking mark just jumped on my back." He then gave me a stiff head mare onto the mat. As I was lying on the mat, I saw him wrapping the chain around his fist and drawing back to clobber me with it. Wide-eyed and scared shitless, I began shouting, "Kayfabe, kayfabe," which is the wrestler's way of letting the other guy know that you're not a mark. He looked at me, kind of perplexed, and I shouted, "Terry Funk told me to run in on the finish." Malenko and Murdoch looked at each other, puzzled, and Murdoch then snarled, "That fucking Terry and his ribs."

At that point, I suddenly found myself surrounded by cops, who handcuffed me and dragged my ass out of the ring. They threw me in the back of their police cruiser and I was contemplating having to spend the night in a southern jail — which, based on movies I'd seen, was nothing to look forward to.

My spirits brightened momentarily when I saw Terry Funk come out the back door of the arena and approach the police cruiser. I figured that he'd tell the cops everything was cool, but he instead launched into an Academy Award–deserving rant about how I'd endangered the safety of thousands of fans, beseeching the cops to lock me up and throw the keys away. He then stormed off in a huff, making out to be incensed and leaving me to ponder how I was going to get my ass out of this sling.

Luckily, just after that, Lord Alfred Hayes — who later gained fame and acclaim in the WWF — came up to the cop car and, in his very proper British accent, pleaded for leniency. He told the cops that I'd got caught up in the heat of the match and attested that he could vouch for me. Much to my relief, the cops agreed to let me go.

I'm not sure if that was some kind of routine initiation for the new kid on the block, but after I had paid my dues, Terry and I had a good laugh. We would go on to become great friends; he remains one of the people I respect and admire most in the business. I might add that I've since pulled more than my share of ribs and practical jokes and would impart the tricks of the trade to disciples of mine, such as my brother Owen and Brian Pillman. A bit of comic relief, I've come to find, is often a good antidote to the drudgery of life on the road and anyone who can't laugh at themselves really doesn't belong in this business.

A few days after the Lubbock escapade, Dory Jr. arrived and took Dean, Bret and me out to his father Dory Sr.'s Double Cross Ranch for a barbecue. Dory Sr. was a lot like my dad — one of those salty, old-school types who are fiercely protective of the business. Beneath the rough exterior, he had a really big heart.

Like my dad's territory, Dory Sr.'s placed a premium on old-school wrestling and they respected the business implicitly. They'd broken in numerous great workers and their credo was much the same as the Dungeon — "fight to survive and survive to fight." Dory Sr. would also test the mettle of guys before deeming them worthy of being broken in. If they came through his trial by fire, they were treated like gold after that. Like in Calgary, they would turn out some marvelous workers, including the likes of Dick Murdoch, Dusty Rhodes, Stan Hansen, Bobby Duncum, Jumbo Tsuruta, Ricky Romero and, later on, guys like Ted DiBiase, Jay Youngblood and Tully Blanchard — all of whom were also people of great character.

At the barbecue, over a steak and a few Coors, Dory Sr. and I had a pretty wide ranging and enlightening discussion about different elements of the wrestling business. He was curious to know about my involvement in the business, back home. I replied that I'd been training for the past year and a half, but since I was still only about 175 pounds, my dad figured I was too damn small. Dory Sr. frowned pensively and said that shouldn't be holding me back and the next thing I knew, he was on the phone to my dad: "Stu, it's Dory Funk, I'm here with your son Bruce and he tells me he wants to get in the ring, but you think he's too damn small." He then proceeded to rattle off the names of a bunch of other stars who hadn't been all that big, including Verne Gagne, Angelo Savoldi, Nelson Royal, Pepper Gomez and Tony Borne, and then asked my dad if, as a favor to him, he could at least give me a shot. I had no idea what my dad was saying from his end, but I heard Senior thank him — which, I figured, must be a good sign.

After he got off the phone, Senior said that my dad had agreed to give me a shot, but he wanted me to remember that just because I was the son of a legend, that didn't mean that I was guaranteed an easy ride. If anything, that should oblige me to try even harder.

He then gave me some advice that made a profound impression on me. He said that he'd seen many a guy who'd been given a push and that they'd let it go to their heads and become big marks for themselves — which was a contradiction of what it was all about. He therefore made me promise him that if I ever did make it in wrestling, I'd keep things in perspective and never become a mark for myself. After I got back from Amarillo, I really began to step up the intensity level of my workouts and, true to his word, my dad assured me he was looking to get me started.

There was one more hurdle in my way though — my dad's booker, Dave Ruhl. Even though I'd always gotten along with him and figured he'd done a decent job with the booking since he'd taken it back in 1966, I'd often heard the wrestlers complain that he was a mark for himself and used to push his own story lines at the expense of young, up-and-coming faces — whom he saw as a threat to his position. Since I'd never been in the ring thus far and had only refereed, I'd never experienced that type of thing myself. During one of the shows I was refereeing, I had a chance to speak to Dave and mentioned to him that I was hoping to get into the ring soon.

Dave kind of looked at me as if I was some little kid and said that he doubted any of the boys would want to get in the ring with a skinny, wet behind the ears punk, as he put it. Because my dad was signing his checks though, he tried to make out as if he was on my side and gave me this sanctimonious pep talk that if I were to say my prayers, eat my vitamins and pump iron — or something to that effect — I could perhaps come back in a few years and he'd see what he could do for me. I wasn't too thrilled with Dave's response, but since he was pulling the strings for my dad, there wasn't a whole lot I could do but bide my time.

A few weeks later though, a funny thing happened on the way to the forum, or actually on the way to the Regina Auditorium, which would put a different spin on everything. While en route to Regina, Dave got into an altercation with another wrestler, Carlos Colon (father of WWE performer Carlito), reportedly over the affections of some ring rat. Dave suffered a fractured skull, which would mark the end of his wrestling career.

11
MAKING MY DEBUT

My dad hired a veteran midcard heel named Joe "Tiger" Tomasso as Dave's replacement. Tomasso was more supportive than Dave Ruhl and a few weeks after he took the book, he pulled me aside and ran a story line by me, one which called for me to come to the rescue of Dan Kroffat — one of our hottest faces. In early December 1972, a tag match would ensue, with Kroffat and me taking on Kendo Nagasaki, a masked heel from England, and his partner in crime, Lord Sloan. To add a bit more fuel to the fire, Tomasso said he wanted the match to be a "hair vs. mask" stipulation — which meant that Nagasaki had to unmask if they lost, but if Kroffat and I lost, we would have to get our heads shaved — and we both had long hair.

We shot the angle that Friday for the following week and, to my pleasant surprise, nearly sold out the Pavilion. In the dressing room before the match, Tomasso came up to me to give us the finish and asked me if I could get some color — which is wrestling parlance for blood. I was a bit taken aback, but told him if he thought it might help get the match over, I didn't mind giving it a whirl. As it turned out, the blood did help to get the match over. I've since gotten color on a number of occasions and, later, when I was booking, I had guys do it when it seemed to serve the purpose. I might add though, that, in the past couple of decades, bookers and wrestlers have gone to the well too often in that regard. Getting juice should never be construed as a compensation for getting heat or selling, because it's not.

Since we drew good houses in both Calgary and Edmonton for my debut matches, my dad let me work weekend shots until the end of my university semester in March — which only whet my appetite to go on the road full time. After I finished my junior year at the University of Calgary, my dad let me work the circuit, full time, for the summer. We had several other young guys breaking in at the time, including Afa and Sika Anoia, Gadabra Sahota (a.k.a. the "Great" Gama), Kim Klokeid, Randy Morse, Ray Stefanko, my brother Smith and Rick Martel. Although none of us were making much money, we probably would have worked for nothing, as it was a great learning environment, in and out of the ring.

One of the guys I really learned a lot from was Dan Kroffat, who was always trying to come up with new angles and concepts; one of his concepts, in fact, was the ladder match, which would go on to become a big thing in the WWE. A lot of the boys, especially the veterans, couldn't stand Kroffat. He was pretty cocky and tended to come across as a smart ass, a know-it-all type, but I always found him to have good insights into the business.

On one of the road trips, Kroffat and I were discussing what set the great babyfaces apart from the average ones and he said that he'd never seen a face draw a dime — regardless of whether he was built like Arnold Schwarzenegger, was a world-class amateur wrestler or whatever else — if they didn't have two key elements of working down pat: selling (getting sympathy) and being able to come back with fire (intensity). Since that time, I've seen (and trained) countless wrestlers and can attest that Kroffat's hypothesis is bang on; if you don't have those two elements down, it's highly unlikely that you'll amount to anything.

Some of the other wrestlers were generous with their insights, as well. When I first started in the business, my matches were always scripted move for move beforehand and I figured I was on the right track. One day though, on the way back from Saskatchewan, I was talking to a couple of grizzled veterans, George Gordienko and Geoff Portz, who told me that scripting was akin to having training wheels on a bicycle and that in order to become a good worker, you needed, at some point, to have enough confidence to "freewheel" or improvise.

Improvising, they pointed out, was what working was really all about, as it enabled the crowd to feel that their cheering, booing or whatever had some bearing on the outcome. Establishing that interactive bond with the fans was what it was all about. Portz, to reinforce his point, icily noted that you wouldn't find any "paint by numbers" renderings in any museum. When he put it that way, I got his point.

The next time I worked, I eschewed the script and decided to ad lib — charting unknown territory. The audience feedback was remarkable and convinced me that Portz and Gordienko were right on the money. Since then, I've become an ardent advocate of improv.

Scripting, unfortunately, seems to be the mode in the WWE these days — which is one reason why a lot of marks have turned off wrestling. It's also one of the main reasons why so few of today's up-and-coming workers have actually learned how to work. If it were up to me, I'd get rid of most of the scripting and spend more time teaching the wrestlers the basic precepts of working — selling, coming back, relating to the fans, making them relate to you and things like that — then let the pieces fall in place from there. If they were to go that route, I have no doubts that the business would be a hell of a lot better — though who am I to cast aspersions upon the gods?

12
BUMPS IN THE ROAD

Heading into summer 1973, I was having a blast; but in the immortal words of Ed Whalen, there was a "malfunction at the junction." We had this spot show near Medicine Hat which was nearly two-hundred miles east of Calgary and during my match, my opponent and I got our signals crossed. I ended up taking a bad bump and really messed up my shoulder. My arm dangled limp, my collarbone protruded through the skin — it was painful as hell.

Seeing as there was no hospital in the town, I had to drive back to Calgary with my arm in a sling. About halfway home, I blew the engine in my car and had to hitchhike. A couple of guys pulled over and offered me a ride — which was nice of them, but it turned out they'd been drinking. They ended up skidding off the road on a curve and nearly rolled. I then had to hobble to a nearby farmhouse where I called my dad, who came out from Calgary to pick me up.

When we got to Calgary, he took me to the Holy Cross Hospital, where X-rays confirmed that I'd dislocated my clavicle, broken my collarbone, torn all the ligaments connecting them and that I'd be needing surgery. It would keep me out of action for a long time — which was pretty discouraging.

I was in my hospital bed later that morning, waiting to be wheeled in for surgery, when one of the nurses appeared and said there was a long-distance call for me. I was wondering who it could be since no one had any idea that I was in the hospital. I'm not sure if he'd found out from my dad or what, but it was Dory Funk Sr., who said that he'd heard about my injury and was just calling to wish me well and to tell me not to let it get me down. I couldn't believe that a legend like him would see fit to call a "wet behind the ears punk" like me just to wish me well. His call meant the world to me. Sadly, a couple of weeks later, I was shocked to hear that he had died of a heart attack. He remains a source of inspiration and wisdom to me.

At the time I was injured, I was being pushed as one of the top faces in the territory, so to sustain the momentum, I suggested to my dad that he use my brother Keith — who'd just started training with me and the others down in the Dungeon. My dad seemed to like the idea and although Keith was pretty nervous and tentative, he eventually began to get the hang of it and would soon both develop into a pretty decent hand and capitalize on the push. All in the family, as they say.

That summer, my dad had my brother Dean and me run his beach for him. The beach had previously been run by these old friends of my dad's, with the main activities out there being swimming and family picnics in the daytime and, on occasion, square dances and company barbecues during the evening. Dean was one of the slickest hustlers I've ever seen and together we convinced my dad to let us run keg parties, which were like something out of the John Belushi movie *Animal House*. Later we would promote rock concerts out there, much to my dad's chagrin. It wasn't exactly the kind of clientele my dad approved of, but by the end of the summer, the beach had become the hottest party spot in town for kids. We ended up making more money from it than we did from wrestling — which was pretty cool.

From doing the rock concert scene I also learned a few things that would help me in wrestling. Most of the bands my brother Dean booked out at the beach were these one-hit wonder types or bands who were on the downhill slide. One time Dean and I booked this old stoner band called Iron Butterfly, who'd had one hit in '60s called "In-a-Gadda-da-Vida." Prior to the show, they appeared to be so wasted and out of it that Dean and I wondered if they'd even be able to drag their asses out onstage, but when the show started, they began to get energy from the crowd — most of whom were probably polluted themselves. They ended up having an awesome concert. Upon further reflection, I came to realize how critical it was for any performer — be it a band or a wrestler — to feed off the crowd and have the crowd, in turn, feed off them. Without that, everything else is kind of moot.

13

WASTING AWAY IN JABRONEYVILLE

Although I had a lot of fun doing the rock concerts and enjoying assorted misadventures out at the beach, I was chomping at the bit to get back into the ring. After several months of arduous rehabilitation, I was finally given medical clearance and was eagerly anticipating making a triumphant return.

On my first night back, I was booked to work against this career jobber named Thunderbolt Cannon, who hadn't won a match ever, I don't think. Since it was my long-awaited return to the ring and since I'd been one of the top faces before I went down, I, naturally, assumed I'd be going over. But before the match, my brother Keith — who had somehow climbed the corporate ladder to become the booker — informed me that he needed me to do the job (lose), because he was intending on giving Cannon a big heel push. I figured he must be kidding — that this was a rib, kind of like something Terry Funk might have pulled. That, unfortunately, didn't prove to be the case. Keith, who never had much of a sense of humor, assured me he was dead serious. My big return turned out to be anything but auspicious, with most of the fans stunned when I got beat by a guy like Cannon. I'm not sure what happened to the "big push" that Keith was planning on giving Thunderbolt. If I recall correctly, that was the only match he won that year and maybe in his whole career. It was one more than I'd win though, as Keith had me doing jobs, night in and night out, for the rest of the year.

I became kind of accustomed to the role of jobber — which is like being a pawn on a chessboard, being sacrificed for the kings, queens (of which there were more than a few, especially in the WWF) and whatever else. Though I wasn't getting my hand raised, I still took pride in being able to get the guys I was working with over. Quite often though, I'd find that the guys I was working with (and busting my ass to get over) had this notion that jobbers were little more than disposable objects — kind of like human punching bags — whose sole purpose was to get their asses kicked and make the stars look good. As such, they'd potato (stiff) you, drop you on your head, give you all kinds of dangerous bumps before finally beating you. Quite often, they were such marks for themselves that they seemed to think you were supposed to be thanking them for the honor of working with them. The whole charade was disheartening at times and later on, when I became a booker, I was always more than empathetic to the plight of the lowly jobber and went out of my way to make sure they were made to feel like integral parts of the team — the old "the chain is only as strong as its weakest link" adage.

Near the end of 1975, I had a rude awakening, of sorts, when Keith had me booked to work a televised match against this pudgy little part-time referee named Rocket Moreau. Moreau bore an uncanny resemblance to the Pillsbury Doughboy. Even though I'd done jobs pretty regularly for the past year or so and had long since checked my ego at the door, Moreau was even lower on the totem pole than me — he'd never won a match in his life and, beyond that, was finishing up that night anyway and heading back to Ontario after the match. When a guy is leaving, it's customary for them to put someone over. As such, I had figured I'd be getting my hand raised, but lo and behold, Keith informed me that he wanted me to put the Rocket over. I went out and did the job, but after the match I got to thinking that if I was doing jobs in my hometown for part-time referees who were leaving the territory, perhaps I should see the writing on the wall — that maybe my future didn't lie on the yellow brick road (as Elton John put it) to wrestling stardom. I decided to hang up my tights, so to speak, and go back to university to complete my teaching practicum. My dad seemed mildly disconcerted, but did not try to talk me out of it. After that, I only worked or went on the road when old buddies, like Terry Funk or Andre the Giant, came up for Stampede Week and other special occasions.

14
NOT GETTING IT

The promotion itself seemed to be going in pretty much the same direction as my career and one of the main reasons was the uninspiring booking. I have no doubt that my brother Keith was trying hard and that he had the best interests of the business at heart, but he never seemed to quite grasp what booking was all about, or — as they say in the industry — he never seemed to "get it."

Booking, I came to find later on, is all about storytelling — coming up with compelling characters and scenarios and being able to gracefully extricate yourself from corners you've unintentionally painted yourself into. It's very intuitive and instinctive, or, as Kenny Rogers once put it, it's about knowing "when to hold 'em" and "when to fold 'em." Like the boy wonder, Eric Bischoff — when he was running wcw into the ground — Keith never quite seemed to understand those things. The results attest to that.

When Keith first took the book in my dad's promotion, he had this idea of making Stampede Wrestling into glorified amateur wrestling, with the emphasis on good sportsmanship and athleticism. On paper, it may have sounded noble, but it got over about as well as someone passing gas in a hot, crowded elevator.

Somebody probably should have reminded him that one of the main reasons why so few great amateurs have ever amounted to much as professional wrestlers is that in amateur it's all about concealing your emotions — kind of like a poker player not showing his hand. It's about never showing your opponents that you're hurt, angry or whatever else. In pro wrestling, though, it's the complete opposite: one's ability to project one's emotions to the audience is what really enables a wrestler to get over.

After several months of unsuccessfully seeking to convert Stampede Wrestling fans into amateur wrestling aficionados, Keith had an abrupt change of heart, and decided to bring in King Curtis, Mark Lewin, Big Bad John, Black Jack Slade, Abdullah the Butcher and associates — the reigning kings of hardcore at that time.

In a matter of weeks, the territory went from Sesame Street to Elm Street, and every nightmare there would be barbwire matches, cage matches, chain matches, no-holds-barred bloodbaths and a proliferation of violence and extremism that would have made Paul Heyman proud. Unfortunately, there never seemed to be any method to the madness, no justifying rationale — just gratuitous violence for the sake of gratuitous violence. Gates continued to be lousy — which is the road to ruin and something my esteemed colleagues in the WWE need to not lose sight of.

During the height of King Curtis' and Lewin's reign of terror, one of the few remaining redeeming elements of our promotion, Ed Whalen, got pissed off with all the blood and quit the show. That seemed to open my dad's eyes and he finally showed Curtis, Lewin and friends the door, but by then things were in an abysmal state.

Keith then decided to go back to his quasi-amateur wrestling and gave the big push to a highly-touted former amateur wrestler from Colorado named Larry Lane. Lane would become Stampede Wrestling's equivalent to Bob Backlund. While Lane was a nice guy and busted his ass in order to get over, he never seemed to grasp what working was all about. Beyond that, he had about as much charisma as Al Gore or Dick Cheney. As a result, our gates, which had already been lousy, went even further into the toilet, which left the future of the whole promotion in increasing jeopardy.

With business in a tailspin, my dad — who usually let the bookers do their thing and didn't interfere — stepped in and brought back a blast from the past, Dan Kroffat. Kroffat had quit wrestling a few years back, mostly due to an inability to get along with Keith and Lane. My dad then had our top heel, Killer Tim Brooks, who'd been working with Lane, drop our top singles title — the North American strap — to Kroffat, who was given the big conquering hero returning push. Kroffat then beat several other top heels, at which point he was supposed to drop the strap back to Brooks, but he suddenly informed my dad that he was going back to selling cars and gave my dad the belt back without dropping it — which caused a furor among the boys, Lane and Brooks in particular.

Things came to a head that Friday night in the dressing room, with Lane and Keith tearing a strip off my dad about putting the strap on Kroffat in the first place. During the course of his tirade, Lane pulled a baseball bat out of his bag and began smashing the drywall and mirrors to pieces. He cussed my dad out, in no uncertain terms — it was beyond disrespectful and unprofessional.

That seemed to be the last straw. A couple of weeks later, in July, it was suddenly announced that my dad had sold the promotion to these two small-timers from Edmonton named Bud and Ray Osborne. I'm not sure what the details of the deal were, other than they'd given my dad a down payment and would pay him the remainder of his money at the end of the year, at which time they would take over the promotion.

I was disappointed to see my dad sell, as it kind of marked the end of the dream, but to be honest, I'd been pretty much out of the business the past few years anyway, so my passion had eroded. Given the amount of money my dad had been losing and all the aggravation he'd incurred, I couldn't really blame him.

15
THE ENGLISH REVOLUTION

I'd been told that the Calgary Board of Education would be hiring in the new year, so I'd have to wait until then to start my teaching career. At the same time my girlfriend Brenda, who was a national gymnastics champion, had just left for a six-month training stint in Russia, after which I figured we'd maybe settle down. Since I had nothing going on, I figured that this might be a good time for me to do some traveling, something I'd been wanting to do for years, but hadn't gotten around to. One of the places I'd always wanted to visit was England, so I booked a ticket over there for the end of August and was planning on staying until Christmas.

Shortly before I was scheduled to leave, I was talking to one of my dad's wrestlers, John Foley, who was from England, and mentioned that I was going overseas. Foley, a leathery old shooter type who'd trained at the infamous Wigan gym (England's equivalent of my dad's Dungeon), told me that I should try to get in a few wrestling matches while I was over there, if only for some walking around money. He said that if I wanted, he could make arrangements for me with the promoters. I told Foley that sounded good. Little did I realize how much of an impact that would make down the road for so many people.

A week or so later, I got a call from Max Crabtree. He was the booker for the British wrestling office, which was called Joint Promotions. Max told me that he'd spoken to Foley and was all pumped about my coming over there. It seemed that the biggest box office draw they'd ever had in England had been a North American Indian star named Chief Billy Two Rivers. With that in mind — since I hailed from Calgary, the home of world famous Calgary Stampede, one of the biggest rodeos in the world — he wanted to bill me as a rodeo cowboy, Bronco Bruce Hart, and capitalize on British fascination with cowboys and Indians. While I wasn't a cowboy by any stretch of the imagination, I told Max that if it might help him sell some tickets, I was game for whatever. I bought myself a cowboy hat and boots to at least look the part.

When I arrived at the airport, I was somewhat surprised that Max had a coterie of media types on hand to interview me. He'd apparently given them some fictitious buildup about me having been a champion bronc rider, who was now looking to ride herd over the British wrestling scene. Mad Max, as the boys used to call him, told me that he'd been hyping me, kind of along the lines of Sonny Steele — the character Robert Redford played in the 1979 movie *Electric Horseman* — and to just go along with it.

I had my first match in Manchester the next day at the world-famous Bellevue arena. It was filled to the brim and my opponent was one of the top heels over there, a six-foot-six menacing monster named Pat Roach, who you may have seen in the first Indiana Jones movie, engaged in a life and death struggle with Harrison Ford on the wing of an airplane. Just before the match, Max — who was a slick-talking P. T. Barnum–style bullshit artist — came up to me with a big Cheshire cat smile on his face and told me that for my grand entrance, he'd arranged for me to ride to the ring on a big stallion, in order to really get my cowboy gimmick over. I kind of swallowed hard and heaved a heavy sigh, but didn't have the heart to tell him that about the only horse I'd ever ridden before was on a merry-go-round. I assured him that everything was cool, but I was wondering to myself what the hell I'd gotten myself into.

I got on the horse, which initially seemed pretty calm, and waited patiently outside the curtain for my cue. When the curtains opened up and the spotlight hit us, there was a big roar from the crowd and that seemed to spook the horse, which went charging down the aisle, full speed, on its way to the ring. I was hanging on for dear life and completely oblivious to the crowd and everything else. As the horse got near the ring, it suddenly put on the brakes and reared up on its hind legs — kind of like Roy Rogers and Trigger, and as nonchalantly as possible — given that I'd just about crapped my pants en route to the squared circle — I waved to the audience, who gave me appreciative applause. Thankfully, that was the only time I had to do the horse entrance.

Although I'd initially been planning on working just a few shots in England, I soon found myself wrestling nearly every night and Max had me going over (winning) most of the time — often over his top boys, many of whom were world-class workers I really had no business beating. Since I'd done nothing but jobs back home, I was kind of sheepish that Max was putting me over. More than a few times, I'd apologize to my opponents for getting my hand raised and assure them that it was Max, not me, who'd called for it.

Most of them were pretty cool about doing the job and assured me that it all just part of being a pro. It's too bad there aren't more guys with that mind-set around today.

In any case, England proved to be an awesome working environment. Some nights I'd work with heavyweights, like Pat Roach, Gwyn Davies or Giant Haystacks; other nights I'd work with guys about my size, like Roy St. Clair, Mark Rocco or Pete Roberts; and still other times I'd work with smaller guys, like Jimmy Breaks, Johnny Saint and Mick McManus. Regardless of their size, almost all the workers over there had this innate ability to make whomever they were working with look good — which is what it's all about. Probably the nicest thing about the English tour was that I regained my passion for wrestling, which I'd lost in the few years prior.

One night I was wrestling in Nottingham and I'm not sure if it was to justify the "star" treatment Max had been giving me, or if I was just trying to show off to the boys over there, but in any case on this night I was doing a lot of flips, fancy moves, cartwheels and whatnot and figuring it would get a good reaction from the crowd and perhaps impress Max and some of the boys.

On the way home after the match, I was riding with these two veterans named Jimmy Breaks and Alan Dennison — both of whom were terrific workers, or "grafters" as they were called in the U.K. Like a lot of the British wrestlers, Breaks and Dennison were always telling off-color jokes, wisecracking and that type of thing, and this night was no exception. Breaks — who bore an uncanny resemblance in appearance and manner to Dudley Moore — related this parable about two bulls: one a young, impetuous horny bull, and the other an older, wiser one. As the story went, the two bulls were reclining at the crest of a hill overlooking the pasture filled with heifers, when the younger bull, becoming aroused, suddenly stood up and proclaimed, "Son of a gun, I think I'll run down there and shag me one of those heifers." To which the older bull sagaciously replied, "Why don't we walk down, son, and shag them all." I laughed; Breaks and Dennison shook their heads, as if to say I didn't get it.

They then told me that from what they'd seen, my approach to wrestling was a lot like the impetuous young bull, in that with all the high spots and irrelevant crap, I was losing sight of my main objective, which should always be getting the match over. I'd never seen wrestling in quite that perspective, but when I thought about it, that made a hell of a lot of sense. Later on, when I was booking, that was another of the fundamental principles I used to impart to other "young bulls": Brian Pillman, Chris Benoit and my brother Owen — all of whom would then "walk down and shag them all" themselves.

A few weeks before I was slated to return home from England, I was wrestling in this place called Cleethorpes and before my match, in the dressing room, this old guy, who looked like the old trainer, Mick, from *Rocky*, came up to me and introduced himself. His name was Ted Betley and he told me that he was well aware of the success that some British stars had enjoyed over in Canada. He had a hot prospect he'd like to send over to work for my dad. I'd already had several other British guys approach me about getting booked in Canada. Most of them knew of the success that guys like Billy Robinson, Les Thornton and Alfred Hayes had enjoyed and seemed to think that Canada was like the land of milk and honey. I didn't have the heart to tell them that my dad was shutting down at the end of the year and that, beyond that, the milk had become somewhat curdled in recent years. In most cases, I used to just tell them I'd put in a word for them to my dad and leave it at that. Funny enough, my impassiveness seemed to only renew their determination to get booked.

I was in the process of giving Betley the same line when he summoned these two skinny, zit-faced kids — neither of whom looked like they weighed more than 150 pounds. He introduced them, first names only, as Tommy and David and divulged that the older of the two, Tommy, was the one he was hoping to send over. He said that while he'd only been working about six months, he saw a lot of potential in him and wanted him to follow in the footsteps of the other great British workers, like Robinson, Portz and Thornton, all of whom had attained stardom in Calgary and then went on to star in the States and Japan after that.

I didn't want to offend anyone, but, quite frankly, I was wondering if this might be some kind of rib. I agreed to watch Tommy in action and let old Ted know what I thought. I really wasn't expecting much, but Betley's protégé — whose ring name was the Dynamite Kid — went out and put on one of the most awe-inspiring performances I've ever seen. Not only did he have an amazing repertoire of moves, sailing around with catlike quickness, but, most impressively, he seemed to have an innate sense of ring psychology that was unbelievable for one so young. I was completely blown away — just about the way trainer Lucien Laurin must have been the first time he saw his colt, Secretariat, rounding the turn.

As I was saying to myself that Dynamite would be a perfect fit for my dad's promotion, it suddenly occurred to me that, of course, my dad was selling the promotion and come January there would be no more Stampede Wrestling, so all of this was irrelevant. I shake my head at the irony of the situation — as I'd first regained my passion for wrestling and now had one of the hottest prospects I'd ever seen literally begging me to get booked in Calgary, it was all for naught.

After the match, Betley and Dynamite came up to me and were eager to hear my impressions. Although the match had been nothing short of mind-boggling, I had no choice but to downplay my reaction and, instead, told them it "wasn't bad" — which would have been like Colonel Tom Parker telling Elvis Presley he "wasn't bad" the first time he saw him, or Berry Gordy telling Joe Jackson that his kid Michael "wasn't bad" after his first audition.

I returned to Calgary a few weeks later, just before Christmas, and the week I got back, the news came out that the Osborne brothers who were supposed to be buying the territory from my dad had lost their asses on a real estate venture and couldn't come up with the money to complete the deal. As a result, my dad would be keeping the territory. My mom was despondent because she'd been counting the days until she could get out of the wrestling business. While I could appreciate how she felt, I was delighted but did my best to suppress my joy at this unanticipated turn of events.

16
DYNAMITE

While I was pleased the wrestling promotion had received a stay of execution, it was still in dire straits. Any decent talent we'd had had already jumped from what they figured was a sinking ship. That left us with a crew of washed-up has-beens, run-of-the-mill jabroneys and unproven rookies. If there was any kind of silver lining to this seemingly dark cloud it was that I, at least, figured I'd have no trouble convincing my dad to book Dynamite.

That wouldn't prove as easy as I thought, as my dad, like most other wrestling promoters in North America at the time, believed heavyweights — guys weighing 220 and up — were the only way to go. To him, the notion that a skinny teenager could turn the territory on its cauliflower ear was laughable, and although I did my best to extol Dynamite's many virtues to him, he was obdurate in his insistence that a 150-pound rookie was incapable of turning around the franchise.

As we limped into spring, my mother stepped up her campaign for my dad to get out of wrestling. With nothing else working, my dad reluctantly consented to bring in the skinny English "messiah" — either to get me off his case or just to prove me wrong, I'm not really sure.

A few weeks before Dynamite was supposed to start, I was talking with my brother Keith — who was still booking — and his assistant, Jack Kruger, about Dynamite. Generally, when a new guy came into a territory, the rule of thumb was to have him go over strong on his first night out — have a "smash" as they call it, and then try to build off that. I was well aware how important first impressions can be and was interested to hear what Keith and Kruger had in mind for Dynamite. Much to my chagrin, Kruger divulged that he couldn't see many of our heavyweights wanting to do a job for a skinny, unproven teenager. Keith agreed and said that, all things considered, he really couldn't see Dynamite being much more than undercard fodder for some of the bigger guys.

I was pissed off at their prejudiced mind-set and figured that I needed to do something to keep Dynamite from being chewed up and spit out before he even had a chance to show what he was capable of.

I was trying to think of a way to present my case to my dad when it occurred to me that the lighter weight divisions in boxing were now the big ticket, featuring dynamic new stars like Sugar Ray Leonard, the original Hitman Tommy Hearns, Roberto Durán and Wilfred Benitez. At the same time, the heavyweights — after the retirement of Muhammad Ali — had gone into the toilet, with a group of uninspiring and charismatically challenged plodders like Larry Holmes, Leon Spinks, Gerry Cooney and Joe Bugner.

I pointed this out to my dad and said that since our heavyweights weren't exactly setting the world on fire, why didn't we endeavor to go the same route that boxing had taken and, rather than having Dynamite work with the heavyweights, make him out to be a champion of his own weight division, which we would call the mid-heavyweight division?

My dad — ever the old-school conservative type — was reticent about going that route, but given that not much else had been working at the time, he finally agreed to bring Dynamite in as the British Commonwealth mid-heavyweight champion. It had a good ring to it, especially since the British Commonwealth Games were scheduled to take place in Edmonton that summer.

We soon began hyping Dynamite's imminent arrival, although there was quite a bit of skepticism. It was much like the response another skinny teenager also launching his career in Alberta at that time — Wayne Gretzky — was receiving. We'd had some smaller guys in the territory, hands like John Foley, Ángel Acevedo (the Cuban Assassin), Norman Charles and Hubert Gallant; most of them had been mired in the undercards because of their size but were decent workers. I persuaded my dad that we could perhaps give them a new lease on life as mid-heavyweight contenders. The smaller guys quickly became the hottest thing in the territory and would also inspire another skinny teenager who was contemplating whether he wanted to get into wrestling — my brother Bret. Later on, as you all know, Bret came to be "the best there is, the best there was, and the best there ever will be," but I'm sure if you were to ask, he'd be the first to tell you that even he couldn't hold a candle to the Dynamite at that time.

Even though Dynamite proved to be everything I'd touted, and then some, our territory, unfortunately, continued to struggle — mostly because our heavy-weights, who were still getting the biggest push, were, for want of a better term, the drizzling shits.

17
OKTOBERFEST

That fall, my brother Smith, Dynamite and I were invited by a German promoter, Edmund Schober, to wrestle in a big forty-five day tournament, coinciding with Oktoberfest, in Hanover, Germany. It was called the International Grand Prix. The tournament would prove to be quite the learning experience. When we arrived, I was pleased to find several other guys I'd crossed paths with in the past over there, including Afa and Sika Anoia, Kim Sakurada, Mr. Hito and Bob Della Serra — all of whom had worked in Calgary. As well, there were a few guys I'd worked with in England: Pat Roach, Dave Cross, Colin Joynson, Caswell Martin and Tony St. Clair.

Upon my arrival, one of the first things I noticed was that the media in Germany treated wrestling as if it was a shoot, which was different than back home. I was intrigued at how they'd have these press conferences where they'd ask all these shoot-style questions — about which factors might enable you to emerge victorious and how you'd prepared for the big tournament and all that type of thing. On many occasions, the American wrestlers would offer tongue in cheek responses — which were dutifully reported the next day in the papers, word for word.

Giving credit where credit is due, the Germans did a hell of a job at hyping and making a big spectacle out of everything. Each night, before the matches began, they would have a marching band play some music and the wrestlers would parade to the ring for formal introductions, bearing their country's flag — much like the Olympics — with the marks getting all caught up in this nationalistic fervor. As well, when the wrestlers came to the ring for each match, they'd play entrance music for them — usually German military marches, which the American boys used to sardonically refer to as Adolf Hitler's Greatest Hits.

At the time, I thought it was all kind of cheesy, but I noticed that, nevertheless, it seemed to get the fans really pumped. Later on, when I took over the booking for my dad's promotion, I had the wrestlers come to the ring in similar fashion — our rock music entrances would later become the norm, not only in our promotion but in the WWF.

Because of the prevailing perception that the tournament was a shoot and perhaps because of all the hype, many of the European wrestlers, in the immortal words of my old friend Dory Funk Sr., became "marks for themselves." Probably the biggest mark for himself of all was the German champion, this haggard-looking old bag of bones named Axel Dieter, who bore a striking resemblance to the Wile E. Coyote character from the Road Runner cartoons. Axel was always stiffing guys and most of the Europeans used to let him get away with it because they didn't want to jeopardize their job security.

One night, Axel stiffed Afa Anoia — who was generally pretty laid-back but not the kind of guy you'd want to mess with. Afa responded by dragging Axel's scrawny ass all over the ring and embarrassing him in front of the countrymen who'd come to perceive him as invincible, like some kind of superman.

After the match in the dressing room, Axel went ballistic and pulled out a big revolver and began shooting up the place and rasping in broken English that he was the only real shooter in the promotion — apparently because he had a gun. Axel's outburst not only pissed off most of the American and Canadians, including Smith, Dynamite and me, it also made him the butt of numerous ribs, courtesy of us North American boys.

As I mentioned before, every night the matches began with a big parade of all the wrestlers marching to the ring. After everyone made their way to the ring, part of the routine was that the ring announcer would present gifts — flowers, chocolates, champagne and pastries— to various wrestlers from adoring fans. One day before the matches, Smith, Dynamite and I, who were living in a trailer on the fairgrounds adjacent to the big tent where the matches took place, noticed Axel sneaking in early with an armful of wrapped presents, which he put on the announcers' table. After he left, we went to check out the gifts. We noticed that they all had tags that read "To Axel." They were from assorted "female admirers." It was Axel's way of making the promoter, who was a big mark himself, think that Axel was really over; in turn, it would compel him to push Axel more.

As a bit of mischief, Smitty, Dynamite and I changed the tags on all the gifts, designating them instead to a bunch of the jabroney types — most of whom had never received a present before and were quite shocked at the unexpected windfall. Axel was seething when the jobbers were given his gifts, while Smith, Dynamite and I were having trouble keeping straight faces.

A few days later, Smith and Dynamite had this ring rat friend of theirs who worked at a local bakery make this really fancy pastry for Axel — the main ingredient was dog food and it featured assorted other ingredients not fit for human consumption. Afterward, in the dressing room, we were half gagging watching Axel and cohorts stuffing their faces with the dog food delight — which they all seemed to think was some kind of Bavarian delicacy called "mincemeat strudel."

Another time, Dynamite got a big bottle of cheap wine and injected this liquid laxative used to deworm racehorses through the cork and then had it gift wrapped all fancy and left it on the table for Axel. For the next several days, Axel and all of his Colonel Klink type comrades were all complaining of acute diarrhea but weren't sure how they'd contracted it.

Aside from Axel and friends being marks for themselves, the trip to Germany had been quite positive, as I learned a lot about hype and marketing — all of which I would put to good use when I became booker in my dad's promotion.

18
YOU'VE GOT TO PAY YOUR DUES

A few weeks before the end of the tournament, I got news from home that an old friend of the family had committed suicide.

This wasn't the first time I'd experienced the loss of a friend or associate, but for some reason — perhaps because I had too much time to ponder such things — I began dwelling on the fact that, to put it into wrestling terms, we all have to ultimately "do a job" for real. It truly affected me.

Before long, I had allowed myself to spiral into an out of control depression and by the time I made it back to Calgary, I was in a hell of a mess. Ringo Starr once lamented that "you've got to pay your dues, if you want to sing the blues" — well, I never had any great desire to sing the blues, but I sure as hell would pay my dues.

In any case, when I got back from Hanover, my dad had hired this new booker named Dick Steinborn: he came with a reputation as one of the sharpest minds in the business. The first time I met Steinborn, he smiled and informed me that, based on television tapes he'd watched and from what he'd heard from other wrestlers, he saw a lot of untapped potential and wanted to give me a big babyface push.

In a matter of weeks, I was going over guys I'd never dreamed of going over and was soon being hailed as the hottest face in the territory. Funny thing, even though I'd done jobs the past number of years, most of the fans seemed to have either forgotten that or didn't care — something guys who have trepidations about doing a job, or two, or one hundred should keep in mind.

What I found to be really weird was that a few years back, I would have been thrilled to win a match, much less go over every night, but instead I was almost oblivious to everything. Most of the time, I was almost entirely on autopilot. When I went into the ring, I usually had no idea whatsoever of what I was doing, but somehow everything would go fine. In fact, I found myself doing crazy, high-risk things I'd never have dreamed of doing before, throwing caution to the wind. In retrospect, I suspect that I may have had some half-assed death wish.

In any case, whatever I was doing seemed to get over. After the matches, most of the wrestlers and even my dad seemed astonished at the things I was doing in the ring and would be giving me high fives, complimenting me on my ass-kicking performances and expressing amazement at my transformation — all of which was cool, I suppose, but I was pretty much numb to everything they were saying.

Funny enough — or, in reality, not so funny — after the roar of the crowd and all of that had subsided and I was back at my place again, alone, the dark cloud would return and I'd return to a state of living hell, often wondering if I'd make it through the night. A while back, when I heard about Heath Ledger, who gave an Oscar-winning performance in *The Dark Knight* but was so messed up while filming that he could barely function and, sadly, didn't live to enjoy the fruits of his labors, I found myself able to relate implicitly.

Christmas was probably the toughest stretch of all. With everyone else in the throes of the joyous festive season, I was close to going down for the count, but I put on my game face so I wouldn't drag everyone else down.

The week after the holidays, my brother Keith and I were coming back from Helena, Montana. We'd had some shows over the holidays and even though I'd been endeavoring to keep my problems to myself I'm sure that he and most of my family sensed I was in a bad state and were trying to help. As we were driving back, Keith pulled out a joint and passed it to me. I'd always been pretty anti-drugs before, but I was willing to try anything as a possible means of escape and had a few tokes. I'm not sure if the joint was laced with something or what, but before long both Keith and I were in this kind of paranoid high. We were flying and freaking out that we were going to crash and burn.

We were so terrified that we had to pull over to the side of the road for a few hours and even after that, we had this slow, white-knuckle drive back. We kind of look back on that now and laugh, but at the time, it was damn scary. In its own way though, it was a blessing in disguise, as it completely turned me against drugs.

Since then, I've unfortunately seen countless contemporaries — who may well have been battling similar demons — choose to use drugs as a means of escape, only to find them a road to ruin. As far as I'm concerned, being high, especially when you're in a depressed state, is like driving down a steep, dark, winding road with no headlights or brakes. It's a surefire recipe for disaster.

Not long after that, my brothers Dean and Ross, my sister Ellie and Dynamite told me that they were planning a mid-winter Hawaiian vacation and invited me along. I initially declined, but they persisted and I finally agreed to join them.

At the time, Dynamite and I were the two top babyfaces in the territory. In order to account for our disappearance, booker Dick Steinborn suggested a story line that entailed Dynamite — who'd been tag teaming with me quite a bit — enlisting the help of a British heel who'd recently arrived to do a heel double cross. The offshoot was that I'd be "injured" and out of action for the next month, while Dynamite, who would turn heel, would be suspended.

I told Steinborn I was game for whatever, so we shot the angle, and as Steinborn had predicted, it got a super hot reaction — making me a martyr, as I supposedly wound up being ambulanced to the hospital, while Dynamite, who'd been one of our most popular babyfaces, suddenly was transformed into the most hated heel in the territory.

I'm not sure if any of you have seen that John Candy/Steve Martin movie *Planes, Trains and Automobiles*, but our Hawaiian vacation was a lot like that; almost everything that could go wrong, went wrong. As soon as we arrived, we found that our travel agent had somehow screwed up our hotel reservations and instead of having separate rooms, we found ourselves all crammed into one room in a second-rate dump. That was just the start of our adventure.

On our first day at the beach, Dynamite and Ellie, who'd been advised by some sun-worshipper to use coconut oil for a really awesome tan, suffered third-degree burns. The sunburns were so severe that for several days they could barely walk. Not long after, Dynamite, Ross and I were walking home from some bar late at night and encountered this girl, in apparent dire distress, screaming hysterically as some guy was assaulting her. Dynamite and I endeavored to come to her aid, but the guy whipped out a switchblade. We were able to disarm him though and he ended up getting the living shit kicked out of him; all the while, this skanky bimbo that had been screaming for help was screaming and swearing at us — for assaulting her pimp. Dynamite snarled at her to make up her fucking mind.

When we arrived back at our hotel later, we found that someone had broken into our room and stolen most of our money. Since none of us had any plastic at that time, we were forced to nickel and dime it and by the end of the trip we were half-starving and running on fumes.

A couple of days before we were supposed to return, my brother Ross contracted a staph infection. An ingrown nose hair got so infected that he looked like something out of *Planet of the Apes*. It was so bad that he wound up in hospital on an intravenous drip. He nearly died.

In its own messed up way though, all the stress and aggravation served to take my mind off my own emotional problems and by the time I got back, I found that I somehow had extricated myself from the emotional quicksand I'd been mired in. I was back on a relatively even keel; it was almost a miracle. It's been said that what doesn't kill you will only make you stronger and that proved to be the case for me — and later on, when I was faced with some pretty serious adversity, I was able to deal with it, because I'd already been to hell and back.

One of the other important lessons I learned from that whole ordeal was that all you can do in life is to concern yourself with the here and now and not incur undue stress by dwelling on what you could or should have done in the past, or by trying to figure out what might happen down the road. Putting it another way, I'd like to relate something my son, Bruce Jr., once told me that sums it up best: "Yesterday's history and tomorrow's a mystery, but today is a gift — which is why it's called the present." Amen. Since then, my philosophy's been to live, love, laugh, enjoy the ride, occasionally raise a little hell — and let the chips fall where they may.

As far as trying to explain the meaning of life or some kind of reason behind its mysteries, I've arrived at the conclusion that, as some jabroney poet once lamented, *Ours is not to reason why; ours is but to do and die.* In wrestling terms, I guess that might mean that we weren't meant to be smartened up in life and that, for all intents and purposes, we're supposed to remain marks — which is, when you stop and think about it, a lot more fun, anyway. Call me a mark if you want, but there's no damn way that life can all be a work or some kind of mere coincidence. Anybody who's inclined to disagree need only take a look at a mother cuddling her newborn, or see the sun rising on a clear day, or have some girl who takes your breath away smile at you. There's no way that could all be an accident or coincidence; by that token, I guess you can call me a mark, and I'm more than happy to remain one.

19
HALF NELSON

When I returned from Hawaii, I was surprised and disappointed to find that Tricky Dick Steinborn had been canned — reportedly because he, Keith and Bret weren't in agreement on schematics. Bret — who'd only been working a few months himself — and Keith were now handling the book.

They had me work with heel Marty Jones on my first night back, in a cage match. The angle we'd shot before I left had been pretty hot and we ended up selling out in short order. Our match went well. That same night, Keith, for reasons known only to him, saw fit to bring Larry Lane back and had him work in a babyface vs. babyface tag against Bret and himself. They had a sixty-minute broadway (time limit draw), which from a technical point of view wasn't bad, but since there was no heat or background story, it had people falling asleep.

That didn't stop my dad, at my brothers' insistence, from paying Lane more than double what Marty and I got that night. Jones, like Dynamite, was a bit of a hothead; he blew a gasket and caught the first plane back to England. Perhaps I should have been pissed too, but at that stage I was happy just to be on the right side of the grass.

With Jones out of the picture, I worked with Dynamite the next week and we turned away close to a thousand fans. It was a barnburner of a match that exceeded all expectations. Even though he was barely twenty, Dynamite had developed into one of the best workers in the business and was only getting better.

I've often been asked what made Dynamite so special. Well, first, he was a phenomenal athlete, remarkably adaptable to virtually any style or format — be it British, North American, or Japanese. What really set him apart was his timing: he seemed to have this innate ability to know precisely when to do things. Beyond that, like all the truly great workers, he was capable of making damn near anyone he worked with look good — in many cases, better than they ever dreamed of looking — myself included.

Even though business remained steady throughout the spring and into summer, there was a fair bit of friction between Bret and Keith. They couldn't seem to agree on methodology and were bickering over who was in charge. Things finally boiled over one night in Calgary when they argued over some finish and ended up getting into an altercation in the dressing room that ended with with my dad having to pull them apart.

My dad then decided to go another direction and hired this crusty old veteran named Art Nelson. Nelson had worked for us back in the early '60s, and since then had made the rounds in a few territories in the States, including Amarillo. The first week that Art was in town, he notified Dynamite and me that he'd never done much business with smaller guys working on top. He pretty much indicated that we'd be relegated to undercard status, as would Keith and Bret — neither of whom weighed much more than 200 at that time either.

Although Dynamite and I weren't thrilled, at least we knew where Art stood. We decided to head to Germany where we'd been invited back for the Hanover tournament. Art then imported a whole crew of these long-in-the-tooth, heavyweight cronies from the States to work in the main slots, including "The Professor" Dale Lewis, Mr. Pogo and Don Gagne, and he put the singles strap on himself.

The second go-round in Germany proved to be even better for Dynamite and me, as we were given a lot better push by the new German promoter, Heinrich Kaiser. Dynamite continued with his practical jokes — something he was gaining notoriety for. He also hooked up with a German doctor, who introduced him to the anabolic steroid Primobolan — which, at that time, was considered the Cadillac of 'roids. Dynamite would definitely get bigger, but, contrary to what they say about 'roids being performance enhancing, I'd vehemently argue that his performance would only decline — as would his health.

When Dynamite and I returned to Calgary in mid-November, Art was still in charge, but business was down and morale was as well. Bret and Keith were not pleased with the way they were being used and a lot of fingers were being pointed. Dynamite and I figured that since Art hadn't been setting the territory on fire with his heavyweight pals he might be inclined to use us a bit more. That didn't prove to be the case, however; on our first night back, he had us in the prelims, working in inconsequential matches.

Around the same time, my brother Dean, who'd been living in Hawaii and helping new promoter Peter Maivia get his outfit off the ground, called and said that business was great and that we could make more down there than we could back in Calgary. He also said that the promotion would provide us a luxury condo on the beach, free of charge. That sealed the deal for me and Dynamite — we were soon headed back to Hawaii.

20
HAWAIIAN PUNCH

Upon our arrival, we found that my brother Dean had stretched the truth a bit. The luxury condo he'd mentioned was a cockroach-infested dump inhabited by derelicts and drunks. Dynamite and I soon found that business, which Dean had told us was great, was in shambles; promoter Peter Maivia had recently lost his television show and gates were abysmal. I probably should have jumped on the first plane out of there, but I felt kind of sorry for Peter and company. Having seen my dad go through similar trials and tribulations, I could relate to what Peter was going through. Dynamite and I decided to hang in there.

Peter lived in the same apartment building — on the floor directly above us, in a slightly larger but equally squalid place. Peter lived with his wife, Lia, his son-in-law Rocky Johnson (who'd wrestled for my dad back in the '60s), his daughter Ata (who was married to Rocky), and their teenaged son Dwayne, or Dewey, as they called him back then. (Today he's better known to most of you as simply the Rock.)

Although we didn't make much money, Peter treated us well and started giving us a pretty good push. For some reason, he had me wrestling as a heel and though I was a fair bit smaller than Peter, Rocky and other babyfaces, such as Don Muraco and Haku, he put the Polynesian heavyweight strap on me and had me going over every night. I also worked a pretty hot program with Dynamite, who was a face over there. Business began to improve.

Unfortunately, they were only running two shows a week, so our salaries were still quite lean. Dynamite decided to head back to Calgary and urged me to do the same, but I had no desire to work for Admiral Nelson. I also wanted to repay Peter and Rocky for having had enough faith to put the belt on me.

In March, my brother Keith came down to Hawaii for a few matches. Like me, he'd been given the big sales pitch by Dean. For a bit of fun in the sun he also brought along our brother Owen, who was on Easter break from high school.

On Keith's first night over there, he and I were booked in some kind of grudge match against Peter, the High Chief of all Samoans, and tag partner Rocky Johnson. Peter set up this finish where Keith and I were supposed to bust him open with a foreign object. He was supposed to do the mega sell and then give Rocky the hot tag — at which point Peter would be helped back to the dressing room to get patched up. In the meantime, Keith and I were supposed to stop Rocky and bust him open also. We'd start getting strong heat on him as well — until Peter, taped up, was supposed to come back and kick our asses. At that point we were supposed to flee — like chicken-shit cowards — and then they'd shame us into accepting a lumberjack tag match.

Anyway, to make a long story short, the match went pretty well according to plan, but when Peter bladed himself, he must have hit an artery and was bleeding so bad that he really did have to be taken back to the dressing room for repairs. When Rocky tagged in, he was supposed to get juice as well — which, given how hot the crowd already was, probably wasn't a very good idea. He, however, gaffed himself shortly after the tag and no sooner than he began his sell, I noticed that the ring was surrounded by irate Samoans — most of whom were the size of Umaga or Rikishi. Making matters worse, nearly all the security guards were also Samoans, so we weren't likely to get any support from them.

As I surveyed the increasingly dire-looking scenario, I recalled something that Abdullah the Butcher had told me when he was heeling for us. He said that the one thing the fans were afraid of and didn't want any part of was someone they figured was completely deranged or crazy and that he always made out to be a lunatic — especially if he had to fight his way through the crowd.

In any case, I turned to Keith — who looked like he was scared shitless — and kind of laughingly asked him if he remembered that scene at the end of *Butch Cassidy and the Sundance Kid* where the Bolivian army had surrounded them. He glared angrily at me and muttered that this was a hell of a time to be talking movie trivia.

I then told him that, just like Butch and Sundance, we were going to make out to be fearless, deranged lunatics, bent on wreaking havoc on the mob. Keith gave me this wide-eyed, disillusioned look, as if to say, "Are you out of your fucking mind?" I reassured him that everything would be cool and to just follow my lead. We then waded out through the teeming throng, acting like a pair of lunatics, and, lo and behold, the lynch mob suddenly began parting like the Red Sea. We made it back to the dressing room, completely unscathed. (I owe you, Abby!)

The only injury we sustained that night was when my brother Owen, who was trying to come to our rescue when the heat was on, got sucker punched by some irate Samoan — something which was noted in the Rock's biography. I felt bad for Owen, but with his typical good humor he laughed and seemed half-proud of his first war wound.

Peter and Rocky began having me handle all the finishes and story lines for them and business began to improve each week out. I'd seen what worked and what hadn't in Calgary and, whatever I did, I always endeavored to have some ostensible rationale or purpose for having done it — which should always be rule number one for any booker.

Beyond that, one of the other things I'd come to learn from having watched other wrestlers who were also booking was to lead by example. Quite often I'd see bookers ask wrestlers to do things that they weren't prepared to do themselves: be it doing a job (losing), getting juice (blood), putting in time or whatever. Having been on the other side of the fence, I used to hear the wrestlers bitching or whining that the booker was asking them to do things that he wouldn't do. I never asked the boys to do anything that I wouldn't do myself and that seemed to go a long way to establishing the respect of the boys — which is essential for any booker to be successful.

While things were going pretty well in Hawaii, I'd been told by my brother Owen — who, even though he was just a teenager, had a pretty good grasp of the business — that things back in Calgary were in a state of flux. To no one's surprise, Art Nelson's my-way-or-the-highway approach to booking had begun to wear thin and he'd been replaced as booker — by Bret.

According to Owen, Bret was trying hard and was having some great matches — in particular with veterans like Leo Burke, Mr. Hito and this big black heel named Kasavubu. Gates, however, remained sluggish. Owen attributed the slump to Art — whose story lines had been pretty tepid — but also to the fact that Bret was going to the well too often by having ladder matches, lumberjack matches, chain matches and, his personal favorite, wrestlers having ten-round boxing matches. Usually these were for no apparent reason, and, as a result, the fans had begun to lose interest.

I was hoping Bret might start getting the hang of things, because I knew from before that if my dad continued to lose money, my mom would be renewing her quest for him to get out of the business, something none of us wanted.

In the meantime, I continued doing my thing for Peter and Rocky.

While we weren't running enough shows for anyone to get rich, the fans had started to respond to our story lines. It didn't hurt that Peter, his wife Lia, Rocky and his wife Ata couldn't have been nicer — always inviting Dean and me up to their place for dinner and virtually giving me carte blanche control over the booking. It was all very gratifying.

In May, I was kind of surprised to receive a call from my dad. He said he was just touching base to see how I was doing. Even though I loved my dad and he loved me (or so I'd like to think), for some reason we never chatted much. Naturally, I was kind of wondering why he was calling.

After some precursory bullshitting, he cut to the chase and told me that several of the wrestlers — including Bobby Bass, Len Denton, Tom Stanton, Luke McMasters, Steve Wright and Bobby Fulton — had walked out. He wasn't sure whether it was because they didn't agree with Bret's booking, or if they were just malcontents, but in any case, our roster was pretty thin.

ABOVE: Sunday dinner, 1961
(All family photos courtesy:
Alison Hart)

BOTTOM LEFT:
Back Row (left to right) Wayne,
Keith, Helen, Stu, Bruce, Smith;
Middle Row Dean, Ellie, Georgia,
Bret; *Bottom Row* Owen, Diana,
Ross, Alison

BOTTOM RIGHT: On my Dad's knee,
with Mom, Smith and Keith

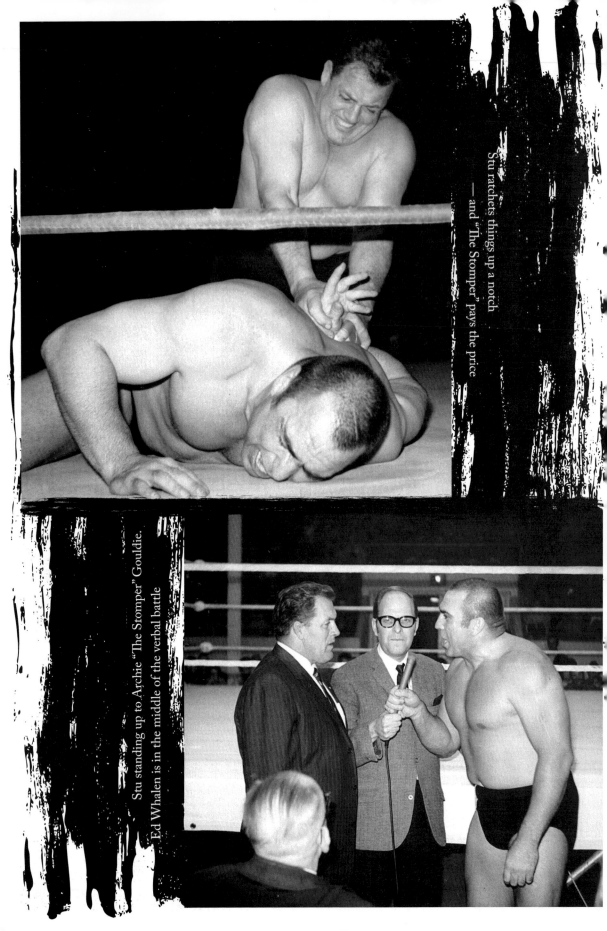

Stu ratchets things up a notch — and "The Stomper" pays the price

Stu standing up to Archie "The Stomper" Gouldie.
Ed Whalen is in the middle of the verbal battle

ABOVE: The Dynamite Kid and Duke Myers

BOTTOM LEFT: Dynamite posing with J.R. Foley

BOTTOM RIGHT: Dynamite with me and Andre the Giant

TOP: I convinced The Giant to join a charity softball team for a tournament in Calgary. Among our teammates were world champion cowboy Larry Mahan (kneeling, next to Andre) and "Mr. Hockey" Bobby Hull at right.

RIGHT: NWA World Heavyweight Champion Harley Race and I do a TV interview, promoting the annual "Tournament of Champions" cards at the Calgary Stampede.

BOTTOM: Me, Owen and Bret — with Stu in the Stampede parade

VOL. 11
NO. 49
25¢

OFFICIAL
WRESTLING
PROGRAM
FOOTHILLS
ATHLETIC
CLUB

Body Press

PRIME MINISTER TRUDEAU — HEAVYWEIGHT CHAMPION DORY FUNK

A world champion meets a prime minister. Dory Funk Jr., world's heavyweight wrestling champion, had t[
opportunity in Calgary recently to meet the top man in Canada's government, Prime Minister Pierre Elliott Trudea[
The occasion was a Liberal barbecue held at Calgary's Heritage Park during the time the PM was in the city for t[
Calgary Stampede. Said Funk, an American: "A most impressive man. And you don't always get First Ladies th[
beautiful."

ABOVE: Dynamite slams me to the canvas with a double-underhook side suplex

BELOW: Owen and I, all business before a rare tag team match

ABOVE: Though we didn't team frequently, Bret and I joined forces on occasion

BELOW: In the ring with Bret and Keith

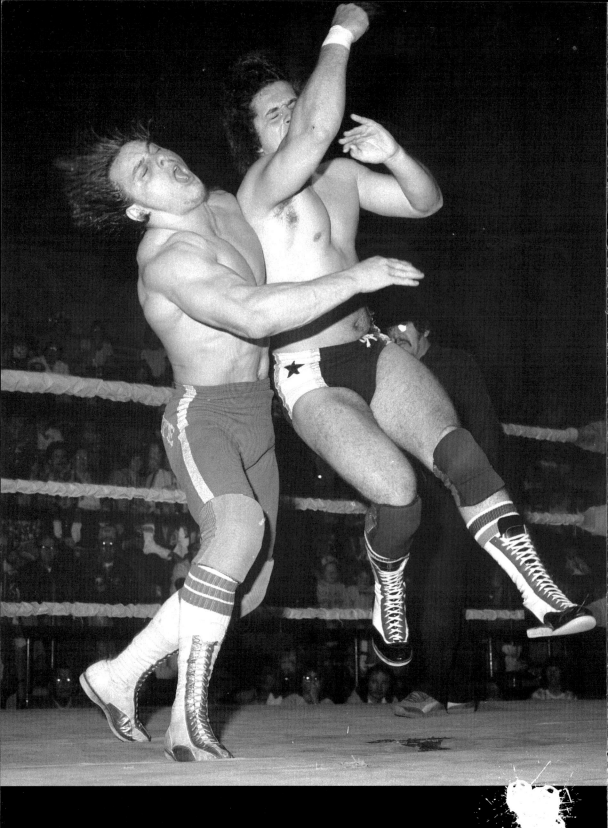

BRET'S UPPERCUT CONNECTS WITH DYNAMITE'S CHIN

Beyond that, he said that Bret had notified him that he was heading to Japan in June, after which he was going to work in New Zealand and Australia. Bret, Keith and my mom were of the opinion that we should shut the territory down for the summer and reopen in the fall — supposedly with a new head of steam. He was curious as to what I thought.

I told him that, in my opinion, if he were to shut down for the summer, not only would he lose Dynamite — who was probably the best worker in the business at that time — but my mom would likely do everything in her power to make sure he didn't open up again in the fall. My dad told me he felt exactly the same way. He then paused, for what seemed like a long time, and said he'd heard, from Dean and Owen, that I'd been handling the book for Peter and reportedly getting good results. He paused again, and I kind of sensed where he might he heading; he inquired whether I might be interested in handling the book back in Calgary.

To be honest, after having been bypassed for several years by unproven younger brothers, overrated old retreads and assorted other nondescripts, my initial inclination was to decline his offer. I sensed though, that if I did, he probably would just shut the territory down and that, unfortunately, would be the end of the line for Stampede Wrestling. As a result, I told him I'd take the book but felt quite bad about leaving Peter and Rocky in the lurch — especially after they'd shown so much faith in me and treated me like family.

RUNNING THE GAMUT

21
TAKING THE BOOK

When I got back, business was as flat as a turd that had dropped from a tall cow's behind — as some esteemed cowboy philosopher once put it — and the roster was about as threadbare as a ten-year-old pair of Levi's. Since things were so lousy, I knew that if I didn't succeed, at least they couldn't lay all the blame on me.

One thing I'd come to learn over the years in the business was that all you can do is play with the hand you've been dealt. About the only guys we had at the time who were marketable were Dynamite (who was an awesome talent but was on the limp, due to a torn knee ligament) and Kasavubu (Jimmy Lee Banks). Kasavubu was a massive black heel along the lines of Kamala, but a lot livelier. He was a pretty fair hand but had just been diagnosed with a debilitating kidney disease that would, tragically, kill him, in less than a year. Aside from them, we had a couple of not bad Hispanics — Ruben Cruz, a.k.a. "Hercules Ayala," and Felix Lopez — neither of whom spoke English, which impeded their ability to get over, as hardly anyone in Western Canada was fluent in Spanish. Beyond that, the cupboard was bare, with another motley crew of non-descripts and castoffs — none of whom had been setting the territory on fire. In taking stock of what we had to play with, I found there were a couple of old guys my dad had pretty much put out to pasture — John Foley and Alexander Scott — who'd been reduced to part-time status, occasionally doing jobs in the opening matches, refereeing and helping set up the ring. They were essentially charity cases, guys my dad tried to find some use for, but who my mom figured were just two more mouths to feed.

Even though they were at the bottom of the proverbial pecking order, I'd always been respectful of Scott and Foley for doing whatever they'd been asked and also — perhaps because of my own tenure as a jobber — I figured that, if given a chance, they could perhaps be of some value.

After giving it some consideration, we came up with this story line where Foley had ostensibly inherited a fortune. He was suddenly transformed into a megalomaniacal George Steinbrenner heel manager type, who was intent on buying all the championships — kind of like a precursor to the role the Million Dollar Man (Ted DiBiase) did a decade later in the WWF. At that time, the hot-test heel on television was J. R. Ewing of *Dallas*, so we changed Foley's name to J. R. Foley. Foley — who was exceedingly grateful for the new lease on life — put his heart and soul into the new role and immediately became one of the hottest heels in the territory.

As for Alexander Scott, just before I returned from Hawaii, I'd seen some late-night old movie about this pious cop who was always sanctimoniously lec-turing everyone but, in actuality, was crooked as hell — kind of like that asshole warden in *The Shawshank Redemption*. Bob Gunton played that role and had done an awesome job; I found myself hating his guts. I got to thinking that perhaps a similar role — as a holier than thou heel referee — might perfectly suit Scott. So I ran it by him.

Like Foley, Scott was grateful for any bone I could throw his way and he, too, launched himself into the role with fervor. In a matter of weeks he would also become one of the most despised heels in the history of Stampede Wrestling.

Even though they were non-wrestlers, Foley and Scott would prove to be invaluable members of our supporting cast — kind of like Robert Duvall's Tom Hagen character in *The Godfather*. What was really cool was that we didn't have to go out and spend money on them, yet they were suddenly transformed into key players.

Our big event every year was in July: the annual Stampede Week show, which coincided with the world famous Calgary Stampede ("the greatest outdoor show on earth"). It was our version of WrestleMania or the Super Bowl. Ordinarily, my dad would pull out all the stops, bringing in the NWA world champion, guest referees like Rocky Marciano, Jersey Joe Walcott and Muhammad Ali, as well as special attractions, like lady wrestlers, midgets, wrestling bears and whatever else. This time around though, with business having been so lousy and the future of the whole promotion in serious doubt, my dad hadn't lined up much of anything. The show was shaping up to be our weakest Stampede Week extravaganza ever and cause for considerable concern.

About a month before Stampede Week, I got a call from Dick Steinborn, who'd been wrestling in the southern states since he left Calgary. He mentioned that he'd recently acquired the NWA world junior heavyweight belt — which, at one time, had been quite prestigious, especially in the South, but with the increasing emphasis among NWA promoters to push heavyweights, they were kind of phasing it out. He said that since Calgary had been pushing junior heavyweights like Dynamite, Bret, myself and Keith, perhaps we might have some interest in having him drop the strap. Seeing as we didn't have much on the go for Stampede Week, I was more than happy to invite Tricky Dick to come up.

To determine an opponent for Steinborn, Dynamite and I worked a match, with the winner earning the crack at the world title — which, by the way, we decided to now refer to as the mid-heavyweight belt, rather than junior heavy-weight (to me, that moniker always suggested underage).

My intent had been to put Dynamite over — with him going on to meet Steinborn — but he told me that he was getting arthroscopic knee surgery after Stampede Week, which would probably keep him out of action for some time. Beyond that, he figured that since both he and Steinborn were heels, it might be a better draw if I, being a babyface, worked with Dick.

I could see where he was coming from, but I told him that in the past when-ever any new person had gotten the book, almost without exception, they started pushing themselves — winning belts and whatnot — and that I didn't want to be perceived that way. Dynamite said he could appreciate that, but the important thing at this critical juncture was to do what was best for the promotion, and, in this case, he felt that meant me getting my hand raised.

Earlier that night, an old face from the past, Dan Kroffat, had dropped by to say hi to my dad. He told me that he'd just finished a stint working as a prison guard and was back in town, selling cars, and might be interested in working a few shots. Even though others in my family couldn't stand Kroffat, I figured that since we had virtually nothing else to work with, why not have him get involved on the finish and shoot an angle to work with Dynamite? It would at least give us one other half-decent match on the card.

That's what we ended up shooting for and the fans popped on the finish — which set us up perfectly for Stampede Week. Even though most of the doubters had predicted a big disaster, we wound up selling out and turning away nearly a thousand fans. The matches themselves went great, with Kroffat and Dynamite having a hell of a match and my match with Steinborn getting one of the most resounding pops I've ever heard. It was pretty gratifying, seeing as only a few weeks earlier everyone had been predicting Stampede Week would be a disaster and imploring my dad to throw in the towel and shut down.

Perhaps the most satisfying aspect for me came the next day when my dad phoned to say Bret had called him from Tokyo, almost as if he wanted to console him and commiserate about what was supposed to be the worst Stampede Week on record. My dad said that when he related the "excellence of execution" — that not only had the show gotten over huge, we'd also had to turn away over a thousand fans — Bret almost seemed deflated. I thought that was kind of cool.

Better still, the world title change seemed to spark a revival within the promotion and our gates took off almost immediately. For the rest of the summer, we drew near capacity crowds — which up until that time was completely unheard of.

When things are going well in the wrestling business, word spreads. We soon began having quite a few pretty big names wanting to come up and work for us, including the likes of Cyclone Negro, Buzz Sawyer, Dave Morgan, Bulldog Brower and Adrian Adonis. However, I'd come to find that most of the guys who'd drawn well up here had been homegrown or developed from within, including guys like Stan Stasiak, the Stomper, Abdullah, Greg Valentine, Buddy Roberts, Killer Kowalski, Waldo Von Erich and, more recently, Dynamite, Bret, Junkyard Dog and Jake Roberts. Consequently, I wasn't keen on importing a bunch of high-priced stars from elsewhere and, instead, figured we could develop from within.

That fall, we were able to build up several up-and-comers but until that time complete unknowns, including David Schultz, Kerry Brown, Mike Sharpe, Jude Rosenbloom, T. G. Stone and Randy Webber. All of them proved to be valuable additions and several of them would go on to become big stars.

22
SILENCING THE CRITICS

Even though we'd enjoyed the best summer on record, there were still a number of people doubting my abilities — claiming, among other things, that it was beginner's luck. Frankly, I've never given a rat's ass what the cynics have to say. As long as I can look myself in the mirror and know I've done the best with what I had to work with, I'm fine. By that token, I was not only pleased with the results, but honestly felt that we had just scratched the surface and could more than sustain our momentum.

When I look back on the amazing run we had that first summer, probably the most amusing thing was how everyone was suddenly taking sellout crowds for granted — as if we'd been turning away fans and garnering rave reviews for years and years, which we certainly hadn't been. I never said much at the time. I just allowed myself to enjoy the ride.

Late that fall, even though I remained the hottest face in the territory and could easily have chosen to keep the world mid-heavyweight strap as long as wanted, I decided to drop it to Dynamite. My rationale was that, in winning it in the first place, it had served to get me and the belt over, but putting it on Dynamite — given his unmatched propensity for getting whomever he worked with over — would better serve the promotion.

When I dropped the title to Dynamite we had a hot finish and got over so well that I gained more glory in defeat than for damn near any match I ever won. To every face who thinks they need a belt to remain over, let me be an example: holding the strap isn't as important as how the fans perceive you. In any case, with Dynamite wearing the strap, J. R. Foley's millionaire manager persona becoming a huge focal point and new faces getting over (such as Davis Schultz, Duke Myers, Kerry Brown, Mike Sharpe and Kelly Kiniski), we headed into what was traditionally our strongest part of the season, winter, in great shape. One of the nice things about that stretch was that, unlike in the past, there were virtually no conflicts, political machinations or any of that sort of thing — which made things so much easier.

Like one of those ill-fated Middle East peace treaties, the tranquility would be short-lived. My brother Bret returned from abroad in the fall and demanded to be reinstated as booker. He claimed that he'd only temporarily relinquished the book because he figured my dad was shutting down for the summer. Since business was now on an unprecedented roll and morale in the territory had never been better, my dad was reluctant to rock the boat.

In an effort to appease Bret, who, as Vince McMahon can attest, can be a "my way or the highway" guy, my dad came up with a half-assed compromise which called for Bret to have complete autonomy over all his own matches, finishes and whatnot, with me handling the rest of the matches and story lines. To be honest, I wasn't thrilled with the new format. To me, it was like letting some egocentric football or baseball player — say, Terrell Owens or Barry Bonds — call his own shots regardless of what the rest of the team was doing. But since I wasn't signing the checks, I didn't have much choice but to go with the flow, as they say, and try to make the best of the less than ideal situation.

While Bret's finishes and story lines didn't always jibe with what the rest of us were doing, I worked around it and our gates remained strong. Eventually the novelty of dancing to his own tune seemed to wear off for Bret and early in the new year, he approached me and told me he'd be willing to work with me doing the finishes, as long as he had some input in how I used him. I told him that any decent booker or coach should be seeking input and feedback from the rest of the team anyway and that my door was always open, as they say. We shook hands on things and proceeded from there.

23
GLORY DAYS

As things turned out, the hottest program in the promotion that winter involved Bret and me. Ed Whalen followed my lead, calling us the original Hart Foundation. We tagged to wrestle against Dynamite and Schultz and we had some ass-kicker matches.

Coming into the spring of 1981, we'd been selling out for close to ten months straight and, with no end in sight, the territory was on the best roll since my dad had opened back in 1948. Around that time, Bret dropped a bit of a bombshell when he announced that he and Dynamite had gotten married to two sisters from Saskatchewan, Julie and Michelle Smadu, in a secret ceremony down at city hall and that they were planning on heading over to Germany for the rest of the year, on a quasi-wrestling honeymoon.

That left us in a bit of a pinch because Dynamite had been our top heel while Bret had been one of our main faces. Ever since I'd taken the book, Dynamite's old trainer, Ted Betley, had been begging me to book Dynamite's cousin, David Smith, whom he rated as a can't-miss prospect as well. When I first discussed this with Dynamite, much to my surprise, he was vehemently opposed to it — claiming that one of the reasons he'd left England in the first place was because he didn't get along with his cousin. He even went so far as to say that if I brought Smith in, he would leave. Since Dynamite was the face of the franchise, I'd always have to kayfabe Betley and tell him we were all booked up, but that I'd keep Smith in mind.

With Dynamite now leaving for an extended period of time, I figured this might be a good opportunity for us to check out his highly touted cousin. I contacted Betley and gave him a starting date for the end of April, which coincided with Dynamite and Bret's departure. When I mentioned to Dynamite that I'd booked his cousin, he wasn't thrilled, but in his typical terse and truculent manner, shrugged indifferently and said that seeing as he wouldn't be here anyway, he really didn't give a shit.

The week before Dynamite and Bret were scheduled to leave for their European hiatus, the German promoter suddenly canceled — reportedly because our old friend Axel Dieter was still bitter about some of the ribs that Dynamite and my brother Smith had perpetrated on previous tours.

In any case, that meant that Bret and Dynamite would be staying put. This was fine with me, because they were two of the best workers in the business. At the same time, we had a bit of a predicament, since Dynamite's cousin, along with a couple of other British guys — Adrian Street and Robbie Stewart, whom Betley had also represented — were scheduled to start the following week. I approached Dynamite and explained that since they'd already bought plane tickets and canceled all their other bookings in England, I was obliged to bring them over and I hoped this wouldn't cause any conflict.

Ever the enigma, Dynamite not only said that he understood the situation and would try to put aside his differences, but he even went so far as to suggest that he'd like to work with Smith on his first night, because he knew his style and could help get him over.

Back in England, Smith had wrestled under the somewhat drab name "Young David." I was endeavoring to come up with something a little catchier when I happened to hear some sportscaster on the radio, hyping an upcoming boxing title bout between lightweight champion Sugar Ray Leonard and up-and-coming British contender Davey Boy Green. I kind of liked the ring of that and decided to change Smith's name to Davey Boy Smith. Much like Steve

Williams becoming "Stone Cold" Steve Austin or Dwayne Johnson becoming the Rock, the name would stick and become an iconic handle.

For Davey Boy's debut match in the territory, Dynamite went out and made his cousin look like a million dollars, which added one more weapon to our already formidable arsenal of young stars.

Although the territory had improved by leaps and bounds since I'd taken the book, it didn't really dawn on me how far we'd come until July 1981 and our annual Stampede Week show, when my dad brought up the legendary Lou Thesz — who's still considered by most to have been the greatest world champion of all time — to be a special guest referee.

I had the chance to ride around the circuit that week with Lou, which was like some wide-eyed hockey junkie getting to ride around with Gordie Howe for a week. I was fascinated by all the stories of the wrestling business of the old days and gained a wealth of knowledge and insight. On Lou's final night in the territory, he came up to me and thanked me for having him up for the week. He said that he'd seen a lot of wrestling the past few decades, but that our brand of wrestling was the best he'd seen since the 1950s. I was completely blown away to receive an endorsement like that — from someone of his magnitude. That remains one of the crowning moments of my career.

That fall, our business hit even higher levels, with gates selling out almost every night in virtually every venue and our television ratings going through the roof. I was especially gratified for my parents — both of whom had endured more than their share of lean years and stress.

24
WAKE-UP CALL

We worked our way into 1982 riding our best season ever. On the night of January 14, I was heading to Lethbridge with Jim Neidhart, Gerry Morrow, Mr. Hito and one of the referees, Kevin Tremblay. As we were motoring along, I noticed this big semi, which had been heading toward us, suddenly begin edging into the intersection, to turn into a truck stop on our right. Given that we were going straight and obviously had the right of way, I naturally figured he'd yield, but instead the moron suddenly began turning his big rig — with two trailers behind him — right in front of us. In a matter of seconds, the whole highway was blocked and we ended up colliding head-on — at close to seventy miles per hour. Fortunately, I had my seat belt on. But I was still badly shaken up. The crash separated my shoulder, smashed my face through the windshield and my chest into the steering wheel so hard that it snapped. It bruised my heart so much that doctors said the impact was akin to having had a heart attack. As for the other passengers, Neidhart went face-first through the windshield, nearly tearing off his nose and lacerating his throat severely, while Hito dislocated his hip and Morrow sustained a broken leg.

After the initial impact, I was dazed and concussive and trying to extricate myself from the wreckage. Since my door was mangled, I had to kick out the window and climb out and just after I'd done that, I felt something brush by my coat sleeve and then heard a huge smash. I turned to see that a pickup truck had nearly hit me and had then smashed head-on, as well, into the semi. Though I was half-dazed, it suddenly dawned on me that I'd escaped death, twice, in a matter of seconds. I quickly got my ass off the highway, but was definitely counting my blessings afterward.

Because of the injuries I'd sustained in the car wreck, the doctors told me that I'd be on the shelf for an extended period of time: a mid-winter break might be advisable. I headed to Kauai for a few weeks, with my brother Dean, to recuperate. While there, I had a chance to collect my thoughts and reflect on things with Dean — who, along with my brother Owen, was the sibling I'd always been closest to. In sharing perspectives with Dean, out on the beach, I related that my brush with death made me realize how precious life really is and that there was a lot more to it than merely the wrestling business. I told him that I'd been putting a lot of important things on hold, including starting up a family and other things, but the accident had served as a wake-up call. From then on, I resolved to not put things on hold but to seize the day, as some wise man once said.

A few days after I got back from Hawaii, I was getting ready to head to Saskatoon, where we had a wrestling show that night. Even though I wasn't in the ring, my dad still had me looking after the shows. When I went out to start my car, I found that my battery was dead. I was kind of cursing the situation, as I was running late, when suddenly these two girls pulled up and politely inquired if they could be of any help. One of the girls, Andrea, was really stunning — so much so that I was almost in disbelief. After getting a boost, I was about to pull away when suddenly the other girl nervously inquired if she could get my autograph — "for her little brother." I was more than happy to oblige and, even though I never thought they'd see fit to show up at the wrestling matches, I nonetheless invited them to come down to see wrestling sometime.

As I drove away, I was trying to wrap my head around what had been happening. First, I'd had this near fatal car wreck, then the seemingly prescient conversation with Dean in Kauai about how I'd always wanted to start a family and whatnot, and now, like some kind of angel, this stunning blonde had dropped in, from out of the blue. As I said before, I'm not what you'd call a religious type, but I found myself thinking that the stars definitely seemed to be lining up in my favor.

That Friday night, I heard a few of the wrestlers in the dressing room discussing — as they're often prone to — this blonde in the ringside audience who was unusually hot, a real eye-catcher. Intrigued, I decided to see for myself what was causing so much attention. I was pleased to find it was the girl I'd seen earlier that week. Much to the amazement and chagrin of the other wrestlers, I strolled up, kind of nonchalantly, and picked up where I'd left off with her. Andrea and I went out that night for a drink after the matches. Soon, we were inseparable — we were married fifteen months later.

As for the wrestling business, at the time of my car wreck, things had been on an unprecedented high, but with me, Neidhart, Hito, Morrow and Davey Boy all out of action, that left us really short of faces, with Bret being about the only marketable good guy left.

As a result, it was obvious we might have to switch one of our heels to a face. Some tend to think that switching a heel to face or vice versa is just a matter of changing roles, whenever and wherever, but, contrary to what they'd have you think, there's actually a method to the madness.

The first thing is the element of surprise, in that when you orchestrate a switch, it should catch everyone completely off guard — if they see it coming, it won't amount to anything. The other key premise to a good switch is the love/hate element. If the fans really love a face — as they had when Dynamite switched to heel — or if they really despise a heel, chances are they'll get over much better upon switching than if they were only half over before.

I got together with my dad and my brothers Keith and Bret — both of whom still regularly gave me input — and we discussed which heels might be best to switch to face. Keith, Bret and my dad were all leaning toward switching Duke Myers — a heavyset big heel, along the lines of Buddy Rose or Adrian Adonis. I had respect for Duke as a worker, but was of the opinion that the heel we should switch was David Schultz — in part because he was a hell of a talker and had a ton of charisma, which I figured would make him more far more appealing as a face than Myers would have been.

Initially, Bret, Keith and my dad were dead set against it and expressed apprehension that Schultz — who was our most hated heel — was almost too despised to get over as a face. I shook my head and told them that was precisely why Schultz probably *would* get over — because the fans did hate him so much. In the past, I'd come to find that the emotional pendulum tended to swing back all the way in the other direction, so that if a guy was really loved and you perpetrated a switch, they'd hate his guts, or, by the same token, if they hated his guts and you orchestrated a plausible swerve, they'd become his biggest fans.

When I put it in that context, they seemed to get the point and we ended up switching Schultz that Friday night. He would, of course, go on to become one of the most popular and iconic faces in the history of our promotion — very much like "Stone Cold" Steve Austin would later become in the WWF.

25
THE ASIAN INVASION

Near the end of February, Mr. Hito, who was still laid up with the injuries he'd sustained in the car wreck, asked me if I could do him a favor and book a couple of young Japanese guys, Hiro Saito and George Takano, who'd been working in Mexico. In his words, they were starving over there. Since we were still short of talent, I told Hito I'd be happy to oblige.

The next Friday night when I walked into the dressing room in Calgary, much to my surprise, Hito had nearly a dozen Japanese guys with him. He gave me a sheepish grin and told me that since business had been so bad in Mexico, the other Japanese guys had all decided to jump ship as well. He assured me that they'd work for whatever we could pay them and promised me that they'd be no problem either. I kind of heaved a heavy sigh, as I contemplated what was I was going to do with the biggest Japanese invasion since Pearl Harbor.

I introduced myself to the new recruits who turned out to be the aforementioned Saito and Takano, Junji Hirada, Shunji Takano (brother of George), Mach Hayato, Itsa Wakamatsu, Rusher Kimura and Toru Tanaka. Even though my dad had employed some excellent Japanese guys over the years, including Kinji Shibuya, Mitsu Arakawa, Chatti Yokouchi, Yasu Fuji, Tokyo Joe, Kim Sakurada, Higo Hamaguchi and Mr. Hito, for some reason, they'd never really appealed to Japanese or Chinese fans in Western Canada — very few of whom ever seemed to come to our shows. By that token, I figured that there wasn't a lot of point in trying to appeal to that market. With my tongue firmly planted in my cheek, as any good booker should be inclined to do on occasion, I decided that a few modifications might be in order.

I quickly got on a creative roll and within the next few minutes George Takano was transformed into the masked Cobra from Uganda; his brother Shunji had became a Cambodian refugee; Mach Hayato — who also wore a mask — became a Filipino; Junji Hirada was given an Iroquois haircut and renamed Sunni Two Rivers. Toru Tanaka was converted into the heinous Ho Chi Lau — supposedly an insidious North Vietnamese insurgent; Hiro Saito, courtesy of Lady Clairol, was transformed into a platinum-blond Singaporean playboy; while Wakamatsu became this dastardly Dalai Lama–type monk from Tibet who preached love, peace and humility but, of course, refrained from practicing what he preached, like some kind of deranged kamikaze throwback to the Second World War.

When my dad walked into the dressing room later that night, he almost did a double take and grunted, dubiously, about what the hell we were going to do with nearly a dozen Japs masquerading as fucking cowboys and Indians — as he put it. To be honest, I wasn't sure myself, but as it turned out, the Japanese newcomers added one more dimension to our promotion and they would all go on to become valuable additions to our roster.

26
THE CARIBBEAN CAPER

By the late spring, Stampede Wrestling was again firing on all cylinders. That may well have been our high-water mark, artistically speaking. Around that time, an *Edmonton Sun* sportswriter named Terry Jones, who covered the Edmonton Oilers hockey team and the Edmonton Eskimos football team, wrote a column in which he claimed there was something wrong with the mind-set of sports fans in Western Canada when an illicit endeavor like Stampede Wrestling was garnering higher television ratings than the Oilers — who, at that time, had the likes of Gretzky, Messier, Anderson, Kurri, Coffey, Fuhr and Lowe and are still considered by most to have been the most prolific offensive team in hockey history.

Quite a few of the wrestlers were up in arms and wanted my dad to call Jones and demand a retraction. My dad though was quite pleased with the article, so much so that he was thinking of sending Jones a thank-you note and perhaps a bottle of Crown Royal instead. I tended to agree with him; father knows best.

In May, my dad called me and told me he had some visitors up at the house who'd just flown in from the Caribbean — he couldn't remember the name of the country. They claimed they wanted to bring a wrestling show down there and wanted to know if I could drive over to meet them.

It wasn't uncommon for wrestling fans from different parts of the world — be it Australia, Japan, Europe or the United States — to drop in at the house, to meet my dad or wanting to have their picture taken in the infamous Dungeon. I figured this was likely just another group of fans but was more than happy to come and meet them and sign a few autographs or whatever.

When I arrived at the house, my dad introduced me to this laid-back contingent of black guys, most of whom were in Bermuda shorts, flip-flops and whatnot — like some ensemble from those Malibu Rum commercials. They reiterated what my dad had already told me. They were enormous Stampede Wrestling fans and our TV show — via pirated transmission — happened to be the number one ranked show in their country, Antigua. Their mission was to convince my dad to bring Stampede Wrestling to the Caribbean. Initially, I figured they were just hardcore wrestling fans, but was soon informed that they, in fact, were high-ranking government officials — including the secretary of state, the justice minister and the deputy prime minister of the country.

In any case, by the end of the afternoon, my dad, who always seemed to have an appetite for adventure, wound up agreeing to send a contingent of our boys down to Antigua later that summer, with the government agreeing to pay airfare, hotel and expenses, and split the gate.

I was initially planning on making the Antigua show. However, it turned out to be on the same day as a special memorial show in Hawaii for my old friend, Peter Maivia, who had recently passed away. In my place, my dad sent my older brother Smith to look after things and to bring our share of the gate back with him. Among the contingent my dad sent down there for the show were Dynamite, David Schultz, Kerry Brown, Duke Myers, John Foley, Jim Neidhart and Charlie Buffong.

I don't think most of the wrestlers were expecting the show to be anything out of the ordinary — perhaps a chance to enjoy some fun in the sun, which was better, most agreed, than having to drive to Saskatchewan. To everyone's surprise though, the gate was well over $100,000, which made it, far and away, the biggest gross we'd ever drawn.

Our cut of the gate, I'm told, was in excess of $70,000 — which meant that most of the boys, especially guys like Dynamite and Schultz, who were the main event that night, could be looking forward to big payoffs. On the way home from Antigua, my brother Smith — who'd been entrusted to bring the money back — decided to stop over in nearby Puerto Rico to hook up with Tricky Dicky Steinborn, who was now booking for the promotion down there. Nobody's quite sure what transpired after that, other than that Smith's suitcase, in which he had the gate receipts from Antigua, disappeared — from Steinborn's hotel room. Despite an extensive search, it never turned up. The common conjecture was that Steinborn, who had a reputation within the business for being light-fingered, had ripped it off. In any case, Smith ended up coming home empty-handed and my dad ended up having to pay the wrestlers out of his own pocket. I'm told that Schultz and Dynamite got around $2,000 apiece, with the others getting about half that. Under normal circumstances, that would have been not a bad week's payoff, but given the size of the gate, Dynamite, Schultz and company were pissed with their payoffs and even went so far as to suggest that it might have been an inside job.

As a result, Dynamite gave his notice and booked himself to Portland, while Schultz, who at this time was involved in a big angle with his old buddy the Honky Tonk Man, jumped ship as well and tried to run opposition against my dad in Calgary and Edmonton.

27
BAD NEWS

The loss of Schultz, Honky Tonk and Dynamite — all of whom were playing key roles for us — would take its toll and, for the first time since I'd taken over the book, business declined. Without Dynamite and Honky Tonk — who'd been our top heel — my dad was on the lookout for someone to pick up the slack. Bret and Davey Boy had just returned from a Japanese tour and were effusive in their praise of this big, black heel they'd seen over there, Allen Coage. He wrestled under the moniker "Bad News" Allen.

Bret described him as a cross between Abdullah the Butcher and the Stomper but bigger and more impressive than either of them. This was pretty high praise, since those were two of the hottest heels in the history of our promotion. That would be like a football scout touting a hotshot college quarterback as a cross between Joe Montana and John Elway, but smarter and more mobile.

As an added selling point, Bret also boasted that News was a bona fide shooter, having won an Olympic medal in judo at the 1976 Olympics in Montreal. With a résumé like that, my dad was sold and he offered Bad News the highest weekly guarantee he'd ever given a wrestler — nearly double what he'd been paying Dynamite, who, at that time, was probably the best worker in the business.

Before he arrived, News was being treated like some vaunted first-round draft choice who was going to revive the franchise. On his first night in the territory, the Pavilion was packed, with fans eager to see the latest big thing.

News made an impressive debut, destroying some jobber and cutting a pretty intense promo afterward, in which he touted himself as the Ultimate Warrior — long before, I might add, anyone had ever heard of Jim Hellwig.

In those days, whenever a new heel came to a territory, the norm was to have him destroy whichever faces he was matched against in his first few weeks — kind of like Mr. T in *Rocky III*. That would establish the new heel's heat and create the anticipatory buzz for him to take on the top faces.

For the first month or so that "Bad News" Allen was in the territory, things went according to plan, with him destroying some pretty decent faces including Mr. Hito, Hercules Ayala and Gerry Morrow. In most cases, they bled for him and ended up being carried out on stretchers — all of which served the purpose of getting him over and priming him for the big title showdown against our current champion: Bret.

At this point, Bret continued to be one of News' strongest supporters — so much so that he said he'd be more than happy to drop the strap to News, to help get him over. I thought that was pretty decent of him. We had News win the strap the next week on a hot finish. Thus far, everything had smoothly established Bad News as our dominant, alpha heel.

Once a new heel has had his initial run in a territory and run roughshod over everyone, he's then usually obliged to return the favor. He's supposed to make prospective challengers look like they're capable of beating him — which is, of course, what compels the fans to buy tickets. All of that is pretty much understood from the get-go, or so I thought. No sooner than we'd put the strap on him and were expecting News to start selling and taking bumps for the faces, though, then he suddenly exhibited this pronounced reluctance to sell or take bumps....

Some of the boys attributed his reluctance to sell to his vaunted reputation as a shooter — something that was relatively common among egocentric amateur champions coming into the professional ranks. I, frankly, never thought that was the problem. In talking to News, I never discerned he had any problem having to sell for the faces.

From what I could see, the problem stemmed from the fact that he was nearly forty when he broke into pro wrestling, which was pretty late to be starting and, since the Japanese office that started him had put him over from the outset as a dominant heel, he had never really learned how to take bumps or sell. In Japan — where monster heels like Allen didn't have to take many bumps or sell that often — News could get away with it. But that didn't cut it in North America.

Adding insult to injury, Allen also informed my dad and me that, because of some congenital disorder, he was unable to get juice.

That, of course, didn't sit well with babyfaces like Bret, Davey Boy, Hito and company — all of whom had gotten juice several times for News. Several of them complained long and loud to me and my dad, claiming that News' congenital disorder was bullshit and it was all just part of his self-serving agenda.

Beyond all else, News' refusal to sell, take bumps or get color made for some pretty lousy matches — but since my dad had invested a lot of money in him and didn't want to admit he might have made a mistake, he was insistent that we keep pushing him as our top heel.

Things, unfortunately, didn't improve. None of the faces wanted to work with News and gates declined by the week.

Making matters worse, News had a propensity for brawling out on the floor and wading into the crowd, using fire extinguishers, chairs and whatever else to batter his opponents. That type of thing was pretty common in Japan. We used to refer to it as the "Godzilla syndrome," after those grainy Japanese monster movies from the '50s. However, fighting in the crowd and beyond the designated ringside area was strictly forbidden by the boxing and wrestling commissions in places like Calgary and Edmonton — for fear of riots or fans getting injured.

In the past, most of the heels complied with that regulation, but News would routinely wade out into the crowd, bowling over spectators and beating the hell out of his opponents. As a result, the commissions began levying heavy fines — which my dad ended up paying. That didn't seem to deter Bad News either. He continued to break the rules — almost defying the commission or anyone else to do anything about it.

Eventually, the head of the commission in Calgary — a guy named Gordon Grayston, who'd been a flunky referee for my dad back in the '60s, but was now on a power trip because of his position — suspended Bad News indefinitely. That put us in an awkward position. Calgary was where we shot our television show and with our lead heel and champ unable to appear on TV, it compromised the hell out of our ability to get story lines over.

At that point, quite a few of the boys, including Bret, Davey Boy and myself, urged my dad to cut his losses and find another lead heel. My dad, however, felt that News had been unfairly treated by Grayston and stubbornly stuck by him. That was noble on his part, I suppose; Grayston had, in fact, been an asshole. Nonetheless, it didn't solve our problem of having no lead heel and gates on the slide. For the next few months, things continued to deteriorate. News wrestled on top in our other towns, but since he wasn't on television, there wasn't much interest.

Being the booker, I soon found myself taking the heat for the lousy gates. I didn't feel it was warranted, and I chose to shrug it off. If there was one thing I'd come to realize the past few years, it was that when things are going well, the boys usually take the bows and when they're not going well, the guy calling the shots is usually the first they point fingers at. As some unemployed football coach once ruefully noted, "It's easier to fire the coach than to replace the whole roster"; that's probably why supposedly great coaches like Mike Shanahan, Mike Holmgren, John Gruden and Bill Belichick have all been fired at one time or another.

28

THE GREAT STOMPER/
"BAD NEWS" ALLEN DEBACLE

With business on its ass and Bad News still getting his high salary even though he wasn't allowed to work, my dad got a blast from the past: Archie "The Stomper" Gouldie said he wanted to return. My dad was more than happy to invite him back — offering him the same exorbitant salary that News had been getting and figuring our problems would now be solved.

Given what the Stomper had accomplished back in the '60s and early '70s, I could see why my dad would think that way, but we were now into the 1980s and not only was Archie on the other side of fifty, but his slow, methodical style had been replaced by faster, more dynamic heels like Dynamite. I expressed my concerns; however, my dad was of the opinion that Archie would have no trouble rising to the occasion.

That, unfortunately, wasn't the case. The fans — most of whom had become accustomed to the high tempo style of Dynamite and the Japanese — didn't take to Archie's methodical, grab a hold and keep coming back to it style. Beyond that, most of the faces that Archie was working with, including Davey Boy, Bret and Two Rivers, began complaining about that same slow, deliberate style. Davey Boy and Bret, in fact, used to refer to Archie as "Molasses" — because, according to them, he moved like molasses in winter.

In any case, rather than being the answer to our problems, Archie's arrival seemed only to make matters worse, as we now had two overpriced lead heels, neither of whom was drawing a dime and neither of whom any of the faces wanted to work with.

With things in a real state of disarray and my dad losing money at an alarming rate, it became imperative that things get back on track, or the whole train might be derailed. My dad and I met with the mayor of Calgary, Ralph Klein, who was a good friend, and we were able to persuade him to have the commission reinstate Bad News, so he'd, at least, be able to wrestle in Calgary.

That seemed to be a step in the right direction, but even after News was reinstated, we still weren't drawing with him on top.

As for the Stomper, unlike Bad News, he seemed genuinely concerned about the state of the territory and was almost apologetic that he hadn't been getting the job done — as he used to put it. He was constantly trying to offer solutions and ideas that he hoped might get things back on track.

One of his ideas was that we bring up this rookie, Tommy Rogers, who he'd apparently been training down in Tennessee and bill him as his son, "Jeff Gouldie." Since Archie and my dad had this long running feud since the 1960s, Archie figured that he and his "son" could challenge me and Bret — who had the tag straps in the territory at the time. The Gouldies vs. Harts family feud might do some business.

On paper, it sounded pretty hot — kind of like Stampede Wrestling's answer to the Hatfields and McCoys. I ran the idea by Bret and my dad, both of whom seemed to like it, so we then brought Archie's "son" up from Tennessee for the big angle.

There was only one snag: Archie's supposed kid — whom he'd touted as a hell of a worker — turned out to be green as grass, nervous and tentative, and he looked like he'd never been in the gym before, much less a wrestling ring. Bret and I worked several tag matches with Archie and his kid — most of which were the shits. After the matches, Bret would be bitching, long and loud, about how lousy the kid was and berating me for having brought him up in the first place.

I finally had to inform Archie that the experiment with his kid didn't seem to be working and that we'd probably have to go another direction.

Archie was apologetic that the kid hadn't lived up to expectations, but in talking with him, I came up with this idea that since his kid would be leaving, perhaps we could work some kind of angle around it. Back in the '70s, Archie had done enormous business working against Abdullah the Butcher. I therefore proposed a heel vs. heel scenario, with Archie and Bad News having a falling out in a tag match — which would then lead to them feuding with each other.

Archie seemed to like the concept, as did my dad and Bad News. So we set up an angle that Friday for a triple tag match, pitting Archie, his kid and Bad News in a triple tag elimination match against three of our top faces — Sunni Two Rivers, Davey Boy and Bret. On the finish, we had News, along with his partners in crime K. Y. Wakamatsu and Kerry Brown, perpetrate this dastardly double cross, which resulted in Archie's kid being piledriven into the concrete floor and supposedly crippled, while his father, Archie, looked on in horror.

Afterward, Archie took the microphone and cut what was probably the most intense and compelling promo I've heard in this business — vowing to get revenge on News for what he'd done to his son.

Subsequent to that, Ed Whalen — who was scheduled to have three weeks off because he had to do two Calgary Flames games and was taking a Christmas holiday — was supposed to make out that he was so disgusted with the whole thing that he was quitting the show in protest. He cut an equally compelling promo, announcing his resignation — all of which had the crowd in a frenzy, which was exactly the desired effect.

Afterward in the dressing room, everyone was ecstatic with how well things had gone. It was kind of like the scene at the end of *The Sting*, when Paul Newman, Robert Redford and company congratulate each other after having pulled off the big sting. It looked like we finally had gotten things back on track.

At that point, my dad came into the dressing room with a grim look on his face and informed everyone that Gordon Grayston — the head of the commission and the guy who'd been at odds with Bad News for the past several months — had blown a gasket at all the heat and was vowing to throw the book at us.

The next day in the newspapers, it was announced that the boxing and wrestling commission (of which Grayston was chairman) was fining my dad over $15,000 and that his wrestling promoter's license had been suspended for the rest of the year. That was a real kick in the nuts.

Because of all the controversy, Ed Whalen, whose initial resignation had been a work, now had no choice but to walk away for real, which was a huge blow, as he was an invaluable member of the team. In light of all the controversy, Stomper, who was pretty high-strung at the best of times, also quit — which meant the whole angle, the one that should have enabled us to turn things around, had now become a complete washout.

Seeing as I'd been the mastermind of the whole thing, I caught most of the heat. I really wouldn't have minded if I felt it was warranted, but what pissed me off was that I hadn't broken any rules or done anything that didn't get over. The only reason, in fact, that there was all this heat was that the whole thing had been executed so well that the fans, heaven forbid, believed it was actually real, kind of like Orson Welles' *War of the Worlds* charade back in the 1930s.

29
PLAY IT AGAIN, SAM

For the rest of the year, my dad had to run his Calgary shows — and shoot our TV program — in a cramped gymnasium on the Sarcee Indian Reservation on the outskirts of town. It kicked the hell out of our gates, especially since there was no access to public transportation. Making matters worse, with Ed Whalen out of the picture, my dad had to come up with a new commentator, in short order. Whalen had recommended one of his cronies at CFAC television, Eric Bishop, who'd done football play-by-play for the Calgary Stampeders broadcast for several years. Having no background in wrestling, Bishop was initially tentative and seemed out of his element, but week by week he was getting better and I figured that once he got the hang of things, he'd be okay.

We got some good news just before Christmas, when Dynamite Kid called and said he'd like to come back in January. It was like when Michael Jordan called the Chicago Bulls after his abortive attempt to play baseball and informed them that he wanted to come back. With Dynamite returning, plus the fact that we still had some awesome babyfaces to feed him including Bret, Davey Boy, Two Rivers, Cobra and even myself, I figured it wouldn't take long for things to turn around. Hope springs eternal, as they say.

The week before Dynamite was slated to return, my dad dropped a bit of a bombshell when he called to inform me that he'd decided to replace Eric Bishop with the late (well, almost), not so great Sam "The Sham" Menacker — the same shyster who'd nearly sunk the territory a couple of decades back.

Aside from ripping off my dad's airplane, sabotaging Ernie Roth and all his other transgressions, Sam was now nearly eighty years old, so our bringing him back would have been like NBC bringing back Steve Allen, rather than going with Jay Leno, when Johnny Carson retired.

No one was really sure what my dad had in mind when he chose to bring back Sam the Sham. Most figured that he wanted to prove to the upstart new generation — me in particular — that anything we could do, he and his old cronies were capable of doing better.

On Sam's first night back, my dad informed me that Sam would be offering input on the booking as well. As a booker, I'd always been receptive to input from anyone and everyone and told him I had no problem with that, but before long, Sam was giving me these shorthand pads full of illegibly written finishes, for each and every match, which I was supposed to impart to the wrestlers.

If any of Sam's worn-out recycled ideas from the '50s happened to get over, which was rare, then Sam was hailed as a genius; if they sucked, which was usually the case, then it was because I'd lost something in the translation.

On Dynamite's first night back, Sam wanted him to do a job in the middle of the show for this midcard Japanese heel named Killer Khan. I'm not sure what Sam's rationale was, but when he was apprised of the finish, Dynamite — who was a hothead at the best of times — began to take off his boots and said if that was all we had in mind for him, then he might as well head back to Oregon. My dad interceded and overruled Sam and had Dynamite go over, but the booking and the state of the territory continued to be stuck in neutral.

30
DOWN UNDER

In February 1984, things were not going well with me and Sam when I got a phone call from a promoter in Singapore named Terrence Priest. He told me he was organizing what he called "the world championship victory tour" in Australia, New Zealand and Singapore in March and April. He'd already signed NWA world heavyweight champion Ric Flair and number one contender Harley Race as part of his main event and, since Stampede Wrestling was syndicated in that part of the world, he was hoping he could get me to defend my world mid-heavyweight title on the same tour.

Given that I was the booker in Calgary, in the midst of our peak season, I would ordinarily have turned Priest down, but since I was sick of being Menacker's fall guy, I eagerly took Priest up on his offer and was soon winging my way to the land Down Under.

The tour was interesting, to say the least. Ric Flair and Harley Race were supposed to be the main event every night — wrestling for the NWA heavyweight strap — while I was just under them, defending my world mid-heavyweight belt against the local challengers. Since most of the fans over there didn't seem to know either Flair or Race — both of whom were cast as arrogant American heel types — their matches never got over the way they should have.

I was cast as an obnoxious, egomaniacal American heel type as well, but since I was defending my title against the local champions — most of whom were faces — there was a lot more interest in the outcome of my matches than in Harley's or Ric's.

I hadn't worked heel since my stint in Hawaii with Peter Maivia and company a few years back, but it didn't take long to get back in the swing. I soon had fans hating my guts and cursing me out and all of that — which is, of course, music to your ears if you're a heel.

The fans in New Zealand and Australia were much like the Samoans I'd seen in Hawaii. In Singapore, the promoters had me working with some local favorite and on the finish I was supposed to perpetrate some typical heel skullduggery in order to get my hand raised — no big deal, or so I thought. But as I was making my way through the crowd afterward, I felt something jab me in the ribs and looked down to see that I was bleeding. I made it back to the dressing room and found that I'd been stabbed. Fortunately the blade had hit my rib and I'd only sustained a superficial wound. The wrestlers informed me that the marks in Singapore perceived wrestling to be on the same level as boxing and, by that token, they bet heavily on the outcomes. Whoever had stabbed me was probably pissed off that I'd cost him a bundle.

I managed to laugh and say that if I'd known that, I would have bet a bundle on the outcome myself.

Aside from nearly getting killed, the world title victory tour went pretty well and proved to be a welcome respite from all the turmoil back home.

There was one aspect of the whole tournament that didn't sit well with me though. Nearly every night of the tour, Flair and Race would drop the coveted NWA world heavyweight strap — which was *the* belt in wrestling at the time — back and forth to each other. I was taken aback because in nearly forty years, the NWA belt had never been dropped even once in my dad's territory and, in fact, since the 1940s there had been less than a dozen title switches. Now, in a month or so, they'd dropped the strap that many times in front of a bunch of marginal fans who seemed to have no clue about the magnitude of the belt. Putting it another way, it would have been about like two NHL teams taking the Stanley Cup to, say, Africa and then switching it back and forth every night.

One night halfway through the tour, I was having a beer with Flair and Race and told them that it almost seemed sacrilegious to see the hallowed NWA world title, which dated all the way back to Frank Gotch, being switched nearly every night so frivolously. They both told me that they agreed, but that since the powers that be in the NWA had authorized it, there wasn't much they could do. To me, it wasn't a good sign. A year or so later, the NWA began to crumble from within. It would soon be replaced as the preeminent organization in wrestling by the WWF. I can't say I was all that surprised.

31
ON THE THRESHOLD

When I got back from the Far East, I was informed that Sam the Sham had been canned. I was handed the reins again; in retrospect, after all the bullshit we'd endured the past year or so, I don't think anyone else wanted the unenviable task.

I was chagrined to find that Sam had switched Dynamite — who'd been one of the hottest heels in the history of the promotion — to a babyface. Other than Bad News, who was still being retained even though he hadn't drawn much, our roster of marketable heels was pretty sparse. In sizing up what we had to work with, I decided to try out a recent arrival from Louisiana named Rotten Ron Starr. He was nowhere near as dynamic as Dynamite but had good ring presence and psychology. Not long after I'd taken the book again, Davey Boy and Dynamite told me that on a recent tour of Japan, they'd run into a rock concert promoter from Vancouver named Bruce Allen, who happened to be a huge Stampede Wrestling fan and said that he might be interested in helping with the promotion on the West Coast. I was intrigued, because Allen was considered a legitimate heavyweight in the rock music business, having launched major Canadian bands, such as BTO (Bachman Turner Overdrive), Loverboy and Bryan Adams.

I gave Allen a call and we had a pretty good chat. He was one of those no-nonsense, cut to the chase types and told me that our marketing and presentation left a lot to be desired, but that he, nonetheless, thought we had an awesome product and with a bit of re-tooling we could be huge. He told me that several of his acts, including Bryan Adams and Loverboy, had come to him as relative unknowns and under his tutelage, they'd seen their careers take off. He was confident the same could be the case for Stampede Wrestling, which was good to hear.

Allen was so confident in his ability to do the job and also in our product that he proposed he handle the hype for our next show in Vancouver out of his own pocket with no obligations. If we were happy with how things went, we could cut a deal and, if not, then that was fine, too; we could go our separate ways, no problem.

Seeing as our gates in Vancouver hadn't been very good thus far, with my dad's old crony Gene Kiniski handling the publicity, I told Allen to go for it and we'd see how it went. With Allen handling all the hype, the attendance for our next show nearly doubled. Even more important, he secured sponsorship deals with outfits like Coca-Cola, Canadian Airlines, Nike and Rainier Breweries — all of which was cause for excitement.

After the show, though, Kiniski — who my dad was still giving a percentage of the gate — had some kind of altercation with Allen and even tried to have him thrown out of the building by security. Allen was steamed and leaving when I ran out and persuaded him to come back. He then told my dad that if Kiniski remained part of the promotion, then he wouldn't. Since most of the wrestlers, including Dynamite, Davey Boy, Ron Starr and myself were in Allen's corner, my dad had no choice but to dump Kiniski. It was no big deal, or so most of us thought, as he'd been getting paid twenty percent of the gate for doing virtually nothing but blowing smoke up my dad's butt.

The week after Kiniski had been shown the door, my dad got word that his old friend Vince McMahon Sr., with whom he'd been friends since the 1940s, had passed away. My dad flew down to the States for the funeral — at the time, no one attached much weight to it, but McMahon's passing would soon prove to have major implications for the promotion.

For the rest of the summer, with Bruce Allen now handling all our publicity and hype, our gates improved dramatically. That August, we set up an angle that had me teaming up with the Vancouver Canucks' resident tough guy, Tiger Williams, and taking on Rotten Ron Starr and the "Great" Gama in a big grudge match.

The match seemed to capture the public's imagination and we drew one of the biggest houses in the history of the promotion. The match went great and the crowd reaction was awesome, with the fans all demanding more after the main event had ended — kind of like when fans at a rock concert demand an encore.

Afterwards in the dressing room, the boys were all pumped and with Allen and his rock music friends onboard, we had a feeling that the promotion was about to take off like never before.

There was one thing that seemed a bit disconcerting to me though: in the past, whenever we'd drawn a huge gate, my dad was always visibly buoyed, but this time around, he seemed subdued. About all I could figure was that he was still pissed off at having to get rid of his freeloading crony, Kiniski, and that he'd soon get over it.

Two days later, back in Calgary, I was heading down to the Pavilion for our weekly Friday night card, which was sold out, when I heard on the radio that tonight was going to be the final show for Stampede Wrestling because my dad had sold out to the World Wrestling Federation. I did a double take and was wondering what the hell was going on. When I got to the Pavilion, I made a beeline for my dad, demanding to know what was going on and why I hadn't been told.

My dad was quiet and then divulged that the deal had been finalized while he was at Vince Sr.'s funeral. He said that, at the time, he was pissed off with having been given the ultimatum to get rid of Gene Kiniski and also hadn't liked the way things had gone with the likes of Sam Menacker and Archie Gouldie. So he'd decided to dump the promotion. He conceded, kind of ruefully, that with the territory suddenly taking off again, with Bruce Allen, Tiger Williams and company, he was having second thoughts about the deal, but that he wouldn't go back on his word.

HOPES, DREAMS AND NIGHTMARES

32
GRASPING AT STRAWS

From what I was told, my dad was to receive a million dollars down payment from the WWF as well as ten percent of the gross whenever the WWF ran in any of our towns, including Calgary, Edmonton, Vancouver, Victoria, Regina, Saskatoon or anywhere else in Western Canada. In addition, the WWF would bring my brother Bret and my brothers-in-law Davey Boy Smith and Jim Neidhart onboard and give them lucrative contracts. That was all well and good as far as they were concerned. I was excluded from the whole deal, reportedly because there were concerns that I would have done whatever I could to block it — which, I have to admit, may well have been the case.

I suddenly found myself unemployed with a wife and a ten-month-old baby to feed. The demise of Stampede Wrestling couldn't have come at a worse time. I'd just plowed most of my money into a new house in upscale Oak Ridge and also had a lot of money tied up in another house in Deer Ridge that I was looking to turn into a revenue property. But the economy in Alberta crashed that fall due to the federal Liberal government's despised National Energy Policy; with the downturn in the economy, the real estate market also crashed. As a result, I wound up not only losing both of my houses, but my car as well, and suddenly found myself broke, out of work and grasping at straws.

I'd been through hard times before — back in the '60s when I was a kid — so while I certainly didn't like it, I was somewhat accustomed to it. The person I felt really sorry for was my wife; when she first hooked up with me, I'd been a pretty high-profile and seemingly successful wrestling star, as well as being the booker for one of the hottest wrestling promotions in the business. Now, I was out of work, we had a new baby girl, Brit, but we didn't even have a place to live — all of which was pretty distressing. To her credit, and my great relief, she stuck with me and didn't lose faith. It really meant a lot.

Later on that fall, I was contacted by Vince McMahon's right-hand man, Jim Barnett. He said that since I knew the terrain, they wanted me to handle their publicity for the WWF's shows in Western Canada. Unfortunately, the WWF's gates in Western Canada initially were lousy — in part because their sedentary brand of wrestling paled in comparison to the balls-to-the-wall style our fans had become accustomed to. After about three tours — none of which were very successful — I had yet to receive a penny for my services and called Barnett to inquire what was going on.

Jimsy — who was kind of like wrestling's answer to Truman Capote — seemed quite disconcerted that I had the unmitigated gall to actually demand my money and curtly informed me that my check, which was for the grand total of $150, was in the mail. He then told me that I'd been fired.

With the wrestling business no longer an option, I tried to find a job with the Calgary Board of Education as a schoolteacher, but they told me they weren't hiring at the time. I finally took a $100-a-week job working at a place called Weightlifter's Warehouse, selling nutritional supplements and vitamins, making protein shakes and that kind of thing. Remember when Mickey Rourke's character in *The Wrestler* was working in the deli — that was pretty close to what it was like for me at the time.

A few months after I began my stint at Weightlifter's Warehouse, my dad called me up and told me that Vince McMahon Jr. had just informed him that he couldn't afford to give him the million dollars he'd agreed to pay for the promotion and that the deal was off. In other words, since the WWF was still running shows in Western Canada and had heisted all our best talent and not paid a cent for any of it, he'd just screwed him — far worse, I might add, than he screwed my brother Bret in Montreal a few years down the road.

My dad was royally pissed and told me that since he had a binding legal contract, he was going to sue Vince for the money. The next day though, my dad called me back and said that Bret and Davey Boy were freaking out that if he sued Vince it would cost them their jobs. They'd begged him not to take legal action. He decided to let things slide. It was just another example of my dad sacrificing himself for the cause, I suppose. Unfortunately, in most cases, there was very little gratitude.

33
KICK-STARTING THE PROMOTION, AGAIN

A few weeks later, my dad — still seething over Vince Jr.'s swerve — announced that he was going to start up the promotion again in the fall. I, honestly, didn't think it was a very good idea, as we had lost all of our best guys to the WWF, not to mention our momentum. I felt he was going back for all the wrong reasons. Nonetheless, I could see where he was coming from and told him that in any case, he could count on my support.

We started training a few rookies down in the Dungeon: Chris Benoit, who'd just graduated from high school and had been hanging around the matches in Edmonton for years; my brother-in-law Ben Bassarab, who'd had a few matches in the past; a big weightlifter/football player named Tom Magee, who'd recently won the "World's Strongest Man" contest in Montreal and looked to have a lot of potential; and a former Stampede football player named Les Kaminski, who had a bit of a local following. In addition, we were able to recruit a few veterans, like the Cuban Assassin (Ángelo Acevedo), Gerry Morrow, Mr. Hito, Kerry Brown and the Honky Tonk Man. It gave us a bit of a nucleus to work with.

About a month before our scheduled startup date of October 24, 1985, my dad called me up again and said he had both good and bad news. The good news was that CFAC, our former TV station, had agreed to give us a one-hour time slot and that Ed Whalen had also agreed to come back to do the show.

The not-so-good news was that since I'd been the one who'd orchestrated the ill-fated angle with the Stomper and "Bad News" Allen back in 1983, Whalen was apprehensive about returning if I was the booker. Since having him back was critical to our chances of success, I had no choice but to withdraw, and my dad installed my brother Keith — who was working as a fireman and therefore could only make weekend shots — and the Cuban Assassin to jointly handle the matchmaking.

Although I wasn't pleased with that turn of events, my main priority at that point was that the promotion got off to a good start. I'm not sure if it was due to the booking or if our talent wasn't that good or what, but when we came out of the starting blocks in November, we came out stumbling: terrible crowds, dull, uninspiring matches and one aggravation after another. Since he was losing a ton of money, my dad probably should have just thrown in the towel at that point, but his stubborn pride wouldn't let him admit that reopening had been a huge mistake, so he doggedly persisted.

In March, after five months of lousy business, Ed Whalen, of all people, called up and apologized for having been reticent about me being the booker and asked if I'd consider taking the book again. I wasn't all that keen about it, as things were a mess at the time, but finally agreed to come back and see what we could accomplish.

I'd love to be able to relate that as soon as I took the book again, business suddenly turned around and everyone lived happily ever after, and so on and so forth, but that, unfortunately, wasn't the case. If anything, things seemed to go from bad to worse, as morale among the troops was at an all-time low, with all of our decent talent trying to jump ship to the WWF and most of the others bitching and pointing fingers at everyone but themselves for all the shortcomings.

The only glint of hope when I took the book was that a few of our rookies, such as Chris Benoit, Ben Bassarab and Johnny Smith, had been making some strides. Aside from that, there wasn't much to get excited about. A few weeks after I took the book back, there was something to get excited about though, as my brother Owen approached me and told me that since the University of

Calgary was scrapping its amateur wrestling program and therefore revoking his scholarship, he wanted to turn pro.

Contrary to some of the bullshit I've heard, Owen had a long and deep-rooted passion for the wrestling business and had already wrestled a number of times in the past, including a tour of England and numerous spot shows for our promotion — usually under a mask, or under some bogus assumed name, to protect his amateur status.

I was more than happy to have him come onboard, as not only was he a terrific wrestler but he had a great attitude and also a marvelous sense of humor.

Owen's first road trip could well have served to turn him off the business for good however, as we had to drive nearly eight hundred miles through a raging snowstorm to wrestle in Winnipeg, only to have most of the gate receipts ripped off by this two-bit conman who was masquerading as a promoter named Tony Condello. We then had to drive back through the same snowstorm, empty-handed, with most of the wrestlers bitching and moaning all the way, arriving barely in time for the show in Calgary.

Our main event that night was supposed to have been "Strangler" Steve DiSalvo against Ron Ritchie, but neither of them showed up. We found that they'd both defected for tryouts with the wwf — which had reportedly been arranged by Davey Boy and Dynamite.

I was working that night with this inept alcoholic named Chick Scott, who blew a simple spot, and I wound up blowing out my knee out so badly that my foot was locked in place pointing backwards — kind of like that grotesque Joe Theismann injury. I ended up having to undergo reconstructive knee surgery and my doctors politely suggested that I should, perhaps, consider retiring from the ring. I sometimes regret not having heeded their advice.

34
REMEMBER THE CORRAL

Not long after the first of two operations I'd undergo on my knee, our old friends from the World Wrestling Federation — fresh off the runaway success of WrestleMania — had a big show in Calgary . . . at the Stampede Corral. They had all their big guns on the card, including Hulk Hogan, Andre the Giant, King Kong Bundy and "Macho Man" Randy Savage as well as former Stampede stalwarts, my brother Bret, Davey Boy and Dynamite — who'd recently been crowned the WWF tag team champions.

My dad, Owen and I decided to drop down to the Corral to say hi to Bret and company, whom we hadn't seen in a while. We figured we'd be well received. Upon our arrival though, Davey Boy — who was never known for his tact — came up to my dad and, in front of the rest of the boys, began ridiculing our struggling promotion, claiming it was an embarrassment and asking why my dad didn't just shut it down as he was fast becoming the laughingstock of the whole industry.

Neither Bret nor Dynamite, who were sitting nearby, came to my dad's defense and we let it slide and left shortly thereafter. Afterwards though, my dad expressed his displeasure and rightfully pointed out that if not for Stampede Wrestling, Davey Boy, Dynamite and Bret would not be where they were then.

Owen, who was irate at the way my dad had been treated, also alluded to the fact that my dad could have sued Vince after he'd been screwed but had sacrificed the whole promotion just so those guys could get into the WWF, and this was their way of showing their gratitude?

In much the same way that "Remember the Alamo" went on to become a rallying cry for Texans against the Mexicans, so too would "Remember the Corral" during the upcoming months for Owen, myself and the rest of the boys in Stampede Wrestling.

35
THE YOUNG GUNS

Although Owen was still just getting his feet wet, he soon began to take the territory by storm, similar to when Dynamite had arrived in the late '70s. Owen soon helped to raise the bar for everyone else in the promotion — especially fellow rookies like Chris Benoit, Ben Bassarab and young Japanese guys like Jushin Liger, Hiro Hase and Shinya Hashimoto. Dave Meltzer, the highly respected publisher of the *Wrestling Observer Newsletter*, described Owen as the "best rookie" he had ever seen in the wrestling business and rated him as better than most of the high-profile stars in the WWF.

Because our crew was so sparse at that time, my brother Keith and I ran our first ever open-to-the-public training camp that summer. There were more than a few stiffs and long shots who never amounted to much, but we also were able to turn out a few pretty decent performers, including Biff Wellington, Ken Johnson, Jacques and Gilles des Fosses, Jeff Wheeler and the irrepressible Brian Pillman.

In the past, my dad had broken in several football players who went on to acclaim in wrestling — Woody Strode, Gene Kiniski, Wilbur Snyder, George Wells and Angelo Mosca — but almost everyone of them turned to wrestling after their football careers had fizzled out. Pillman, on the other hand, was the

Stampeders' starting linebacker when he decided to turn his back on football and go into wrestling — something that was virtually unheard of at that time. Like Owen, Pillman had an infectious enthusiasm that served to inspire others in the promotion, as did his outrageous personality. He would quickly become one of the key cogs in the revival of the promotion.

With Owen, Pillman, Bassarab, Benoit and Keiichi Yamada (later Jushin Liger, in the wcw), leading the charge, the quality of our matches began to improve by leaps and bounds. Unfortunately, that still didn't really translate into any great jump at the gates though, as they were all faces and we didn't have anyone to fill the vital lead heel role.

In late September, I received a call from Mike Shaw, a big "Crusher" Blackwell–style heel who'd worked our territory in the past as an undercard wrestler. Shaw would later gain some notoriety in the wwf as Bastion Booger. Mike told me he'd just finished a stint in New Brunswick. He was looking for work and wanted to know if we could use him. Since we were in the market for a heel, I was happy to give him a starting date.

Later that week, in the van on the way to Saskatchewan, Owen and I were kicking around ideas as to how we might use Shaw, especially in light of the fact that when he'd worked the territory before, he'd mostly done jobs and it would be nice if we could give him a new persona or refurbish his image — much like the wwf did, years later, when they converted Dr. Isaac Yankem to Kane.

As we were talking, we heard something on the news about how Pakistan-based terrorists were suspected in the bombing of an airplane and other acts of terrorism against the Canadian government. Owen, who had this sardonic sense of humor, suggested that we could perhaps capitalize on all the prevailing anti-Pakistani sentiments by converting Mike into a "born-again Pakistani" — kind of like a takeoff on those born-again Christian types.

In any case, with tongue firmly planted in cheek, on Mike's first night back, we had this really over the top ceremony in the ring with this Ravi Shankar music blaring full blast throughout the arena while some taxi driver friend of the "Great" Gama's posed as a holy man. Mike was formally ordained as Makhan Singh — kind of along the same lines as when Cassius Clay became Muhammad Ali or Lew Alcindor had become Kareem Abdul-Jabbar. Even though the whole charade was more of a spoof than anything else, it got surprisingly good heat. We now had Makhan and his new heel associates, including Gama and a few others, who came to be known as the Karachi Vice — a cheesy takeoff on the hit TV show *Miami Vice*.

After having Makhan "squash" a few faces in his first few weeks back in the territory, we set up the big showdown between him and Owen, who was now our reigning champion. Their match was slated to take place on Friday, October 31, in Calgary. Since it was Halloween, we announced beforehand that any fans who wore costumes that night would get in for half price. That resulted in a big jump in attendance and also served to enhance the atmosphere, with a lot of off-the-wall types dressed up in bizarre costumes.

That night, as part of the story line, I had several of the guys who were in our training camp dress up in masks depicting politicians such as Richard Nixon, Ronald Reagan, Brian Mulroney and Pierre Trudeau and sit ringside to heckle and harass the heels; it served to get the crowd into things.

At some point during Makhan's match, I had his partner in crime, Gama, wade into the crowd to confront the hecklers. After a heated verbal exchange, Gama slapped a couple of them around. This resulted in my dad — who was always freaking out about the wrestlers assaulting the fans, because of the potential for lawsuits — running up and trying to break them up himself.

After that match, there was an intermission — at which time I had the training camp marks leave their seats. They changed places with Gama and several other heels. Then, during Owen's big showdown with Mike, I had the same "marks" suddenly pull the top rope down on Owen as he was hitting the ropes at full speed. Much to the crowd's horror, he took a wild "ass over tea kettle" type bump onto the concrete floor and appeared to be seriously hurt.

Mike then jumped out of the ring, grabbed Owen, rolled him back into the ring and pinned him to win the North American heavyweight title. I then had the "marks" who'd pulled the top rope down on Owen come into the ring to join in the celebration, at which time they took off their masks — revealing themselves to be Gama and assorted other heels, all of whom had been involved in the earlier altercation with the supposed marks at ringside. The fans were stunned and the angle got a huge reaction, which helped get Mike's title reign off to a good start. With Owen and Makhan leading the charge, our gates finally began to climb. It was good, because my dad had been losing a ton of money since we reopened and the possibility of having to shut down was always in the back of everybody's mind.

36
BILL AND TED'S BOGUS ADVENTURE

Just as we'd begun to emerge from the abyss, it seemed to be the case all too often back then, there was something else threatening to drag us down again. This time, it was what came to be known as the "great musclehead migration."

Around that time, the WWF was really emphasizing bodybuilder types, with guys like Hulk Hogan, Big John Studd, Tony Atlas and that lot. Perhaps to curry favor with the WWF brass or to appease my dad (who seemed to have a thing for big, mesomorphic types), Bret, Davey Boy and Dynamite kept sending these anabolically enhanced, athletically challenged stiffs up to Calgary for us to break in.

By the fall of 1986, the territory seemed to almost be overrun with them, including Ted Arcidi, the reigning world record-holder in the bench press; Bill Kazmaier, who'd won the world power lifting championship several times and was considered to be the Babe Ruth of the power lifting set; Dave "The Barbarian" Barbie, another big juice freak who was nearly as big and impressive as Kazamier; and last and probably least, the one and only Outback Jack, who was also big but as graceful as a kangaroo with two left feet.

Making matters worse, for some reason my dad had been coerced into paying all the power lifter types more than damn near anyone else in the territory, which would become a serious bone of contention among the rest of the crew when they found out.

Because my dad had invested a lot of money in them and also because he was trying to appease Davey and Dynamite who'd sent them our way, he kept admonishing me to push the muscleheads, which proved to be an exercise in futility as their work was the shits and they were also routinely injuring the smaller guys, including Pillman, who sustained a separated shoulder that would keep him on the shelf for several months.

After a while, with most of our smaller guys reluctant to work with the muscleheads, I had to eventually begin pairing them against each other — which was kind of like watching those godawful Godzilla vs. King Kong monster movies from the 1950s.

Since that wasn't working and my dad was still insistent on keeping them around, it was back to the drawing board. I figured that since Kazmaier and Arcidi were bona fide legends in the weightlifting realm, perhaps we could have a weightlifting contest, which might garner some interest and, from there, we could perhaps shoot some kind of angle, for them to start a feud.

My dad, Kazmaier and Arcidi all seemed to like the idea, so we had Arcidi, a heel, challenge Kazmaier, a face, to a weightlifting contest to determine once and for all who was the strongest man in wrestling. Because both of them were legitimate legends, at least among weightlifting aficionados, we drew a pretty good house to see the big showdown. Unfortunately, the weightlifting contest — which for some reason has since come to be called "Bill and Ted's Bogus Adventure" — would turn into a comedy of errors, with almost every conceivable thing that could go wrong, going wrong, including Kazmaier fainting. If you ever get a chance to watch that abortion, perhaps on YouTube, you'll know what I mean.

In its own way, that skit actually had a positive effect, as it seemed to open my dad's eyes to the folly of pushing the muscleheads. He soon sent Arcidi, Kazmaier and the rest of the musclehead misfits packing. We were finally at liberty to begin really concentrating on the young up-and-coming guys in the territory — much like in the early '80s, when guys like Bret, Dynamite Kid and Davey Boy had been given the ball and allowed to run with it.

37
"HAVING TOO MUCH FUN"

Around May 1987, after undergoing exhaustive rehabilitation on my injured left knee with the Calgary Stampeders' physiotherapist, Pat Clayton, I was finally given medical clearance to return to the ring. Before I started back on the main circuit, I wanted to do a few test matches in spot shows, just to get rid of some ring rust and to see how the knee held up. On one of those cards, in Claresholm, a small town about an hour south of Calgary, I tag teamed with Brian Pillman, who was just returning himself from a shoulder separation.

The match went surprisingly well and afterward, on the way home, Brian and I kicked around the possibility of forming a tag team.

For years, I'd been giving thought to this concept, along the lines of Dirty Harry or Rambo, in which the babyfaces were badder than the heels and used whatever tactics they felt were necessary to see that justice was served. I mentioned this to Pillman — who enthusiastically threw out the name Bad Company and, after a few more beers, we'd even come up with this radical look for the team, which called for wraparound sunglasses, biker jackets and bandannas. We even came up with a distinctive new color scheme — black tights with pink lightning bolts. A few years later, my brother Bret and my brother-in-law Jim Neidhart would adopt the same look, which brings to mind that old saying: "imitation is the most sincere form of flattery."

A couple of weeks later in Calgary, we were having a tournament to determine new tag team champions and Pillman and I unveiled the Bad Company concept. Since I'd always been kind of an understated babyface type in our territory and had never really manifested my heel alter ego before, I was a bit apprehensive about how the crowd might react. Pillman also had some apprehensions, but as anyone who later saw him in the wcw and wwf during his legendary loose cannon days can attest, he seemed to have a natural affinity for being a heel. Our biggest concern was that we might make fools of ourselves, but we decided to throw caution to the wind and see how it went.

Though our heels in faces' clothing persona was a radical departure from what the fans were accustomed to, they immediately embraced us, and Pill and I would become one of the hottest face teams in the history of our promotion.

A few years later, while he was in the wcw, Pillman tagged up with an unproven newcomer named Steve Williams as the Hollywood Blonds, and he would later impart the ass-kicking bad guy under the guise of being a face concept to Williams and he'd take it to new heights in the wwf as the Texas Rattlesnake, "Stone Cold" Steve Austin.

With Bad Company starting to get over, I was on the lookout for some dancing partners: a heel tag team to work with. In June, I received a phone call from Butch Moffat, a big heel we'd broken in a couple of years back. He told me he'd been testing out a new persona in Puerto Rico called Jason the Terrible, which was modeled after the hockey goalie mask–wearing psychopath from the *Friday the 13th* movies. He said he'd like to give it a shot up in Calgary. I was a bit dubious, but I'd always liked Moffat's work ethic and told him I'd give it some thought.

The next day, I got another call from former wwf midcarder Barry O, whose older brother Bob Orton Jr. was then one of the wwf's top heels. He told me he was looking for a new start and mentioned this persona he wanted to try: a masked heel with dark overtones named Zodiac. I'd never been a big fan of witchcraft, hocus-pocus or that kind of thing, but as Barry was running things by me, I got to thinking that perhaps Barry's Zodiac character could be tied into the Jason the Terrible persona that Moffat had been pitching me the day before. The more I thought about it, the more I liked it, and I ended up putting Moffat and Orton together — which would prove to be a match made in heaven, or should I say, hell.

Their success, combined with Owen, Makhan Singh, Chris Benoit, Ben Bassarab and Keiichi Yamada (Jushin Liger) as well as Bad Company, all contributed to a remarkable turnaround and our business that summer was the best since the glory days of the early '80s, when a similar crew of dynamic young stars, like Dynamite, Davey, Bret, Schultz and Honky Tonk, had ignited the territory.

Overall, we probably drew more back in that earlier era, but the summer of 1987 has to rate as the most satisfying stretch of my career — mostly because we'd overcome so many seemingly insurmountable obstacles in order to finally get back to the top of the mountain again. As an added bonus, my wife gave birth that year to our first boy, Bruce Jr. — all of which made that year probably the best of my life.

Things appeared to be in great shape heading into the fall, especially since we were able to add a few more useful pieces to the puzzle, including Corporal Mike Kirchner and Garfield Portz (a.k.a. Scotty McGee). Corporal Mike Kirchner was a kind of cross between Sgt. Slaughter and John Cena; he wasn't a great worker but had a ton of fire. Portz was a Dave Finlay–type heel from England who fit in nicely as well.

I fondly recall one story from 1987 that probably best reflects that memorable run. In November, we had a ten-man elimination tag team match in Edmonton with Pillman, Owen, me, Benoit and Kirchner taking on Makhan and Gama Singh, Jason the Terrible, Barry Orton and "Champagne" Gerry Morrow. Most times when we wrestled in Edmonton, the boxing and wrestling commission, which was quite anally retentive, didn't let us get away with much, but for some reason none of the commission members showed up that night — which kind of inspired this "when the cat's away, the mice will play" mind-set among the boys.

Since we had more than half of our roster in the ten-man tag match and only had three other matches on the card that night, we needed to put in some time.

The match was supposed to go about fifty minutes or thereabouts. Before the match, as I was giving the boys their finishes, I was addressing Barry Orton, who was supposed to be the first guy eliminated, and I told him that we'd probably put him out around twenty-five to thirty minutes.

In most cases, whenever you have battle royales, elimination matches and that kind of thing, most of the boys are eager to get in and get out as early as possible and I initially figured that might be the case that night. As the match began to unfold though, an incredible pace was being set, with every guy out there doing awesome moves and things snowballing from the get-go.

When I heard the timekeeper announce that we'd reached the fifty-minute mark, it dawned on me that no one had even been eliminated yet and since I was in at the time with Barry Orton, I asked him if he was ready to be eliminated. He gave me this kind of reluctant look and asked me if he had to leave so soon. I told him that since we'd gone past fifty minutes and hadn't even eliminated anyone yet, it was about time and he gave me this kind of sardonic smile and replied, "I'm not ready to leave yet; I'm having too much fun!" In retrospect, we all were; no one wanted to leave.

As 1987 drew to a close, the prevailing feeling was that we'd only just scratched the surface and we were confident 1988 would be even better, as most of our young guys had improved by leaps and bounds and things were just starting to really mesh.

38

THE GREAT CRASH OF '88

Unfortunately, another amazing season would not prove to be the case, as we soon would encounter an almost unbelievable stretch of bad luck. First off, my brother-in-law Ben Bassarab, who'd been tag teaming with Owen and was really starting to come into his own as a babyface, was stabbed in a bar-room altercation and lost half of his liver in the process, which marked the end of his career.

Next, Nobuhiko Niikura, who along with Hiroshi Hase had formed the hot heel tag team the Viet Cong Express, suffered a brain aneurysm, which left him partially paralyzed and also marked the end of his career.

Only a week or so later, Scotty McGee, who was just coming into his own, suffered a debilitating stroke — kind of like the one my brother Bret had years later — which paralyzed him and also finished his career.

Shortly after that, Corporal Kirchner, who'd gotten over surprisingly well as a G. I. Joe type babyface, got into a bar-room brawl, was arrested and charged with aggravated assault. After posting bail, he skipped out of the territory and wasn't heard from again.

Next, Barry Orton, who might have been the hottest heel in the territory at the time, divulged to me that before he'd come to our promotion, he'd been involved in a car wreck in which his female companion had been killed. Initially, the district attorney had decided not to press charges, but the case had since been reopened and he was now being charged with vehicular manslaughter. He had to return to Arizona for the trial. He wound up getting sentenced to three years in jail, which, of course, put an end to the Zodiac persona and without him Butch Moffat's Jason character lost much of its appeal as well.

As if all of that wasn't enough, we next found ourselves having to contend with the 1988 Winter Olympics in Calgary, which were, at that time, probably the biggest thing ever to hit Canada. Making matters worse, we were kicked out of our regular building, the Stampede Pavilion, because it was being used for the Olympics. As a result, we ended up having to run for the months of January and February in this cramped bowling alley out in the industrial out-skirts of town, which decimated our crowds; because the seating and lighting were so lousy, our ambience suffered big time.

Beyond not being able to run in our usual building during peak season, the Olympics proved to be a huge distraction: everyone in the country was caught up with Olympic fever, with wrestling relegated to the back burner.

By the time the Olympics were over, we then were beset with Stanley Cup fever, specifically the "Battle of Alberta." Back in those days, as any hockey fan can attest, the two best teams in the National Hockey League were the Edmonton Oilers and the Calgary Flames, with the Oilers at the time the defending champions, while the Flames would finally dethrone them in 1989. That spring, the Oilers would once again go all the way to the finals, in May, and win the Cup again, while the Flames proved to be their toughest challenge.

In any case, after having had to contend with Stanley Cup fever, the Winter Olympics and all the other aforementioned trials and tribulations, we were already halfway through the year and into June before things kind of leveled off and people were ready to get into wrestling again. Although we'd lost some good talent and had been through all kinds of unexpected losses, I nonetheless figured that, like any babyface worth his salt, we could make the big comeback.

39
THE DINOSAUR

Just around the bend, there was another pothole on the highway to hell — this time, the great dinosaur debacle. In early June, we had a show in Drumheller, Alberta — which is called the dinosaur capital of Canada because many dinosaur remains have been unearthed there. Whenever we were in Drumheller, as a rib on the rookies, the wrestlers would begin talking about this famous statue of my dad that was located there — making out as if it was Alberta's answer to the Statue of Liberty. As we got closer to Drumheller, the rookies would be getting excited and when we finally got into town, we'd come around this bend and there it was — a thirty-foot-high Tyrannosaurus Rex. The boys would then all launch into their Stu impersonations, while the rookies would enjoy a good laugh. The rib — originally conceived by another reptilian, Jake "The Snake" Roberts — had been going on for years and had always been good for some harmless fun. We pulled it that night on a big bodybuilder named Jeff Beltzner — who looked like Ron Simmons but came across more like Richard Simmons — who'd been sent to the territory by Davey Boy and Dynamite. At the time, everyone had a good laugh — no big deal, or so we thought.

In any case, the following Friday, Pillman and I, who'd driven down to the Pavilion together, pulled into the parking lot behind the building and noticed

Davey Boy's and Dynamite's vehicles parked there — which was kind of strange, since both were in the WWF at the time and hadn't been to any of our shows in several years. Pillman and I made our way to the dressing room, stopping, as we usually did, for a coffee on the way in. Pillman came into the dressing room first and before I could even enter, I heard this loud crash and saw Pillman hit the floor — the result of a sucker punch from Beltzner, the musclehead friend of Davey and Dynamite who we'd pulled the rib on. I endeavored to intercede, but Dynamite pulled a gun out of his jacket pocket and snarled, "Let them fookin' fight."

Before he could even get the words out of his mouth, Pillman — who'd been an All-American linebacker at Miami of Ohio — showed his form by spearing Beltzner, driving him into a set of lockers. Pillman began raining punches and kicks on Beltzner, in one of the most one-sided utter shit-kickings I've ever seen. When the smoke had cleared, Beltzner's face had been pounded into a bloody pulp, with his cheekbone protruding grotesquely through his skin and both eyes swollen shut. I noticed Davey Boy and Dynamite — who'd been so keen on having them settle their differences — had also disappeared, probably disenchanted that their steroid-supplying flunky had gotten his ass kicked.

My dad showed up shortly after and told me he'd run into Dynamite and Davey Boy in the parking lot and that, according to them, Beltzner had merely been defending Stu's honor, because Pillman, Owen and I had been implying that he was a senile old dinosaur. I shook my head in consternation, amazed that something as harmless as the Tyrannosaurus rib could be taken so far out of context. Before I could even explain that to my dad, he informed me that I'd been relieved of my duties as booker and that Keith — who was pretty much retired from wrestling and was now working as a fireman — would be replacing me.

Within a few weeks, Keith systematically scrapped almost everything we'd done in the past two years, including disbanding Bad Company (which resulted in Pillman quitting and heading back to the States). Keith then converted Jason the Terrible, who'd been one of our most frightening heels ever, into this Shrek-type babyface, which was about as lame as when the WWF took the mask off Kane and turned him into the bald-headed buffoon type he plays now.

Keith wasn't finished though. Next, he took Mike Shaw (Makhan Singh), who'd been our lead heel, and had done an awesome job, out of the ring and tried to turn him into a Jesse Ventura–type color commentator, which was a waste of his talent and my dad's money.

His last master stroke was to take Kerry Brown, who'd long been a valuable midcard heel — kind of like a Val Venus or Arn Anderson type — and converted him into this working class–type babyface, kind of like this lame character the WWF was endeavoring to introduce at the time named Duke "The Dumpster" Droese. Brown's working class hero persona would get over about as well as some lowlife pinching a loaf in a crowded swimming pool.

After a few months of declining gates and wrestlers looking to jump ship, the novelty of being a booker seemed to wear off and Keith resigned. I was asked to take the book again.

All things considered, I probably should have given my dad the classic Johnny Paycheck line: "Take this job and shove it." But because the promotion was on the brink of going under, I found myself back in the saddle again. It didn't turn out to be a particularly enjoyable ride though, as most of the story lines and personas I'd put in place had been scrapped. It was tough sledding, trying to put the pieces back together.

I put Mike Shaw back in the ring and turned Kerry Brown and Jason the Terrible back into heels and gave Chris Benoit — who'd recently returned from a sabbatical in Japan — a pretty good push. I also recruited a few promising prospects from the States, including a highly touted black heel named "Lethal" Larry Cameron, and set about trying to get things back on track.

40
MASTERS OF DISASTER

Just before Christmas, word came out that my old cronies, Dynamite and Davey Boy, had been fired by the WWF, after what one-time WWF manager Jimmy Hart referred to, in his book, as their "reign of terror," which included Ex-Laxing assorted unsuspecting rookies, allegedly date rape–drugging and sexually assaulting groupies, assorted bar-room brawls, trashing hotels and missing bookings. The last straw had, apparently, been a violent backstage altercation between Dynamite and Jacques Rougeau, in which Dynamite had gotten several teeth knocked out and had threatened to shoot Rougeau in retaliation.

Since the Bulldogs both still lived in Calgary, had family ties and were still considered to be marquee attractions, my dad welcomed them back with open arms, seemingly oblivious to the potential problems they might cause.

On their first night back, we sold out the Pavilion and, as they'd been huge stars in the WWF for the past five years or so, there was a great deal of buzz surrounding their return. They were booked that night against Mike Shaw and Gary Albright (alias Makhan and Vokhan Singh — the Karachi Vice). Before their match, I came up to them in the dressing room to give them their finish. Dynamite snarled that, just like Bret back in the early '80s, my dad had given him and Davey Boy complete autonomy over their finishes and they didn't have to take "fookin' orders," as he put it, from me.

After all the bullshit I'd already encountered that year — with the dinosaur debacle, Keith's abortive stint as the booker and trying to put the pieces back in place — I was pissed off with this latest aggravation. I informed my dad, who was trying to make out as if we could all work together, that I was through. I submitted my resignation on the spot. My dad's response was to appoint Dynamite the booker — which, as things would turn out, was like appointing the Taliban to handle peacekeeping detail in the Middle East.

As good a worker as Dynamite was — in my mind, one of the top five ever — he may have been equally bad as a booker.

Being a booker, at first glance, doesn't seem all that hard. Initially, it seems like it would be kind of a hoot to be telling guys who's winning and losing and concocting finishes, off-the-wall scenarios and all of that.

For the shallow types, I guess, having people kiss their asses and blow smoke up their sphincters is also kind of appealing. I'd also venture to say that damn near any idiot can draw a house or two, the first few weeks that they have the book, if only by conjuring up some type of gimmick scenario — like a cage match, ladder match, lumberjack match or something out of the ordinary. It's a totally different thing though to sustain things for weeks or months at a stretch, without losing your momentum.

After drawing not bad for the first few weeks, things began to quickly unravel with Dynamite and his trusty sidekick Einstein (Davey Boy) calling the shots. One of the most common blunders neophyte bookers are guilty of is immediately resorting to gimmick matches — cage matches, scaffold matches, chain matches and whatnot. That was my brother Bret's weakness when he was a rookie booker a decade earlier and the same was the case for the Bulldogs. Seeing as there was no method to the madness, or discernible reason for having most of the gimmick matches, the novelty quickly wore off and before long our gates hit the skids.

The Bulldogs' next brainwave was to have my dad import, at considerable expense, all their washed-up old cronies from the WWF, like the Moondogs, Magnificent Muraco and a bunch of other ass-kissing associates, such as the

Power Twins and Sandy Beach, whom they'd befriended while in the WWF. When those moves didn't pan out, they began importing — also at considerable expense — midgets, girl wrestlers, wrestling bears and other so-called special attractions, none of whom drew a dime.

Beyond their shortcomings as bookers, Dynamite and Einstein continued right where they had left off in the WWF, perpetrating practical — or should I say impractical — jokes: defecating in wrestlers' bags, padlocking suitcases to the pipes, cutting the crotch out of wrestlers' pants and — their stock in trade specialty — Metamucil Slurpees and that type of highbrow frivolity.

One of their crowning achievements, as far as ribs go, came in Kelowna, British Columbia, when they roofied this rookie from Florida named Tom Nash and after he staggered back to his hotel room and passed out, Einstein snuck in and set fire to his bed while he was sleeping in it. Fortunately, the smoke detector in Nash's room went off; otherwise Nash probably would have died of smoke inhalation.

After a few months, the Bulldogs had more than worn out their welcome and, perhaps sensing it was imminent, saved themselves the embarrassment of getting fired by informing my dad that they'd accepted an offer to do a tour of Japan in April. They also related that, upon their return, they were planning on going to Florida to wrestle. The news was greeted with a sigh of relief by my mom and dad, not to mention most of the wrestlers. With those two out of the picture, my dad once again turned to . . . drum roll, please . . . you guessed it, none other than yours truly to pick up the loose ends again. It was kind of like wrestling's version of Billy Martin and George Steinbrenner in the 1980s — hire me, fire me, hire me, fire me. . . .

When my dad approached me this time around, I was probably more dubious about accepting than I'd ever been — with good reason. As usual, the prevailing pretext was that if I didn't take the job, he'd probably just shut the territory down, which none of us wanted to see. So, once again, like some misbegotten masochist, I took the reins.

When I'd briefly taken the book after Keith's stint, the crowds had been bored to tears and needed to be kick-started, but after the British Bulldogs' relentless stretch of gimmicks, hotshotting and overkill, it was about trying to get back to the middle of the road — and I'm not really sure which was harder to follow.

In taking stock, about the only heel the Bulldogs hadn't destroyed was this big, black guy named "Lethal" Larry Cameron — mostly because they were half-racist and didn't want anything to do with him, but also because they knew he was too impressive to just be jobbed. As such, they just left him in the under-card in essentially meaningless singles or tags.

Because of all the bullshit the past year or so, I hadn't really worked the terri-tory for most of 1989, which was almost a blessing in disguise. It almost made me a new face. On my first night back, I launched an angle with Lethal Larry and we got a surprisingly good pop and tried to build things from there. Aside from that, we still had a few other good faces on our roster — most notably Benoit and my brother Owen, both of whom had been spinning their wheels under the Bulldogs' assbackward booking. All things considered, given all the turmoil the territory had endured the past year or so, I was pleased that things were at least headed in the right direction.

41

THE NORTHWEST NIGHTMARE

At the end of May 1989, after a not so triumphant tour of Japan, Dynamite and Davey Boy returned. To everyone's chagrin, they informed my dad that since their sojourn to Florida had been canceled, they'd like to resume working for Stampede Wrestling. No one was that keen on having either one of them back, but since they were family, we were kind of stuck with them.

This time around though, at least my dad didn't mince any words as to who was giving the orders and both of them seemed okay with that — at least at the outset. In retrospect, I think they were relieved, as handling the book had become more of a chore to them than anything else and I don't think either of them wanted to admit they were in way over their heads as bookers.

When the Dawgs came back, I was kind of unsure as to how we could get any mileage out of them. They'd already chewed up and spit out most of our heels and there didn't appear to be anyone left for them to work with. In considering our options, I got to thinking that back in the early '80s, they'd drawn us a lot of money, with Dynamite working as a heel and Davey as a face. I, therefore, proposed to my dad that we could perhaps shoot some kind of angle calling for Dynamite to double-cross Davey and, from there, have him work heel — have them reprise their hot feud from the early '80s.

Somewhat to my surprise, they both seemed to like the idea, so we set things up for Dynamite to perpetrate the big swerve on Einstein.

Other than maybe the Road Warriors, there probably hadn't been a more iconic tag team in the business in the '80s than the Bulldogs and their breakup elicited a huge buzz, not only within the territory, but all over the business.

The Dawg vs. Dawg feud became a hot ticket in Stampede Wrestling, drawing huge gates all over the territory. Suddenly things appeared to be in good shape again — the best, in fact, since our breakout summer of 1987.

Even though they were drawing good crowds, though, I discerned that Dynamite and Davey Boy kind of resented the fact that I was getting credit for the turnaround.

Near the end of June, my dad sent us on this extended safari to the Northwest Territories, which is Canada's answer to Alaska. I think the journey was close to 2,500 miles round trip and, unlike the superstars in the wwf, we didn't get to fly, but instead had to drive, which proved to be quite the ordeal.

According to our itinerary, we were supposed to leave after our Saturday night shot in Edmonton, then head about 500 miles due north to a place called High Level, which is near the Alberta/Northwest Territories border, for our first show of the tour on Monday. We then were supposed to set off right after that and make the eight hundred miles' or so run to Yellowknife, where we would wrestle on Tuesday night. From there, we had a shot in Hay River on Wednesday, which was about five or six miles south of Yellowknife. We would then have Thursday off, in order to make the 1,100-mile return to Calgary in time for our Friday show.

We had a good house in Edmonton on the Saturday and everyone appeared to be in pretty good spirits as we set out on the road. I took the first shift behind the wheel and just after we got on the road, my old buddy Dynamite gave me a beer. Since I was driving, I refrained from drinking it. I didn't want to appear to be disdainful so I accepted his seemingly magnanimous gesture and took the beer and put it in the cupholder, figuring I might have it after I turned the wheel over to someone else.

I later on gave the beer to this Japanese rookie named Sumu Hara, who was riding shotgun, and didn't give it any further thought until we stopped to get coffee and gas at this truck stop in Fox Creek. Hara was so fucked up that he couldn't even crawl out of the van. I immediately deduced that the beer Dynamite had given me had been spiked and that if I'd drunk it while driving, we all could have been killed. I tore a strip off Dynamite — who was half-plastered and drugged out. He, of course, denied spiking the beer. No one believed him.

About an hour or so later, we blew the engine in the babyface vehicle and had to abandon it on the side of the road. Fortunately, the heel van was behind us. We then all had to pile in it, about eighteen of us crammed in like sardines. Finally on Sunday afternoon we dragged our weary asses into High Level. Mercifully, we had a day to rest up before our first show. We drew a good house and then embarked for beautiful Yellowknife.

Since there were no Hertz or Avis rental outlets or anything of that sort up there, the van was still uncomfortably crowded, but we were able to ease the situation a bit by putting a few of the boys in the ring truck. A few others rode with our road agent, Bob Johnson, who had gone up earlier in the week in his Ford.

The haul to Yellowknife was close to seven hundred miles of mostly gravel and dirt roads. You had to navigate a slalom course, dodging humongous buffalo and moose that I swear must have been on steroids. It was like one of those automobile rallies from Khartoum to Dakar.

Still, Yellowknife drew a huge gate and the show went great. I endeavored to show my appreciation afterward by picking up the tab for the boys at Yellowknife's poshest restaurant and when I left them that night, most of them appeared to have been grateful and in pretty good spirits.

The last show of the tour was Hay River and seeing as I had to do a radio interview the next morning, I left that night with Bob Johnson. I left instructions for the boys to be on the road by noon. Most of them had done hundreds of road trips, so there was no need to take them by the hand or chaperone them, or so I thought. The next night we had our best gate yet — another standing-room-only crowd in Hay River, which was a relief, as poor old Bob Johnson had incurred a lot of heat for having arranged the trip in the first place. Since we'd drawn good gates, he was kind of vindicated.

That night, I was supposed to work with "Lethal" Larry Cameron, but by 7:30, no one other than myself, Johnson and Kerry and Bob Brown, who'd come down early to indulge in some fishing, had arrived. As a result, I had to first work with Kerry for close to forty minutes and, with the rest of the boys still not there, as a contingency, I had Bob Brown interfere and cost me the match, at which point I challenged him to a match — all of which was just a means of playing for time. After working over eighty minutes in both matches with the Browns, much to my relief, the rest of the crew finally arrived and Bulldog Bob and I went into our finish, pleased that we'd been able to save the show.

When I got back to the dressing room, I was half-exhausted and in the process of asking the faces why they'd been so late, when, out of the blue, I was sucker punched from behind by Dynamite, which knocked me on my ass and dislocated my jaw. As I staggered to my feet, I was then head butted in the mouth by Davey Boy, which drove my teeth through my lower lip and knocked me on my ass again. At that point, my brother Dean and a few of the other wrestlers interceded and they then escorted me out and I ended up having to go to the hospital to have my jaw put back in place.

I was told later that Dynamite and Davey Boy had ambushed me because I'd supposedly been making fun of them for having to ride 2,500 miles round trip in a crowded van — which was a radical departure from flying first class in the wwf. I don't recall having made such a comment, but even if I had, it would have been kind of funny and certainly shouldn't have warranted me getting sucker punched, or all the other bullshit.

I'm sure the real reason for their attack, beyond drugs and alcohol, was that they were pissed off that I'd snatched them earlier for trying to give me the spiked beer. When they were in the wwf, Dynamite and Davey had similarly sucker punched Jacques Rougeau, Outback Jack and others after they'd accused them of having pulled ribs on them — which, I should note, they had.

42
THROWING IN THE TOWEL

The weekend after the Northwest Territories travesty was my brother Owen's wedding. I'd been asked to be his best man and was eagerly looking forward to the big occasion, but in light of all the bullshit that had taken place up north, I told Owen that if either of those two A-holes — Davey or Dynamite —were at the wedding, I wouldn't be there.

Owen implored me to reconsider and we had a big meeting up at my dad's place. At my dad's and Owen's behest, the Bulldogs were invited to come over and account for their transgressions. Einstein showed up and sheepishly apologized, claiming he was drunk and that he and Dynamite had been stirred up by this shit-disturber newcomer, Ricky Rice, who claimed I'd been making fun of them for having to ride eighteen guys in the van on a gravel road for 5,000 klicks. I accepted his apology and we shook hands and made peace, but Dynamite never did show up and never put in an appearance at Owen's wedding either, which was just as well.

The wedding went quite smoothly and there were no problems or issues. A couple of days after the wedding though, there was another "high spot," as we call them in the wrestling business. The boys were supposed to heading west to Prince George, British Columbia, on the Fourth of July for a show. The past three or four years, on the Fourth of July, there had been serious accidents involving wrestlers, including Brutus Beefcake nearly being killed in an accident on the beach involving a paraglider; the following year, three wrestlers, including Adrian Adonis, were killed in Newfoundland when their car swerved to avoid hitting a moose and went off the road; the next year WWF referee Joey Marella, son of Gorilla Monsoon, was killed in a car wreck in New Jersey.

When the wrestlers left that day in '89, someone sardonically made reference to the Fourth of July curse — which may have been a bad omen. True to form, this time around, my brother Ross was driving the faces' van on some stretch of mountain road. He had a head-on collision with a motor home and nearly went down the side of the mountain. Several of the wrestlers were seriously injured, including Jason the Terrible (broken leg), Sumu Hara (broken hip), Davey Boy (separated shoulder and facial lacerations), and Chris Benoit (concussion). Thankfully, no one was killed, but the accident unfortunately marked the end of Jason's career, and also put an end to the Davey Boy vs. Dynamite story line, which we'd been expecting to be our big ticket for the summer.

Even though the promotion limped along for a few more months after that, that plus the Hay River melee and all the other unfortunate incidents took their toll. My dad decided to pull the plug on the promotion at Christmastime — which didn't exactly result in "Joy to the World" or any festive celebrating.

After all the crap my dad had been made to endure the past few years, no one could blame him for pulling out. On the one hand, I was sad to see him close, as I had put my heart and soul into the operation and it marked the end of the dream. I was proud of a lot of what we'd accomplished the past couple of years — especially the development of rookies like Owen, Pillman, Benoit, Liger, Hase, Hashimoto and others, all of whom would go on to become major stars in the next decade.

On the other hand though, all the bullshit had eroded my passion considerably and my dad's decision to shut down was almost like the plug being pulled on some terminally ill patient who'd been suffering far too long.

The person I felt saddest for at the demise of the promotion was my dad. I probably never realized, until then, just how much the wrestling business meant to him. It hadn't just been a job or occupation, but his passion and such a part of his whole being. It had taken him from a life of punishing poverty and oblivion and made him one of the most well-known and respected people in Canada. (This was later recognized when he was inducted into the Order of Canada.) Wrestling had also provided a pathway to fame and fortune for many others in our family, including my brothers Bret and Owen. I'm sure that something inside my dad died when he had to close down the promotion.

Not to digress, but I read some years later in Dynamite Kid's not particularly well-written book, *Pure Dynamite*, that when my dad shut the promotion down, Dynamite was pissed off that no one had thrown him any bouquets or given him any props for all he'd done for Stampede.

I found that kind of amusing, because most people will tell you his (and Einstein's) return to the territory in 1989 was one of the main reasons why Stampede Wrestling went out of business. There's no arguing that Dynamite was one of the primary reasons for the rise of the promotion in the late 1970s — his performances were cutting-edge and razor sharp. By 1989, though, he was like a rusty, dull blade who could no longer "cut it" and because of that the promotion had gone down. We may have lived by the sword, but we would die by it as well. *C'est la vie.*

PRAYERS AND PROMISES

43

FAREWELL, NEVERLAND

If you've seen the Mickey Rourke vehicle *The Wrestler* — which, in my opinion, should have won the Academy Award for Best Picture, hands down — you may recall that one of the most pervasive themes was how addictive the wrestling lifestyle is and how difficult it is to go back to the real world afterward.

From one who's been there and done that, I can certainly attest to that. In its own twisted way the wrestling business is kind of like a real life Never Never Land in that wrestlers are allowed to extend their childhood: dressing up in costumes and playing cowboys and Indians, cops and robbers or whatever else. I can certainly see now why guys like Ric Flair, Hulk Hogan and Terry Funk have kept at it for so long. I suspect the same is the case for athletes from other sports, like Brett Favre, Mark Messier, Chris Chelios and Nolan Ryan, as well as entertainers, like Mick Jagger and Rod Stewart.

One of the toughest things for me to adjust to after I got out of wrestling was dealing with the inherent cynicism. In wrestling, where everything's a work and everyone seems to always be working everyone else, you tend to become cynical and figure everyone's working you, or that they're all marks and need to be worked by you.

Either way, you tend to have this skewed take on everything and don't take anyone at face value. When I eventually came to realize though that most people outside the wrestling realm didn't seem to have any overriding agenda, my cynicism abated — which made things a lot better. After my dad shut down the promotion, fortunately, I was able to hook on with the Calgary Board of Education as a substitute teacher and though the money wasn't great, there wasn't much stress. I was also delighted to find out in February 1990 that my wife was expecting our third child in September and I'd be able to spend some quality time with my family — something I'd missed out on while I was on the road.

Later that summer, my dad was asked by an old friend named Richard Kessler if he could promote a Stampede Wrestling retro show at a rodeo in the small town of Rockyford, Alberta, about fifty miles east of Calgary. My dad readily agreed and recruited a few of former Stampede guys, including Gama, Gerry Morrow, Cuban Assassin, Phil La Fon, Leo Burke, my brother Keith and myself, as well as a few rookies he'd been stretching in the Dungeon. The show came off surprisingly well.

I rode back from Rockyford with my dad and he was pumped with how well the show had gone, but also lamented the fact that the WWF had wiped out all the smaller promotions, such as Stampede Wrestling — which was where all the good workers had developed their craft. He said it was a shame the WWF didn't see the merit in re-sowing the seeds at the grassroots level. He suggested that I drop our old friend Vince McMahon a line, pointing out that wrestling was the only major sports entity that didn't have a farm system or viable means of replenishing its talent pool and that perhaps they could see fit to revive Stampede Wrestling for that purpose. Although I was dubious that I'd get a reply, I figured nothing ventured, nothing gained, and therefore dropped Vinnie Mac a line, extolling the virtues of starting up a farm system, so to speak.

A few days after I'd mailed the letter, I ran into my brother Bret up at my dad's. Bret was still working for the WWF and I mentioned the letter to him. He shook his head and smirked. Sardonically, he posed the rhetorical question: if Vince had gone to such great lengths to systematically wipe out all the regional promotions, such as Stampede Wrestling, back in the '80s, why the hell would he want to give any of them life again?

A couple of weeks later though, much to my (and Bret's) surprise, I received an extremely pleasant reply from Vince, thanking me for my letter and extending an invitation to me to fly down to the upcoming Survivor Series, at which time we could discuss things in more detail.

44
"ONLY THE GOOD DIE YOUNG"

A few weeks later, I flew down to Hartford for the big pay-per-view. The night of my arrival, I was sitting in the ringside watching the matches when one of the referees came up to me and said there was a message for me to call home. I went into the back and made the call and was saddened by the news that my brother Dean had died that afternoon in Calgary.

Even though Dean had been having health issues the past few years and had been on dialysis, his death still came as a shock. Of all my brothers, the two I was closest to were Dean and Owen. Although Dean was the smallest, physically, of the eight boys in the family, he probably had the biggest heart and wouldn't back down from anyone.

After I got off the phone, through tears and laughter, I found myself reflecting on the many misadventures Dean and I had been through together, including the trip to Amarillo, the rock concerts we'd promoted and the escapades in Hawaii, among other things, when I felt a big arm draped around my shoulder and turned around to see it was Kerry Von Erich. He told me he'd just heard about Dean's passing and offered his condolences; he then told me that he'd said a prayer, asking his brothers David, Jack and Mike — all of whom had died in the past few years themselves — to look after Dean up in heaven. The next thing I knew, Kerry was sobbing and getting quite emotional and I soon found myself, instead, having to console him. In any case, I was greatly impressed with his sensitivity and compassion.

The next night, the WWF had a show in New York at Madison Square Garden. After the show, Curt Hennig, Rick Rude and Mike Hegstrand (Hawk from the Road Warriors/Legion of Doom) took me out on the town. We went to the China Club and then the Hard Rock Café and they went out of their way to show me a good time, which I thought was an incredibly nice gesture on their part, especially since I'd only just met them. While we were at the Hard Rock, Curt asked the deejay to dedicate a song to me — Billy Joel's classic "Only the Good Die Young." Sadly, Kerry, Curt, Rick and Mike would all leave us far too early themselves. Whenever I hear that song, those guys come to mind.

As for my meeting with Vince, he came up to me after the show in New York and told me that he'd been busy as hell with a number of other things and hadn't really had much of an opportunity to give any thought to the farm system concept yet. He said that we could perhaps discuss it some other time. On the flight back home from New York, Bret asked me how the meeting with Vinnie had gone and when I told him, he gave me one of those smug "I told you so" smiles and said that Vince liked to just pull people's strings like that and that rarely did he deliver on most of his promises.

Bret then reiterated what he'd said in the first place: that, in his opinion, Vinnie really didn't give a rat's ass about developing new wrestlers, that he figured all you really needed to do was take a prospect — be he a bodybuilder or football player or what have you — and teach him a few holds and leave the rest to the scriptwriters, which is pretty much what they'd done with guys like the Ultimate Warrior. I figured Bret — who obviously knew Vince better than me — was probably right.

45
HITMAN'S GHOST

In early May, my brother Bret, whom I remained on good terms with, called me up and said that the *Calgary Sun* had approached him about writing a syndicated weekly wrestling column. He told me that he'd like to do it, as it would enhance his exposure and might help kick-start his singles career, which had been stuck in neutral since the Hart Foundation tag team with Jim Neidhart had been disbanded. The only problem was that he'd never done much writing before. He wondered whether I might be able to ghostwrite the column for him — as I'd ghostwritten most of his English and Social Studies essays for him back when he was in high school.

I told him I'd be happy to give it a shot, but that my writing style tended to be tongue in cheek and satiric. Bret said he was fine with that and the column — which was often outrageous and had people wondering whether Bret was serious or not — turned out to be a big hit.

In one of the early columns, I paid my respects to the revered, or should I say, reviled, Australian wrestler (I use the term very loosely), the one and only (thankfully) Outback Jack:

A lot of fans have — okay, I won't insult your intelligence — one foul-tempered and foul-mouthed, toothless skank, looking to file a paternity suit, asked me what's become of him. Some of you may recall him as the colorful Australian wrestler whose unique wrestling style resembled that of a kangaroo with two left feet. Well, we were recently able to track Jack down in his native Australia. He relates that after being injured in the ring (probably from tripping over himself), he was forced to retire and went back to school, where, after several unsuccessful attempts, he persevered and was finally able to obtain his degree — as a sanitary engineer. He's now stationed at Moroganga, a sheep station in Australia's remote Western Desert region where he rides herd over a raunchy group of volatile, unruly and at times, highly unpredictable portable latrines. He tells us, quite proudly, that friends now call him "Outhouse Jack" — which, when you stop and think about it, is probably what he should have been called in the first place, since his performances in the ring usually stunk to high hell.

With the column quickly becoming a hit, Bret's popularity also took off. Each week, he would call me from wherever he was on the road and give me the lowdown on what he'd like me to write about in the column and then I'd take it from there. Quite often, during our weekly confabs, he'd also seek input from me on finishes and angles — since I had a wealth of them from my days as a booker in Stampede. In the past, I'd given him ideas, such as the pink and black attire, as well as the wraparound shades and biker jackets that Brian Pillman and I had worn during our Bad Company days. During one of our conversations, he told me he was looking for a new signature finish and wanted to know if I had any suggestions. When I was booking in Calgary, I'd had one of the Viet Cong Express use a cross-legged version of the Boston Crab that we'd devised down in the Dungeon as a finish; it had gotten over pretty well, so I suggested that to Bret. He wasn't all that keen on it, initially, but said he might give it a whirl and see what the reaction was. He called me back the next week though and was quite stoked at how well it had gotten over — so much so that the WWF had given it the new name "the sharpshooter" and wanted him to use it as his signature finish. As most of you probably know, it would go on to become one of the most celebrated finishes in the history of the WWF.

46
TRIALS AND TRIBULATIONS

In July, the WWF came to Calgary for a big show and TV taping. After the show my parents hosted a barbecue for the WWF brass and the boys. I ran into Vince McMahon and he seemed to be in pretty good spirits and he said that he'd been tied up with a myriad of things lately but was still keen on pursuing the farm system concept we'd discussed in New York. He wanted to have me fly down in August for SummerSlam and said that we could meet afterward.

I was fine with that and flew in for SummerSlam — which featured Randy Savage and Elizabeth's wedding, as well as Bret going over Mr. Perfect (Curt Hennig) for his first singles title, the intercontinental strap. I was seated at ringside with my parents, watching the matches, when one of the WWF agents came up to me and said there'd been an emergency and that I needed to call home immediately. Naturally I was apprehensive about what might have happened this time. I rushed to the pay phone adjacent to the dressing rooms in Madison Square Garden and, after ringing busy several times, I finally got through to my mother-in-law. Half-hysterical, she related that my wife, who was six months pregnant at the time, had been rushed to the hospital, hemorrhaging. It didn't look like she or the baby would make it; I needed to fly home, immediately.

As I was straining to hear her, the WWF was staging this over-the-top skit — only about ten feet away — in which Jake "The Snake" Roberts had just crashed Randy and Elizabeth's so-called wedding with a bunch of poisonous snakes. There was all this screaming and shrieking — which was really weird, having my mother-in-law's anguish on the phone and all this feigned anguish right beside me.

As soon as I got off the phone, I ran into the dressing room and told Bret there was an emergency and I had to fly home. I asked him to convey my regrets to Vince. I'm not sure if Bret didn't grasp the gravity of the situation or what, but I was astonished when he replied that Vince wouldn't be happy that I was standing him up, and that I should reconsider. There was no time for any of that and I reiterated that I had to fly out immediately. Bret shook his head, disapprovingly, and informed me that I was likely blowing my big opportunity. I could only stare in disbelief and finally told him, so be it, and took off for the airport.

When I arrived home, my wife gave birth prematurely to our son Rhett. He'd been due in early December, but was born on August 31. He weighed less than two pounds, with all kinds of complications, including a hole in his heart and collapsed lungs; the prognosis for his survival was pretty grim: the doctors were doubtful he'd make it through the night.

Being a Hart though, he was a fighter and hung in there. Each night, for the next several weeks, my wife and I would sit outside his incubator in the neo-natal intensive care unit at the Foothills hospital, beside his bed, hoping and praying that he'd make it.

Every night, his heart would stop six or seven times, which would set off these alarms and the nurses would come running over and use a defibrillator or some such thing to kick-start his heart again — all of which was extremely nerve-wracking, especially since, on any given night, two or three babies, in similar circumstances, wouldn't make it. It was pretty heartbreaking and gut-wrenching to be seated nearby, while the doctors, who were almost devoid of emotion, broke the news to the devastated parents that their baby hadn't made it.

What was really strange was that whenever my wife or I made our way to or from the neo-natal intensive care unit, which was always an emotional hell, we would have to walk through the maternity ward where it was high season for celebration, with proud papas beaming at their healthy newborns, handing out cigars and flowers, completely oblivious to the trials and tribulations ensuing just down the hallway.

After several months of struggling to survive, Rhett began to hold his own and was allowed to go home just before Christmas — which was one of the best Christmas presents I've ever received. During that tough stretch, I received an incredible amount of support from several members of my family, including my parents, my mother-in-law and family, as well as my sisters Ellie and Georgia, in particular. I might add that Bret, his wife Julie, her sister Michelle and Dynamite couldn't have been nicer.

47
"THERE, DIGNITY BEGINS"

Throughout that difficult stretch, I continued to write Bret's column and each week he would call me up from the road to give me some general idea of what he wanted to talk about. In January, he called me up for our weekly confab and was quite bent out of shape because the WWF brass wanted him to drop the intercontinental strap to Jacques Rougeau.

He said that he didn't mind doing the job, but that in his estimation Rougeau was nowhere near as good as he was and the only reason they were putting the strap on him was because he was kissing ass and doing whatever else to appease and curry the favor of some of Vince's homosexual bookers — whom he not so affectionately used to refer to as "the Gay Mafia." As a result, Bret said he was seriously considering jumping to the WCW (World Championship Wrestling). They had made him a lucrative offer and he wanted to know what I thought.

I told him that regardless of what he thought of Rougeau personally, he was still obliged to do the job — that was what being a professional was all about. Beyond that, if he were to walk, he'd most likely be permanently burning his bridges with the WWF — which, I cautioned him, might not be a very good career move, considering there were only two promotions up and running at that time.

Bret seemed half-pissed that I wasn't more empathetic to his situation, but told me he'd sleep on it and decide what he was going to do. I'm not sure whether I had any influence on his decision, but he decided to do the job for Rougeau and stay put, even though he wasn't happy about it.

A couple of months later, at WrestleMania, the WWF put the intercontinental strap back on him, having him beat Roddy Piper (who'd since dethroned Rougeau). Funny enough, after winning the strap back, Bret, who'd been routinely knocking Pat Patterson's booking since having to drop the strap, was suddenly effusive in his praise, touting him as a brilliant manipulator.

A few months down the road, Bret called me up again for our weekly chat from London, England — the site of SummerSlam — where he was slated to defend his intercontinental belt against Davey Boy. He'd been in pretty good spirits for a while, but this time around, he seemed down. When I asked if anything was wrong, he informed me that the WWF wanted him to drop the strap to Davey Boy.

Bret claimed — not that convincingly — that it wasn't doing the job that bothered him, but that losing to his brother-in-law (Davey Boy was married to our sister Diana) was a deliberate slap in the face, and he figured the WWF was just doing this to insult him.

He said that since there was still a standing offer on the table from the WCW, he was once again seriously thinking of telling the WWF where to go, and heading to the other promotion.

I figured he would have already learned his lesson the last time, but painstakingly pointed out to him that, lest he forget, Davey and Dynamite had dropped the tag straps to him and Neidhart back in 1987 with no qualms and that he shouldn't read too much into having to do the job, as it was all just part of the job description. Once again, he seemed half-pissed that I didn't put him over or tell him he was doing the right thing, but he kind of tersely said he'd think things over and decide what to do.

To his credit, he put Davey Boy over in front of nearly 80,000 ecstatic fans at Wembley Stadium in what many in the know consider to have been one of the best matches in WWF history. Watching the match back home on pay-per-view, I had goose bumps as it unfolded over nearly an entire hour of incredible back and forth action. I was as proud of Bret (and Davey Boy, too, I might add) as I've ever been of any two wrestlers. After that match and that weekend, on Bret's behalf, I wrote the following, in his weekly newspaper column:

"Where boasting ends, there, dignity begins"
— Edward Young, *Night Thoughts*

> I'm not going to offer any hollow excuses for my intercontinental title defeat at the hands of my brother-in-law, Davey Boy Smith at SummerSlam. There's no shame in having lost if you've given it your best and I can take solace in knowing that I did. On this night, the decision went to the better man — so be it. I congratulate Davey Boy on a job well done, but, in the immortal words of General Douglas MacArthur, "I exit with my head held high, but shall return."

Losing to Davey Boy at SummerSlam may have been the best thing that could have happened to Bret, because he gained more glory and recognition from that defeat than for any match he ever won and he was suddenly being mentioned in the same breath as legendary workers like Ric Flair, the Funks, Harley Race and Rick Steamboat.

48
THE SASKATCHEWAN MIRAGE

The week after his epic encounter with Davey Boy, Bret called me up and divulged that the WWF brass were so pleased with his match at Wembley that they were going to put the world title on him a couple of weeks hence, in Saskatoon. He also mentioned that WWF booker Pat Patterson had been given an indefinite leave of absence because of some sexual harassment indictment and that Bret had recommended me for the job. He said that he'd pointed out to Vince how many stars had been developed up in Calgary while I was running things for my dad, as well as the many cutting-edge concepts we'd introduced to wrestling. He said Vince wanted to fly me out to Saskatoon to discuss the possibilities and that, as far as Bret was concerned, the job was mine. I thanked him for having touted me and though I'd long since come to realize that talk was cheap, when dealing with the WWF, I figured something might come of it.

A few weeks later, I flew out to Saskatoon with my dad for Bret's coronation as champion and to discuss the booking gig with Big Mac.

The first day there, I was told by one of the agents (or "stooges," as my old buddy Harley Race used to call them) that Vinnie was tied up finalizing details for Bret and Flair's title bout and that he couldn't see me until Tuesday night in Regina, at the TV tapings. No big deal, or so I thought.

As for the big title tilt that night between Flair and Bret, for whatever reason, it never really seemed to live up to expectations. In fact, in his autobiography, *To Be the Man*, Flair described it as "the shits" and even though it was a historic occasion with a hometown hero — Bret — becoming the first Canadian ever to win the WWF world title, the crowd reaction was pretty subdued. It was almost like when Buster Douglas beat Mike Tyson for the heavyweight boxing crown. Despite all that, I still was pretty happy when they presented my brother with the world title, as it was, in its own way, an affirmation of what Stampede Wrestling had been all about. One thing that was kind of hard to fathom was that, for some reason, the WWF chose not to show the match on television; that made no sense to me, considering the magnitude of the belt at that time.

After the show, my dad and I were back at our hotel, in the lounge having a beer with Owen and Davey Boy, when one of the WWF agents, J. J. Dillon, who'd worked for my dad back in the '80s, dropped by to visit. He and my dad were discussing Bret's match with Flair and my dad — who wasn't really being critical, just frank — said he thought the title change should have been on TV and that it didn't make any sense why they wouldn't have shown it.

My dad also said that while it was nice to see Bret win the strap, he was kind of disappointed in the match itself, as it never seemed to get off the ground, as he put it. Davey Boy, who was half out of it due to his usual post-match mix of Jack Daniels and Percodan, interjected and described the match as a "fooking abortion." He knocked both Flair and Bret and said that since he'd already beaten Bret at SummerSlam, it would have made a hell of a lot more sense if they'd put the strap on him instead. At the time, I was engaged in a conversation with Owen and had already been around the block enough times to know when not to be knocking people, so both of us pretty much stayed out of things.

The next day, we all flew to Regina for one of those interminable TV tapings that the WWF used to shoot in those days. They spent about five hours shooting promos for every town the WWF was going to in the next month or so, which was about as exciting as watching paint dry. I was hanging around the back with my brother Owen, waiting for my summit meeting with His Royal Highness King Vincent II, when one of the agents approached me and told me that I needed to call home, urgently.

In the past couple of years, I'd flown down twice to WWF shows to meet with Vince and each time I'd been called to the phone: the first time I was informed that my brother Dean had died; the second, I'd been told that my pregnant wife had been rushed to the hospital and likely wouldn't survive. With a great deal of trepidation, I found the nearest pay phone and called home. My wife, who was quite upset, tearfully related how she'd taken our son Rhett in for his twelve-month evaluation at the Children's Hospital — which I hadn't anticipated to be anything to be overly concerned with — and that the prognosis wasn't good. She said that after having undergone CAT scans, MRIs and whatnot at the neuromotor clinic, the doctors had informed her that he had suffered brain damage — likely due to oxygen deprivation during birth — and, as a result, he would be confined to a wheelchair and would be severely handicapped.

This all was, as you can imagine, pretty disheartening, because even though Rhett had been slow developing, I'd always been under the impression — or perhaps wishfully thinking — that it was mostly due to him having been born so premature and that, in time, he'd catch up and would be okay. After receiving that devastating news, the big meeting with Vinnie Mac suddenly seemed quite trivial and I, honestly, would rather have not even bothered with it at that point.

My brother Owen was standing nearby when I was on the phone and could tell by my expression that something was wrong. He came over and asked and when I mentioned the grim prognosis for Rhett, he seemed genuinely troubled and gave me a supportive hug. He said if there was anything he could do to let him know. I trudged back into the half-empty arena, watching an endless series of squash matches and promos, preoccupied with thinking about Rhett, but also, in the back of my mind, wondering when my meeting with Vince would finally take place. I ended up spending the rest of the afternoon and damn near the whole night, sitting up in the stands, being ignored and treated like some kind of fucking mark, happy to just be hanging around the superstars.

Near the end of the night, Owen came up to me and asked me if I'd spoken to Vince yet. I told him that I hadn't and that by this time, I didn't really give a damn whether I spoke to Vince anyway. Owen seemed quite pissed off and stormed off into the back, behind the curtain, where I could hear him tearing a strip off Vince. He told him to stop playing fucking games and that if he had no intention of meeting with me, then he should say so and stop dicking me around.

Vince then had one of his flunkies come out and tell me that Mr. McMahon — as all the ass-kissers actually call him (which is probably why they parody that name on TV) — would see me now. I, frankly, was in no mood to discuss wrestling at this point, but went back anyway.

I was escorted to Vince, who was standing by his limousine, making out as if he was in a hurry. He asked, "You wanted to see me?"

I tersely replied, "No, I was told, by Bret, that you wanted to see me about taking over the book because of Pat's legal problems — which is why, I presume, you flew me out here."

He made out as if he now remembered having sent me the ticket, but said that since he was in a hurry to catch a plane, could I perhaps send him my résumé and he'd look it over and get back to me. At this stage, given all the games and bullshit I'd already incurred, not to mention the decimating news about Rhett, I, frankly, felt like telling him to go fuck himself, but because Bret, Davey and Owen were still working for him and also because I was in no mood for confrontation at this point, I kept my mouth shut and just left — wondering to myself why Vince, Bret and whoever else continued to play all these fucking games.

I saw Bret on the plane, when we were flying back from Regina, and asked him what the hell was going on. He informed me that the reason why Vince had been such an asshole was that J. J. Dillon — the WWF agent/stooge who'd dropped by our table in the bar the night before — had told him that my dad, Davey and I had been criticizing the WWF for not having broadcast the title and that we'd also been knocking his match with Flair, claiming that it had been "the shits."

I rolled my eyes and said to myself, "Here we go again." I then told him I'd barely spoken to Dillon and that my dad and Davey had been kind of outspoken about the match not being on TV and whatnot, but even so, it was true and they shouldn't be so thin-skinned or immune to criticism. Bret, however, was impassive and gave me this sanctimonious sermon that I should have known better than to be knocking the office. He said that I'd likely blown my chances of getting hired.

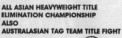

Dave Ruhl mangles Sweet
Daddy Siki's face in the late '60s

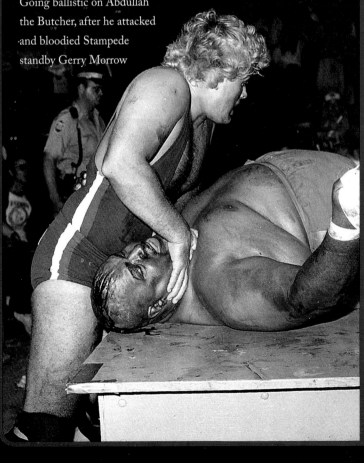

Going ballistic on Abdullah
the Butcher, after he attacked
and bloodied Stampede
standby Gerry Morrow

"Dr. D" David Schultz
with a bloody Bobby Burke

Dynamite gets the "Bad News"

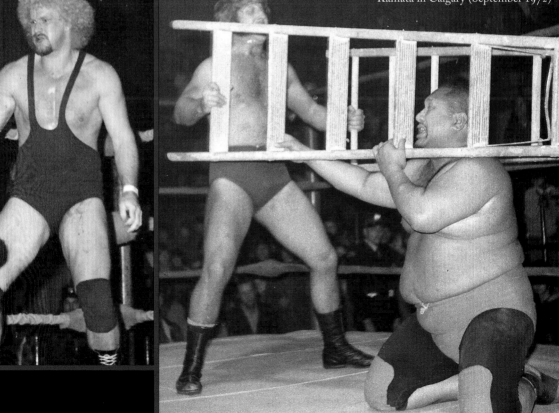

The world's first ladder match: Dan Kroffat batters Tor
Kamata in Calgary (September 1972)

FLYIN' BRIAN PILLMAN FLIES THROUGH GERRY MORROW

Makhan Singh (Mike Shaw) tortures my good friend and partner Brian Pillman

Bad Company

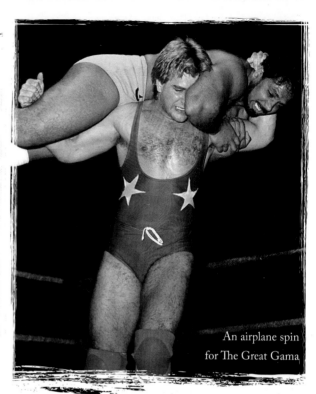

An airplane spin
for The Great Gama

Dynamite Kid is headed for a hard
landing, courtesy of a piledriver

Before becoming the "Phenom" known as
The Undertaker, a young Mark Calaway
learned the ropes with Stampede

LEFT: I was the best man at Owen's wedding

RIGHT: My brother Owen

BACKGROUND:
Owen soars toward the masked Viet Cong Express No. 1

Stu receiving the Order of Canada from Governor General Adrienne Clarkson, May 31, 2001 (Courtesy Sgt. Julien Dupuis)

Passing the knife to Stu for the ceremonial cutting of his 80th birthday cake, as several hundred family members and friends surround us

TOP LEFT: Stu and Helen on their back veranda in 2000

TOP RIGHT: *Training in the Dungeon*: "Kwik Kick" Kirk Melnyk hoists Rob "Highlander" McManus for a body slam, as I look on

BOTTOM: *From left* Lou Thesz, Harley Race, Ross Hart, Chris Benoit, Danny Hodge

and I flank Stu at the Cauliflower Alley Club reunion in 2002

I was a bit pissed with that but had far bigger things on my plate, what with the distressing prognosis about Rhett. When I arrived back home in Calgary, I found myself indulging in a bit of self-pity — the old "why me" lament. I suddenly put the brakes on though and cursed myself for being such a narrow-minded jerk, because it occurred to me that I had no right, whatsoever, to be feeling sorry for myself as it wasn't me who'd been dealt the lousy hand, it was Rhett. I made a pledge that I would endeavor to do everything in my power to make his life better and to help lighten his load — which is what I've strived to do ever since.

Even though Rhett has had to deal with a lot more than most of us can even conceive of, he remains one of the happiest, most fun-loving kids I've ever known and has been a source of inspiration to me and everyone else in our family. Anytime my kids or I have had a bad day or are feeling sorry for ourselves, all we need to do is to take a look at Rhett, who's still smiling in spite of everything that's on his plate, and our spirits are suddenly brightened. This may sound like bullshit, but I feel truly blessed that he's graced my life.

49
WCW FOLLIES

In the spring of 1993, I got a call from Davey Boy, who'd been canned by the wwf — I'm not sure if it was for having knocked the office or for drug abuse. This was not long after the Saskatchewan trip and Davey Boy was now in the wcw. He informed me that the wcw had just fired their booker, Bill Watts, for having made some ill-considered racial remarks on television and they were looking for a replacement. My name had come up and the Turner Broadcasting brass wanted to fly me down to discuss it.

The wcw flew me down to Orlando where they shot their television show. The day that I arrived, my sister Diana (Davey's wife) picked me up at the airport and drove me to the beach at St. Petersburg where the wcw was doing a television shoot involving Davey Boy, his partner Sting (Steve Borden), Van Vader and Vader's manager, Colonel Parker (Robert Fuller). They were setting up the story line for their upcoming Summer Slamboree pay-per-view.

I'm not sure what the ostensible story line was supposed to be, but while Davey and Sting were playing beach volleyball, they had a dwarf wearing a shark fin on his back sneak onto their boat, which was docked nearby, to plant a bomb on it. Shortly thereafter, just as Davey and Sting were about to start up the engine to go for a ride, someone came running up and informed them that a midget dressed up as a shark (I'm not making this shit up) had planted a bomb on the boat, at which point Davey and Sting then both jumped into the water — which was only about two feet deep. Sting nearly broke his neck and Davey landed on some bed of coral and badly gashed his knees. There was then a deafening explosion, with the boat being blown to smithereens.

Since this was on a crowded public beach and the public apparently hadn't been forewarned, there were people running for cover and little kids screaming, while toxic fumes were billowing all over the place. All the while, Eric Bischoff, who was directing this fiasco (later described by Dave Meltzer as the worst angle in wrestling history) was congratulating everyone and making out as if he was the second coming of Steven Spielberg.

Davey and Diana later told me that Bischoff had recently done another equally lame skit in which Mick Foley was cast as a homeless person in the ghettos of Atlanta out begging for nickels and dimes, at which point Teddy Long and a limousine full of black heels, made out to be pimps and drug dealers, pulled up and mugged him. Davey said that since about eighty percent of wcw's fan base was black, there was a huge outcry of protest from the NAACP, which was threatening to boycott Turner Broadcasting because the angle was racially stereotyping.

The TV tapings at Disney World were a Mickey Mouse performance — pun intended. Before the show started, the ring announcer told the audience — most of whom were tourists who'd been bribed with free T-shirts to come to the taping — that they were supposed to boo or cheer on cue, depending on which sign this moron wearing a clown outfit held up. As Davey Boy and Sting (who were wcw's top two faces) were coming out, the clown — who must have got his signals crossed — was holding up the *Boo* sign, so all the fans started booing them. One of the wcw flunkies then came running out and was dropping F-bombs on the fans — mostly kids and their parents — for being smart-asses, because they were booing the faces. One of the parents then pointed out that the clown had been holding up the *Boo* sign, which was why they were booing. The wcw guy then started chewing out the clown — in front of all the marks. He then had Davey and Sting re-enter, while the clown now held a *Cheer* sign. I was in the back watching this gong show with my old buddy Brian

Pillman and he told me that this type of thing was a pretty regular occurrence, which, I must admit, gave me second thoughts about the whole gig.

After the TV taping I had dinner with Bill Shaw and Bob Dhue, who were the TBS executives running the WCW, and they asked me what my impressions were. I told them that while the WCW had some awesome talent, including up-and-coming young stars like Steve Austin, Eddie Guerrero, Chris Benoit and Brian Pillman, as well as established stars like Barry Windham, Arn Anderson, Bobby Eaton and Davey Boy, not to mention the whole network at their beck and call, the whole promotion was a gong show, as evidenced by the beach blast, the Mick Foley ghetto mugging and the clown holding the boo/cheer signs. Shaw and Dhue — who I was later told had been the creative geniuses behind a lot of that crap — didn't seemed too thrilled with my candor and told me that they'd get back to me. I wasn't surprised when I never heard back from them.

They ended up hiring as their booker the ubiquitous Eric Bischoff, who proceeded to run the promotion into the ground and serve up future superstars like Austin, Benoit, Pillman, Booker, Foley, Jericho, Guerrero and Mysterio to the WWF on a silver platter. I have no doubt, whatsoever, that I could have done a hell of a lot more with that crew and the resources at hand than Bischoff ever did, although that's not saying much as damn near anybody could have.

50

THE "REALLY BIG" STORY LINE
(OR "I COULDA BEEN A CONTENDER")

After the exercise in futility down in Orlando, I figured, once again, that my wrestling career was over and was prepared to get on with other things. I'd just found out that my wife was expecting our fifth child (Rhett and Tory had already joined Brit and Bruce Jr.), Lara — due near Christmastime. I was more than ready to do the family guy thing.

Near the end of August, out of the blue I received a call from Pat Patterson, who had beaten the sexual harassment rap and was back working for the WWF. He asked if I'd like to come down to SummerSlam in Detroit — as his and Vince's guest. The event was only two days away. I wasn't sure what he had in mind but told him pretty bluntly that the past few times I'd been flown down to WWF gigs, it had been a waste of my time and that I wasn't that keen on flying to SummerSlam unless I got paid for it. Pat seemed quite taken aback that I wasn't marking out just at the opportunity to fly down and hang out with all the superstars, and kind of tersely replied that I'd be paid for coming down. I had no idea what Pat or Vince had in mind, but figured that if they were paying me, they must have something in mind.

Pat and Vince — who'd kind of kayfabed me on previous trips down to the WWF — couldn't have been nicer this time around. They told me that they had a "really big story line" in mind, which called for me to be planted in the crowd, like a mark, and then, at some point, when Bret was in the main event, defending his world title against Doink the Clown (Matt Borne), Jerry Lawler was supposed to hit the ring and they were supposed to kick Bret's ass. At that point, I was also supposed to hit the ring and kick their asses and brawl back to the dressing room with them.

The whole charade was easy — much like Stampede Wrestling–type fare — but got a hell of a pop, with the fans really getting into it. In fact, Dave Meltzer later wrote that there was something seriously wrong when a walk-on wrestler, who'd never been in the WWF before, got the biggest pop on the biggest pay-per-view of the summer. I'm not sure if he was putting me over, or knocking the WWF, but I took it as a compliment and was pleased that, at long last, things had gone without a hitch.

I still wasn't sure exactly where the story line was going, but Vince and Pat assured me they had something really big in mind for me at their next pay-per-view — the Survivor Series in Boston — which was going to catapult me to stardom.

As it turned out, they had me, Bret, Owen and my brother Keith tag billed originally to wrestle Jerry Lawler, Doink, Shawn Michaels and my old crony, Terry Funk, in what was billed as the Family Feud. I, honestly, wasn't sure how the hell Lawler and company could be construed as family, but then, on the other hand, Charlie Manson and his "family" weren't exactly blood either.

A few weeks before the match was supposed to take place though, Lawler got into some kind of trouble with the law in Louisville and Doink was apparently fired for being drunk and disorderly. Terry Funk also pulled out the day before, so the match ended up being the Harts vs. Shawn Michaels, Greg Valentine, Barry Horowitz and some big rookie named Jeff Gaylord.

Before I flew down to Boston for the match, I'd been led to believe by both Vince and Pat that they had some hot angle in mind for me, which was going to set the stage for something really big for me, but the night of the show, Vince and Pat were both conspicuous by their absence and we were given our finish, instead, by Bruce Prichard (Brother Love).

The script called for Owen to be eliminated first, after which he was supposed to be pissed off at me, Keith and Bret for having allowed him to get pinned. After that, the script (which was kind of flat) then called for Bret, in succession, to beat each of the heels — all with the sharpshooter, while Keith and I didn't do much but cheer him on.

I got a decent payoff for the match, but to say it was an anti-climax would be an understatement, as the supposedly really big plans that Vince and Pat had alluded to certainly didn't materialize. I was wondering if their definition of "really big" and mine were different, or if they were both simply full of shit.

A number of years later, though, I came to find out "the rest of the story," as Paul Harvey used to say. In 2000, on the first anniversary of my brother Owen's death, my beloved brother Bret divulged, in his weekly column in the newspaper, that "in September 1993, Vince McMahon . . . wanted me to wrestle my brother Bruce . . . who, as the story was going to go, would challenge me to a match . . . and our angle would build from there. I sat listening and finally told Vince McMahon that if I do wrestle any of my brothers, it had to be Owen, not Bruce. The WWF didn't like the idea, but I simply refused to do it any other way."

When I read the article, I finally realized that Vince and Pat had actually been on the level and not full of shit, as I'd long surmised, but that Bret had been the one who'd kiboshed things. What really pissed me off was that my having a "run," as they call it, in the WWF wouldn't have hurt Owen, as he was already in the WWF, making decent money at the time, while I was struggling to scrape by on a sub teacher's salary, with a ton of expensive medical bills, including wheelchairs and whatnot for Rhett. As well, at that time, I was still ghostwriting Bret's hit column, free of charge, and figured he was in my corner. Apparently not.

51
THE HART ATTACK TOUR
(MONEY FOR NOTHING)

After the less than rewarding Survivor Series charade, naturally, I figured that I'd run my course in the WWF. I wasn't expecting to hear from them, but about seven months later, in June, I was at home, watching O. J. Simpson and the bizarre white Bronco chase on the Los Angeles freeway, when my wife handed me the phone and said it was somebody from the WWF. It turned out to be Bruce Prichard and he asked if I'd be interested in tagging with Bret against Owen and Jim "The Anvil" Neidhart on a big, nationwide summer tour, to be billed as the Hart Attack Tour.

I hadn't been all that pleased with Survivor Series, but seeing as school was out and I didn't have any income over the summer, yet still had bills to pay and a family to feed, he didn't have to twist my arm too much. What's that old saying? "Money tends to make whores out of damn near everyone."

A couple of weeks later, I was on my way to southern California for the Hart Attack Tour. Our first shot of the tour was in San Diego. I flew into Los Angeles that morning to hook up with Bret, Owen and Anvil — who were already down there.

Seeing as we had the afternoon off and San Diego was only an hour's drive, we went to Gold's Gym in Santa Monica — where the owner, Pete Grymkowski, a big wrestling fan, used to comp the WWF boys. After our workout, we were upstairs hanging out with him, when in walked football player Al Cowlings, who just happened to have been driving the white Bronco during O. J. Simpson's bizarre cruise down the L.A. freeway a few weeks before. I was told that Cowlings was a big wrestling fan and he seemed to be a pretty regular guy. We hung out for about fifteen minutes and I was dying to ask him what was the inside scoop on O.J. and all of that but decided not to — not only because it was none of my business, but I didn't want to commit the cardinal wrestling sin of coming across like a mark. Funny enough, later on, Owen and Anvil told me that they, too, had been itching to ask big Al the same question but also didn't want to come across as marks.

When we went into the ring for our match that first night in San Diego, the building was half-full and most of the fans seemed pretty flat — probably, in part, because most of the matches thus far had been lame and uninspiring. Although the WWF agent for the tour, Jack Lanza, had given us a move for move script to follow, it was kind of lame and I figured why not freewheel or improvise a bit, just for the hell of it. I tried some of the standard Stampede Wrestling spots with Owen and Jim and they got an instant reaction, so we did some more and ended up having a pretty hot match. Afterward, most of the boys came up to us and were giving us high fives and complimenting us on having gotten the crowd, which had been pretty dead all night, off its ass.

The next night, we were at the "Fabulous" Forum in Los Angeles. Being a big Lakers fan, for years I'd heard of the Forum — Kareem, Magic and "Showtime" and all of that — but when I was sitting in the dressing room, I saw a big rat crawl out, almost nonchalantly, from under one of the benches and meander to the other side of the room. After that, I saw these humongous cockroaches conducting 100-centimeter dashes on the wall, and I came away with a decidedly different perspective on the Not-So-Fabulous Forum.

That night, the matches in Los Angeles were — move for move — pretty much the same as what I'd seen the night before in San Diego. Since San Diego is less than an hour from Los Angeles, there were probably more than a few fans going to both shows and I mentioned to Bret that doing the same things again might be an exposé. He and several other of the WWF wrestlers looked at me as if I was crazy or, perhaps, a mark, and one of them said, "They already know it's a work, so who cares?" I was taken aback at the cavalier attitude and told Bret that in Stampede there may have been some prevailing skepticism about the business being a work, but that through hard work and well-conceived schematics we'd made believers out of the cynics and we should be endeavoring to do the same down here. Bret shrugged indifferently and said he wasn't planning on doing things much different than he had the night before.

The crowd was pretty listless most of the night, so I decided to take things into my own hands a bit with Owen and Jim. We did a bit of brawling on the floor and standard Stampede Wrestling–style ass-kicking and wound up getting a pretty decent response. The next few nights, Owen, Jim and I continued doing more improvisational spots in the ring or out on the floor and each time, the fans really got into it.

In Denver, at the McNichols Sports Arena, we had our best crowd so far on the tour — around 10,000 people. The crowd seemed pretty lively from the get-go, so Owen, Jim and I decided to do some of our balls to the wall routines from Stampede Wrestling and the crowd ate it up. We ended up having our hottest match to date. After the match, when I arrived back in the babyfaces' dressing room, I was amazed at how many wrestlers were coming over and giving me high fives, which, I thought, was pretty cool.

I noticed that Bret wasn't in the dressing room, which was kind of odd, because most times, he'd come back with me, since we were a team. I thought that maybe he was talking to some marks or whatever and didn't give it much thought. After I showered and had changed, Bret finally returned and just after he came in, the wwf agent Jack Lanza came into the dressing room as well. Thus far on the trip, Lanza had been pretty nice, but this time around, he came over and began berating me, saying that since I was a "fucking schoolteacher" and not a wrestler, that I should be strictly following the script and not pretending that I was a fucking worker. I'd been ribbed in the past by guys like Terry Funk and initially figured Lanza — who was a seasoned old pro himself — was maybe pulling some kind of rib on the new kid, so I let him run his mouth off, without saying anything back. Like the Energizer bunny, he kept going and going . . . and going. He was also kicking garbage cans and slamming doors and whatnot. He then launched into this diatribe about the WWF being a family show and that the type of bullshit we'd done back in Calgary didn't cut it down here and all of that.

I continued trying to be diplomatic, but he continued his rant and began getting personal, making out as if I had no business even being in the ring.

When I realized he wasn't ribbing, I finally began to defend myself and angrily fired back at him, kind of like Steve Martin in *Planes, Trains and Automobiles* unloading on the rental car women. I said, "Hey Jack, if I'm just a fucking schoolteacher and not a fucking wrestler, as you keep insisting, why the fuck did you bring me down here in the first place? And why the fuck do you have me working in the fucking main events on the whole fucking tour and why the fuck did you fly me down to fucking Detroit for SummerSlam and fucking Boston for fucking Survivor Series, if I'm not a fucking wrestler?" I was eagerly awaiting Jack's reply, as were most of the boys in the dressing room, but he was suddenly at a loss for words and muttered that he didn't have to take shit from a fucking schoolteacher — as if that was akin to being a criminal — and stormed out of the dressing room.

Afterward, Bret shook his head mournfully and laid this sanctimonious lecture on me that you *never* talk back to the office and told me that, once again, I'd blown it. Funny enough, a few years later, when Bret punched out Vinnie Mac in the dressing room after the Montreal screwjob, I was half-tempted to lay the same lecture on him.

In any case, after Lanza's big tirade, I was treated like some kind of mark for the rest of the tour and wasn't allowed to do much but stand in the corner and once again act like a half-assed cheerleader. Typically, Lanza would now come in and blow smoke up my ass, telling me how much better the matches were going and making out as if he was happy with the performance. I felt like telling him not to lay the bullshit on too thick but most of the time just went along with it, because that's the way it goes in the WWF — the Wonderful World of Fantasy, as my old friend Barry Orton used to call it. Overall, the Hart Attack Tour reminded me of that cynical Dire Straits riff — "Money for Nothing."

52
DRUGS, 'ROIDS 'N' WRESTLING

While I can't say I learned a whole hell of a lot about wrestling on that tour that I didn't already know, it was quite a learning experience in other ways — especially about the proliferation of drugs and steroids. In light of the many drug- and steroid-related tragedies that have beset the WWE in recent years, I've been asked many times, why drugs and steroids have become so pervasive down there.

I've heard over and over that the "brutal" schedule in the WWF is one of the prevailing reasons for the rash of drug abuse, overdoses and whatnot. That might sound like a good excuse, but as far as I'm concerned, that's essentially a horseshit cop-out.

From what I saw, their schedule is nowhere near as grueling as the schedule we used to have in Stampede Wrestling — where we were on the road for six, sometimes seven, days a week, averaging nearly 2,000 miles a week. We were driving, not flying, everywhere — often through brutal winter weather — and staying in dumps, not five-star hotels. Usually we wound up eating at greasy spoons and fast-food joints, not five-star restaurants, like the boys in the WWF.

In its own way, our schedule in Stampede Wrestling actually served as a deterrent to taking drugs, because, since we were driving everywhere, everyone had to take their turn at the wheel, so there was no way you could be stoned or wasted.

Beyond that, in Stampede, even if you were inclined to do drugs, none of us were making enough money to indulge in coke, heroin, crystal meth or any of the so-called good shit that they seem to be using these days. As well, if you were stoned or had a drug problem, because you were among the boys all the time, it was pretty hard to do it for any length of time without everybody noticing it.

From what I could see, the two main reasons for the ongoing drug problems in the WWE are time and money. In the WWE, the wrestlers seem to have way too much time on their hands — on any given day, they have five or six hours before the matches and probably near that after the matches, which is a lot of time to kill. As well, since they're making way more money than we used to make back in Stampede Wrestling, they seem to be able to afford all the expensive drugs. I need not point out that most of those drugs are highly addictive and have all kinds of dangerous side effects. Before long, they take over, and the results, all too often, are extremely tragic.

Another contributing factor is that a lot of wrestlers have come to equate being a worker with doing high-risk stunts — the Jeff Hardy/Sabu syndrome. Because they're all doing these dangerous moves on such a regular basis, they're getting hurt a lot more and often have to wrestle injured rather than allow their injuries to heal. As a consequence, they've been resorting to heavy-duty pain-killers — OxyContin, Halcions, Demerol, Placidyls and even morphine and heroin — all of which are highly addictive and have proven to be lethal.

One of the other things I noticed down in the WWF that's a major factor in the ongoing drug problem is that the wrestlers really need to be "on" or normal for maybe fifteen minutes per day. By that I mean the only time they really need to be somewhat clear-minded or coherent is when they're in the ring.

Since most matches in the WWF rarely go past fifteen minutes, that's the only time they really need to have their shit together, and since most of their matches are scripted as well, even if they're half out of it, most times they can stumble their way through or have the other guy carry them and still get away with it. In any other normal line of work, except maybe for being a rock musician, you couldn't get away with that. Because the body soon develops a tolerance for drugs, users invariably have to increase the dosage to achieve the desired effect, and so on and so forth — to the point where things invariably seem to just spin out of control. This is pretty much what happened, I'd venture to say, with Pillman, Guerrero and so many of the other poor bastards you keep reading about in the obits.

What's really twisted is that when one of the wrestlers overdoses, even though damn near everyone around them was well aware that they were on drugs, everyone — probably because they're either covering their own asses or are in some fucked-up state of denial — makes out to be stunned and claims that they never saw it coming. It is a classic case of a head in the sand attitude.

While I'm on the subject of drugs and whatnot, the other major one that continues to be a problem in the WWF is anabolic steroids, which in many cases are intertwined with the other forms of drug abuse we've already been discussing. In recent years, there have been an alarming number of wrestlers who have died prematurely and damn near everybody in the business knows that it was due to steroid abuse, but more often than not, the cause of death is reported as a heart attack or natural causes — which is bullshit.

Even though the WWE supposedly now has regular, state-of-the-art steroid and drug testing, there seem to be more anabolically enhanced guys on their roster than ever and the list of former WWE stars who keep dropping dead way before their time continues to grow.

I'm sure that the powers that be will tell me that I'm way off base, but I have no doubt whatsoever that if the WWE truly wanted to get rid of steroid abuse, it could do so in short order — simply by not pushing guys because of their look and by putting in place some legitimate educational programs about steroids and the damage they cause. As the old cliché goes: an ounce of prevention is worth a pound of cure. If they practiced what they so sanctimoniously preach, the steroid problem would have been eliminated a long time ago.

In any case, I apologize for my somewhat lengthy dissertation on drug and steroid abuse in wrestling. It's something I felt I had to address, somewhere and somehow in this book.

After the conclusion of my own version of *Dancing with the Stars* on the Hart Attack Tour, I once again figured that was the end of the line. As Ol' Blue Eyes, Frank Sinatra, once so poignantly rhapsodized, "Regrets, I've had a few, but then again, too few to mention." That's about how I felt at that stage; even though I unfortunately hadn't scaled the heady heights that Bret and others in the family had, I'd still been lucky enough to bask, if only briefly, in the spotlight, which was a lot more than I can say for many of my poor, hapless colleagues.

53
A NIGHT TO REMEMBER

After the unfulfilling Hart Attack Tour, I was pretty much out of the wrestling business and can't say I was really having any great withdrawal issues, as my wife had given birth to our fifth child — my daughter Lara — and I was also coaching my sons in baseball and hockey. I was inadvertently drawn back when my brother Ross and I ran into our old Stampede Wrestling commentator Ed Whalen just before Christmas 1994. Ed asked how my dad was doing. Ross mentioned that he was doing fine and that his eightieth birthday was coming up in May. Ed suggested a nice way to honor the occasion would be to have a commemorative wrestling card and invite back former Stampede Wrestlers from the past — for one last hurrah.

Ross and I agreed with Ed that it would be kind of cool and I suggested that the proceeds from the show could go to some good cause — which turned out to be the Calgary Quest Academy, a school for special needs kids such as my son Rhett.

Whalen — who'd worked tirelessly for years for the Children's Miracle Network and Easter Seals and whatnot — was all for that and we shook hands on it and agreed to make it happen. I soon began contacting wrestlers and was amazed by how many people wanted to be part of the show, including my brothers Bret and Owen and brother-in-law Davey Boy. They were headlining in the WWF. We also invited back other Stampede alumni, like Brian Pillman and Chris Benoit, who were stars in the WCW.

Our original intent was to have the card on or around my dad's birthday in May but, because the WWE was on a European tour at that time, it wouldn't work for Bret, Owen, Davey and the other WWE guys. We ended up trying to come up with other dates through the summer or fall, but for one reason or another, nothing seemed to work with everyone's schedule. We finally had to book the show in December, because that was the earliest date we could get the building and the boys and everything else at the same time.

Ross and I were amazed at how many guys wanted to appear on the card, including WWF stalwarts like Razor Ramon, Shawn Michaels, X-Pac, Shane Douglas and a star-studded cast from the WCW including Terry and Dory Funk and Mike Shaw. We also were able to line up an impressive array of old-timers, including Dan Kroffat, Tor Kamata, Gil Hayes, Archie Gouldie, Dynamite Kid and Angelo Mosca, among others.

In addition to the wrestling luminaries, we also extended invitations to surviving members of my dad's 1938–1939 Edmonton Eskimos football team, as well as to other football and hockey stars, and dignitaries, such as the prime minister, the premier, the mayor and other prominent Canadians. We hoped all of this effort would make the show "a night to remember."

While it was exciting to see so many wrestlers and others onboard, the whole venture was, nonetheless, quite costly. By the first of October I'd already laid out over $40,000, out of my own pocket, to pay for building rental, airfares, hotel reservations, advertising and assorted other expenses — and that didn't even cover the talent. I was confident that we would draw a good house, but for some reason, our initial advance ticket sales were pretty sluggish. Since I'd pretty much mortgaged the farm, my wife was starting to panic.

Thankfully, ticket sales began to move in the first week of December and by December 10, we'd passed the break-even point and my wife and I could finally breathe a bit easier. Much of the credit for the success of the show, I should point out, was due to the work of our tireless group of volunteers, including Bonnie Pacaud, Jude Heyland, Marge Gudmandson, Carson Ackroyd, Jim

Wilde, Georgie Fixler, Gerry Forbes and Linda Slobodian — all of whom worked long and hard.

A few days before the show, I got a call from my brother Bret. This wasn't unusual, since I was still writing his weekly column for him and figured he might be giving me some material for that week's piece. That wasn't the reason why he was calling this time though, as he tersely informed me that it had been brought to his attention that the wcw guys would be on our show. Since the wcw and the wwf were at war at the time, he demanded that I remove them from the card immediately or else he, Owen, Davey Boy and the other wwf guys would boycott the show.

It had been no secret, from the get-go, that former Stampede stars such as Pillman, Benoit, Shaw and the Funks — who were now working for the wcw — would be on the card. I couldn't fathom how Bret hadn't been aware of that. Beyond that, I stressed to him that this show wasn't a wwf or a wcw show, but that it was about Stu. The boys were on the card because they wanted to pay tribute to him — plain and simple. Bret, however, stubbornly refused to change his mind and reiterated that if the wcw guys were on the card, the wwf guys wouldn't be, and angrily hung up on me.

About twenty minutes later, Carl De Marco, the figurehead president of the wwf, called and said that it had been brought to his attention that non-wwf performers were going to be on the birthday card for my dad and that this was a contravention of wwf policy and that if they weren't removed, he'd have no recourse but to remove the wwf guys from the show. I endeavored to explain the situation to him, but, like Bret, he was completely unbending and told me to govern myself accordingly.

A few hours later, I had to drive out to the airport to pick up my old crony, Brian Pillman, and I related my dilemma to him. He was quite pissed off and said that he'd taken time off from his wcw schedule to fly up, strictly because of his high regard for Stu, and that so had the other guys, and Bret should understand that.

Later that night, I got a call from Owen — who told me that De Marco had called him and had decreed that he boycott the show. Owen sneered that De Marco was merely a figurehead flunky — about like Vickie Guerrero being the manager of *SmackDown!* Owen said that he had told De Marco he was going to be on the show, regardless of what he said, and that was that.

Owen also told me that De Marco had tried to give the same ultimatum to the other WWF guys, including Davey, Razor Ramon and Sean Waltman (X-Pac) and that they had no intentions of boycotting the show either. As it turned out, by showtime, the only guy who looked like he'd be a no-show was Bret — who still was refusing to change his stance.

The show, I'm happy to report, proved to be an unqualified success, and though it was a tribute card, the matches, in typical Stampede Wrestling tradition, were intense, with the wrestlers pulling out all the stops. It was a dream come true for me and Pillman to have the opportunity to work against two of our all-time idols: Terry and Dory Funk Jr. We had an old-fashioned ass-kicker of a match that was rated "match of the year" by longtime wrestling journalist Dr. Mike Lano. I'm pleased to also report that, at the last minute, my obdurate brother Bret finally did show up and worked against Davey Boy.

The highlight of the night was when all the wrestlers, from the past and present, a veritable who's who of wrestling legends, assembled in the ring while Alberta Premier Ralph Klein delivered a moving tribute to my dad, which had many in the crowd misty-eyed. After paying all the expenses, I was also able to write a check for nearly $10,000 to my son Rhett's school, which was an added bonus.

After all the hard work and assorted trials and tribulations, I was pleased and relieved that the show had finally been an unqualified success, but early the next morning, I was awakened by a phone call from Bret. I figured that since his match had gone well and that he'd not only received a decent payoff for it, but also a $1,200 commemorative biker jacket that Harley-Davidson motorcycles had custom-made for each of the WWE and WCW wrestlers, that he might be calling to perhaps bury the hatchet. Instead, he launched into a profanity-laced tirade, claiming that the only reason he'd worked was because it would have made him look bad if he'd been the only one to boycott his own father's show. He then informed me that since I'd defied his request to get rid of the WCW guys, he no longer wanted me ghostwriting his syndicated newspaper column for him. His Christmas greeting to me, as he was bidding me adieu, was for me to go fuck myself — thanks, bro, whatever happened to "'Tis the season to be jolly" or whatever else? Although my dad's eightieth birthday show was a resounding success and certainly lived up to its advance billing as "A Night to Remember," some aspects of it I'd just as soon forget.

54
MORE FUN AND GAMES

After the smoke had cleared from my dad's birthday bash, I sent Vince McMahon a thank-you note for having allowed the WWF boys appear on my dad's birthday bash. A few weeks later, Vince's son Shane McMahon called me and said he and Vince were pleased to hear the show had gone well. He then related that he was now handling talent development for the WWF and, given the number of great workers that had emerged from Stampede Wrestling, the WWF was interested in working with us to establish a developmental territory in Western Canada. I mentioned to him that I'd proposed this several years ago to Vince and that nothing had materialized, but that if he was serious, I'd be more than happy to work with them on it.

He assured me he was quite sincere this time around and said he'd like to fly up to Calgary to meet with me and my dad. I made arrangements to hook up with him. The day that he was supposed to arrive, I drove out to the airport to pick him up, but he was nowhere to be found, and I found myself wondering what had happened. I later on ran into Owen, who told me that Bret had intercepted Shane and had convinced him to let him run a training facility for the WWF out of his house instead.

I was perplexed, because Bret had never trained anyone in his life, but even if he had been the world's greatest trainer, he was still wrestling full time in the WWF, so he wouldn't be able to devote any time to it anyway. Owen said he totally agreed, but that for some reason Shane and Vince had changed their minds and decided to go that direction and that was that.

As things turned out, the only two wrestlers of any note who did eventually come out of Bret's so-called training camp were Mark Henry and this big bodybuilder named Brakkus (Achim Albrecht), which pales in comparison to the number of world-class performers who had come out of the Dungeon. As far as I'm concerned, that was a huge blown opportunity for the WWF. I don't think that too many people in the know will argue that the lack of a viable means of supplying talent not only continues to be a major cause for concern in the wrestling business today, but is the main reason why the WWE has had to continue to resort to sex, violence, second-rate comedy and other bullshit as a means of compensating for the dearth of decent talent.

Since Bret's tantrum at my dad's eightieth birthday show and his subsequent swerve with Shane, I didn't have much to do with him, but in July 1996, our family was beset with a life-and-death situation: my thirteen-year-old nephew, Matt (the son of my sister Georgia), was suddenly stricken with deadly flesh-eating bacteria. We were all summoned to the hospital where he was fighting for his life.

When I arrived at the hospital, various members of our family were gathered there for the grim vigil and I ran into Bret. There was an uneasy pause on both of our parts, but I decided it would only add to an already stressful situation by continuing to grind my ax with him, so I extended my hand and we embraced, putting aside our differences out of respect for the situation. Sadly, Matt would pass away a couple of days later — the first in what would become a rash of tragedies and misfortune for our family over the next few years.

55
THE NOT SO BIG APPLE

Just before Christmas 1996, my brother-in-law Jim "The Anvil" Neidhart called me and told me he was now working for a new promotion called UCW (Ultimate Championship Wrestling) that was running shows in and around New York. They were looking for a booker and he'd recommended me for the job. Since I was still working for the Calgary Board of Education and had justifiable misgivings about the stability of any wrestling endeavor — the old bird in the hand being worth two or three in the bush adage — I wisely declined the offer. Jim persisted though and said that since the UCW was only running every second weekend, the promoter would be willing to fly me down for those shows and I could still keep my day job, so to speak. Since I was barely making enough to get by teaching, I was happy to have the extra income and decided to take them up on the offer.

The UCW gig was interesting, to say the least. The shows were along the lines of what was shown in *The Wrestler*, with a few out-of-work ex-WWF stars like Jim Neidhart, Marty Jannetty, King Kong Bundy, Tony Atlas and Tatanka headlining the cards. The rest of the roster consisted of self-trained local guys, who wore homemade outfits and had to set up the rings, take down the chairs, do all the grunt labor chores and got paid next to nothing for working, but were happy just to be able to have a chance to work — something I could relate to, having come from Stampede, where we often ran on a shoestring budget ourselves.

When I first arrived down there, the shows were pretty pathetic, with most of the WWF guys just going through the motions and collecting their salaries, while the UCW guys worked strictly in the opening matches and had no clue as to what they were doing and weren't given any guidance. The crowds were small and most fans had come out to see the so-called names from the WWF, but after seeing the lackluster performance, they usually didn't come back. Even so, I sensed that if we gave the fans decent shows — along the lines of what Stampede used to have — the fans were ready to come onboard. I therefore endeavored to light a fire under the local guys and also told the WWF guys that it would be in their best interests if the promotion got off the ground, because it would provide them a long-term employment option if other things didn't materialize.

I came up with this concept of casting the ex-WWF guys as arrogant, fat-cat heels, looking down their noses at the inferior local guys and built up this feud between the two. The fans seemed to get into it and would be chanting "U–C–Dub" loudly, and booing the ex-WWFers. In time, the story line began to take hold and our gates began to improve each time out. By springtime, things had improved to the point where the gates were pretty good and the promoter was close to getting a television show and looking to expand — which was encouraging.

Around about that time though, my brother Bret — who was still the WWF champion and was in the midst of launching the revival of the Hart Foundation to stoke his feud with "Stone Cold" Steve Austin — called Neidhart and invited him to return to the WWF. Even though Neidhart had recently signed a two-year contract with the UCW, he headed back to the WWF. I couldn't really blame Jim for jumping, but the way he handled it wasn't very good. He didn't explain his situation to the UCW promoters, who'd invested a lot of time and money into him, only to see him suddenly walk. Since I was Jim's brother-in-law (and Bret's brother), it was assumed that I'd been behind Jim's defection, so I was let go as well. I couldn't blame the promoters, but it was too damn bad, as the promotion was just starting to finally get off the ground.

That seemed to mark the end of the UCW; it would shut down a month or so later. I felt bad because it was just starting to get off the ground. It could have become a good place for guys to learn how to work and been a viable feeder territory for the WWF.

56
THE RAW DEAL

A month or so after the demise of the UCW, my old buddy Brian Pillman called me up. Since I'd last seen him, he'd jumped from the WCW to the WWF and had joined the reformed Hart Foundation — which consisted now of Bret, Owen, Jim Neidhart and Davey Boy — all of whom were now cast as anti-American heels. Although they were all great workers, none of them had been that strong on the mike, but with Pillman (one of the best mike men in the business) onboard, they were now the hottest heel aggregation in the industry. Their feud with the All-American redneck "Stone Cold" Steve Austin and fellow American iconoclasts like the Legion of Doom (Hawk and Animal) was now the big ticket in the WWF. It was selling out all over North America.

In any case, Pillman told me the reason he was calling was that he'd been pitching Vince McMahon to bring me down to the WWF to join the Hart Foundation and that, as part of that, we could perhaps reprise our highly successful Bad Company tag team. He told me that Vince and Pat Patterson had been receptive and that they were coming to Calgary in a couple of months for a big pay-per-view called the Canadian Stampede and wanted to introduce me on that card.

I was pumped at the prospect of reuniting with Pillman. He and I had not only enjoyed great synergy in the ring, but he'd always been a great friend. At the same time though, since we were talking about the WWF here, where talk is exceedingly cheap, I wasn't about to count any of my chicks (or should I say, checks) until they hatched.

A couple of weeks later, my brother Bret — whom I was now on pretty decent terms with — called me up. Unaware that Pillman had called me, he made out as if he'd been the one who'd gone to bat for me with Vince, but, in any case, divulged that they wanted me to come down for the big pay-per-view and were going to shoot some kind of angle on that card that would bring me into the Hart Foundation — and things would unfold from there. Bret said they were either looking to have me go after the cruiserweight belt, which would give the Hart Foundation all the title belts in the WWF, or, more likely, wanted me to tag up with Pillman. In any case, he said that they were quite keen on having me on the team and to prepare to raise a little hell with him and the boys.

When the WWF hit town that July for their first pay-per-view ever in Calgary, there was a huge buzz. On the finish of the match, which was a ten-man tag pitting the Hart Foundation (Bret, Jim, Owen, Davey and Brian Pillman) against Austin's redneck army (Steve Austin, Hawk, Animal, UFC star Ken Shamrock and Golddust), they had me interfere with Austin, thereby costing him the match — and setting the stage, or so I thought, for some hot angle with Steve and company.

When the Harts went over on the finish, there was a huge pop among the 20,000-plus rabid fans in the Saddledome. Cheering went on and on, afterwards. As the crowd continued to cheer, my brother Owen and Pillman invited my dad and me into the ring to join in the post-match celebration. As we were getting in the ring, some of the third-generation Harts, including Owen's son, Davey Boy's kids, my kids, Bret's and others started climbing in the ring and soon there must have been about forty family members and friends in the ring, while the crowd continued cheering. I thought that was pretty cool — the Stampede Wrestling fans showing their love for the Harts, especially my dad — and never had any idea that it would be any kind of problem or issue.

I'd been told before the Canadian Stampede pay-per-view by Pat Patterson that, as a follow-up to what we'd done in Calgary, my dad and I were supposed to go up to Edmonton the next day for *Monday Night RAW*, at which time we were supposed to be guests of Jerry "The King" Lawler for his King's Court segment. "Stone Cold" Steve Austin was supposed to come out, supposedly angry that we'd cost him the match the day before. We were supposed to then shoot some kind of angle between him and me — which would lead to my being brought into the mix. Since Austin was the hottest thing in the WWF at the time, it sounded like a great opportunity and I was pumped about the possibilities.

After having driven the three hours up to Edmonton the next day, my dad and I were kayfabed at the back door by the same security guys who'd embraced us with open arms the day before. They said that the WWF had told them no backstage access for anyone but the wrestlers. I explained to them that Pat Patterson and Vince had instructed us to come up because we were supposed to be appearing on *RAW* to shoot the angle, but they refused to let us in. I finally asked them to get Owen, Bret or Pillman to come out and they'd vouch for us. After close to an hour's wait outside, Pillman finally came to the back door. He was steamed that Bret had vetoed the whole thing because he was pissed off that all the kids had come in the ring the day before and figured I'd invited them in just to upstage him — which was so ridiculous that it was laughable, except that unfortunately, it wasn't actually funny.

While I was pissed off at having gotten my hopes up only to have them dashed again, by now I'd almost come to expect getting swerved — like Charlie Brown having the football pulled away by Lucy. I felt bad for my wife and kids though — who, for the past few years, had seen Bret, Owen, Davey, Neidhart, Pillman and several other guys whom I'd helped launch in Stampede Wrestling all making big money, driving hot cars and living in fancy shacks, while we continued to struggle to make ends meet. After the rousing success the day before in Calgary, they'd been excited about the supposed angle that was going to take place on *RAW* and had all gathered in front of the television with their friends to watch their pop in action. Once again though, nothing happened and I suspect they must have figured that I'd maybe made the whole thing up. In any case, when I came home the next day, nobody said much, but I could see they were really disappointed, my wife especially — which would have a major impact on things down the road.

HART BREAK

57

ANOTHER ONE BITES THE DUST

Two days after the *RAW* deal in Edmonton, I received a frantic call from Brian Pillman's wife, Melanie, who said that Brian was supposed to have arrived back in Cincinnati on Tuesday afternoon after the *RAW* taping. She hadn't seen or heard from him yet. I told her which hotel the boys stayed at up in Edmonton and about fifteen minutes later, she called me back and said that Brian had been found, apparently still sleeping in his hotel room in Edmonton.

I was happy to hear he was okay, but the fact that he was still asleep nearly two days later was pretty worrisome. I asked her if Brian, like a number of other wrestlers I'd known, had a drug problem.

She kind of broke down and told me that this hadn't been the first time something like this had happened and that the past few months he'd been taking Percodan for a leg injury he'd sustained in a car wreck. She said that they seemed to be getting out of hand.

She intimated that she was worried sick that he might wind up like Eddie Gilbert, "Quick Draw" Rick McGraw and other wrestlers who'd died of drug overdoses. She said that she suspected one of the reasons Pill had been hoping I'd get booked into the wwf was because he hoped I could perhaps help him get back on track.

I called Pill the next day and he initially denied that he had any kind of drug problem, but after talking to him for a while, he acknowledged that he'd been taking some heavy-duty painkillers and was concerned that they were becoming a problem. I told him that he should take some time off and get checked into a drug rehab clinic, but he told me he had an expensive mortgage, car payments and a stack of bills to pay and couldn't risk getting fired — which he figured would likely happen if the WWF found out that he had a drug problem. I called Owen afterward and asked him if he could perhaps room with Pillman or try to get him into rehab, but he told me that his wife, Martha, would blow a gasket if she found out he was rooming with a womanizing playboy like Brian. He said that he'd talk with Pill and try to convince him to get some help.

I spoke to Brian a few more times over the summer and while he still didn't sound great, he assured me that he was weaning himself from the heavy drugs (like Percodan, Placidyl and Soma) and that he was getting back to normal. I had my doubts, but he assured me he was okay. I told him, in any case, to feel free to call me, anytime, if he needed someone to talk to, or whatever else.

On the afternoon of Friday, October 3, I came home from school and my wife told me that Brian had called that afternoon from the "sky phone" on the plane, en route to Minneapolis where the WWF was wrestling that weekend. When I asked her what he wanted, she told me that it was kind of strange — that he didn't really seem to have any reason to have called but nonetheless kept her on the phone for over half an hour, just talking about nothing, as if he needed to talk to someone. I had no idea how to get a hold of him, but made up my mind that I would call him when he got back to Cincinnati after the *RAW* taping on Monday night. I told my wife that I might take some time off from teaching to fly down and see if I could be of some help.

Two days later, my brother Owen called me from St. Louis and told me the distressing news that Brian had just been found dead in his hotel room in St. Paul, Minnesota; the cause of death, he said, was an apparent heart attack, but most figured it had been due to a drug overdose.

I flew down to Cincinnati later that week for his funeral and the night before the funeral, I had a chance to hang out with some of his longtime wrestling buddies, including Les Thatcher, Mike Mooneyham, Kim Wood, Joey Maggs

and Dave Meltzer. Though there were a few tears in our beers, as some senti-
mental cowboy poet once ruefully remarked, we had a nice time, reflecting on
the life and times of one of wrestling's most colorful characters.

The next morning, just before we were leaving for the service, Brian's wife
came up to me, upset, and told me that Steve Austin, who was supposed to be
one of the pallbearers and was also supposed to deliver a eulogy, had just faxed
her this note, which she showed to me. It said, "Hey Mel, sorry I couldn't make
the funeral, a few things came up. Talk to you later, Steve."

Eighteen months later, when my brother Owen tragically died, the only WWF
star not in attendance then was Steve Austin. Not to knock him, because he's
always been a nice guy to me, personally, but I wonder if that's why he's called
"Stone Cold."

As a pinch hitter for Austin, Brian's wife asked me if I could deliver the eulogy
for him. Although it was on exceedingly short notice, I told her I'd be honored to
give it a shot and scribbled down the following on the way to the funeral:

> In the dog-eat-dog world of pro wrestling, where backstabbers,
> liars, ass-kissers and egomaniacs are the rule rather than the
> exception, true friends are few and far between. Through thick
> and thin, ups and downs, the good times and the bad, Brian
> Pillman was a true blue friend all the way.
>
> I can recall, as if it were yesterday, the first time we met. It
> was the summer of 1986 and an acquaintance on the Calgary
> Stampeders football team called me and told me that one of his
> teammates — a linebacker named Pillman — had been having
> trouble getting along with the hard-ass defensive coach and
> was looking to get into wrestling instead. I arranged to meet
> him and Brian the next day up at my dad's infamous Dungeon
> — which was where many other future stars also got their start.
>
> Based on what I'd been given to believe, I was anticipating
> some kind of cocky, arrogant loose cannon type, with a chip
> on his shoulder, but instead encountered this self-effacing and
> quietly determined guy who respectfully asked whether I'd

consider breaking him into wrestling, as it had been a lifelong dream of his to train in the Dungeon. We shook hands on it and that marked the beginning of a great friendship.

Though he was plagued by injuries, including recurring shoulder and ankle problems, and was also thought by many to be too small to make it big in the then heavyweight-dominated world of big-time wrestling, Pill tackled wrestling with his usual fierce determination and within a matter of months was ready for his ring debut — which was attended by all his teammates from the Stampeders.

Brian's career took off from the get-go and he soon was receiving rave reviews. However, shortly afterward he messed his shoulder up quite badly, so much so that the doctors weren't sure if he could wrestle again. That type of conjecture served to only fuel his fire more though and within a matter of weeks, he returned to the ring — even better than before.

I later came to learn that the shoulder injury had been just one of many seemingly insurmountable hurdles that he had to overcome. When he was only four, he was stricken with life-threatening throat cancer and would endure several operations for the recurring condition. Later on, despite not being offered a scholarship because scouts deemed him too small, he — as a walk-on, which is almost unheard of — would go on to become an All-American linebacker at Miami University of Ohio and would go on to play in the NFL for his hometown Cincinnati Bengals, as well as the Grey Cup champion Calgary Stampeders in the Canadian Football League. Time and time again, in his all too short life, he stared adversity squarely in the eye and then would throw it for a ten-yard loss.

In wrestling, he not only rose to the very top of the ladder, becoming a superstar in both the WCW and the WWF, he also became the only non-family member to be welcomed into the Hart Foundation. To me, my brothers Bret and Owen, my brothers-in-law Davey Boy and Jim Neidhart and my father, Stu, he was family, in every sense of the word.

Because of his often unconventional performances in the ring, many perceived Brian as some kind of certified loose cannon, but, in actuality, he was nothing like that. To those who knew him, he was a caring, compassionate friend who would unhesitatingly give you the shirt off his back. He was respected and held in high regard throughout the business and, in the very best sense, was "one of the boys." Beyond that, he was a devoted family man, with an enormous heart.

Although this is a very sad occasion, rather than mourn Brian's passing, I'd like to take this opportunity to celebrate his life — the triumphs, his beating of the odds, his unsinkable zest for life and for all the things he did that so enriched our lives and the wrestling business. This past week, I've found myself repeatedly running the gamut of emotions, from tears to laughter and back again — remembering the awesome matches and a few awful ones, too, the road trips, the ribs, the hopes and dreams we shared, and I shall cherish those memories.

Somewhere up yonder, I know there's a raspy-voiced new recruit, with just a touch of hell in him, who has just drop-kicked wide open the Pearly Gates and has likely admonished a startled St. Peter with his signature greeting, "You'll do nothing, and like it!" Take it from me, folks — heaven will never be the same. In closing, to paraphrase Elton John, "It seems to me, Pill, that you've lived your life like a Roman candle in a hurricane — your candle having burned out long before your legend ever will!" Rest easy, old friend.

58

THE INFAMOUS MONTREAL SCREWJOB

Only a few weeks after Pillman had been laid to rest, another decimating blow was dealt to the Hart Foundation and, all things considered, to the entire wrestling business, with the infamous "Montreal screwjob," as it has come to be known. For those of you who are unfamiliar with that whole tawdry affair, it goes something like this.

In the fall of 1997, the Hart Foundation (consisting of my brothers Bret and Owen, and brothers-in-law Jim Neidhart and Davey Boy Smith) was still riding high in the WWF, holding most of the major titles, with the world title held by Bret. That November at Survivor Series in Montreal, Bret was scheduled to defend his title against his old nemesis, Shawn Michaels. Based on what I've heard, Vince McMahon and his advisers wanted the Hitman to drop the strap to Shawn. Bret, however, was about as fond of Shawn as Donald Trump is of Rosie O'Donnell and also felt that having to lose to him in his native Canada was a deliberate slap in the face. As a result, he informed Vince that he simply couldn't see fit to put Shawn over. Although McMahon and his chief booker at the time, Vince Russo, did their level best to get Bret to oblige, he reiterated his abject disinclination to lose to Shawn, claiming that in his humble opinion the Heartbreak Kid simply wasn't fit to wear the title. Finally, with things at a protracted impasse only days before the big show, McMahon and Russo made out as if they had capitulated to Bret's refusal to lose to Shawn and instead came up with some kind of compromise finish, which would have enabled Bret to retain the title — or so he was given to believe.

McMahon and Russo, of course, subsequently reneged on their promise to Bret (that he didn't have to drop the strap) and then proceeded to orchestrate this sneaky double-cross which involved referee Earl Hebner making out as if the Hitman had submitted to Michaels (who, to add insult to injury, had Bret in his own signature submission hold — the sharpshooter). Hebner then ordered the timekeeper to ring the bell and raised Shawn's arm and handed him the belt.

When Bret got up and realized he'd been royally screwed (without even being kissed), he went totally ballistic — he contemptuously hawked a big loogie in Vince McMahon's face at ringside and later punched him out in the dressing room. Bret was so bitter and enraged afterward, in fact, that he was quoted in Vince Russo's book *Forgiven* as saying that he "felt like showing up at the building the next day with a gun and blowing people away!"

The Montreal screwjob remains one of the most controversial incidents in the annals of our business. Not only as Bret's brother, but also as one who's been on both sides of the proverbial fence in the wrestling business — as a wrestler and also as a booker/promoter — I've been asked many a time what my take on the whole sordid scenario is. I've spent a fair bit of time endeavoring to see it from both sides and will now attempt to render an objective and hopefully insightful assessment — straight from the Hart!

As for Vince McMahon and his cohorts in the WWF, I honestly don't know whether they could have perpetrated a more poorly executed fuck job if they had tried. I say that for a number of reasons. First, the half-assed and illicit way the title was switched certainly didn't do much for the new champion, Michaels. As a rule, when a major title changes hands, one of the primary objectives is for the new title holder to be able to get off to a good start by going over strong or getting a good reaction when he wins the belt. That usually involves a hot finish — something impressive and well-conceived, which sets things up nicely for the new champion's title run. That, obviously, wasn't the case here, as the shoddy manner in which the belt was transferred got over about as well as someone passing gas on a subway car at rush hour. As a result, it essentially reduced Michaels to lame duck status as champion — which, of course, considerably compromised his drawing ability.

Beyond that and probably even more damaging, the shoddy title switch cheapened the hell out of the image of the belt itself. It's important to keep in mind, regardless of whether wrestling is perceived to be a work or not, that at that time the WWF title was still regarded as wrestling's Holy Grail — our sport's equivalent to the Super Bowl, Stanley Cup, World Series or whatever else. In the eyes of wrestling fans, it was every bit as sacred as those prestigious titles. That changed in Montreal though. As major league baseball fans can ruefully attest, if the perceptible integrity of your ultimate championship is compromised or tarnished — which is what happened in 1919 when Shoeless Joe Jackson and his crooked Black Sox teammates threw the World Series — it can place the whole sport in jeopardy and take years to recover. The Montreal debacle had a similar effect on pro wrestling and left the WWF with a pronounced black eye and made it the object of all kinds of derision and ridicule.

On a purely personal level, the whole unseemly affair certainly didn't do a whole hell of a lot for Vince McMahon's image either. Prior to Montreal, while there may have been some conjecture about him being ruthless, arrogant and, at times, unethical, he was nonetheless respected by most as a shrewd, savvy operator whose vision and entrepreneurial acumen had transformed the WWF from a regional promotion into a huge worldwide phenomenon. Not only did the Montreal miscarriage cause the public to see him as a devious, profligate swerve artist, but the heavy-handed and incompetent way it was carried out made him look like a bumbling screwup who couldn't even pull off his own ill-conceived treachery. That sure as hell isn't the type of image the CEO of a multibillion-dollar publicly traded corporation wants to cultivate.

In a lot of ways the whole surreptitious scandal reminds me of Watergate — what with the sneaky, devious intent and the remarkably amateurish execution. Surely Vince and his coterie of supposedly clever and resourceful co-conspirators could have come up with a more subtle, fool-proof plan of attack that, at the very least, would have kept the commander-in-chief from being incriminated or caught up in the middle of things — just as most people would have figured the same for Richard Nixon. We all know what Watergate did for Nixon's career and his legacy. Fortunately, the WWF isn't held to the same type of circumspect scrutiny as the White House and, because *Wrestling Observer* publisher Dave Meltzer doesn't quite carry the same cachet as Bob Woodward and Carl Bernstein did, Vinnie Mac couldn't be impeached or run out of town on a rail. The whole botched comedy of errors nonetheless still compromised Vinnie Mac's image in much the same way as it did Tricky Dick's.

Aside from all the negative publicity Vince incurred, I would imagine that the whole fiasco must have adversely affected his working relationship with a lot of the boys as well. I would have to think that stars like Steve Austin, Undertaker, Mick Foley and others must have been thinking to themselves, as they watched the whole charade unfold, "If Vince is capable of screwing one of his longest serving, most loyal and dedicated stars in this manner, then he's just as likely to screw any one of us in a similar fashion." Breaching the sacred trust of the boys, upon which the success of any promotion is predicated, is, in my humble estimation, one of the worst transgressions a promoter can be guilty of.

Beyond making Shawn Michaels a lame duck champion, compromising the all-important image of the world title, irrevocably tarnishing his own image and that of the whole company and seriously jeopardizing his working relationship with much of his talent, the Montreal screwjob also served to make Bret a major martyr, which, of course, considerably enhanced his marketability with the rival WCW — which, I suspect, wasn't what McMahon and Russo had in mind either.

I've heard a number of excuses put forth as to why the WWF felt they had to orchestrate things the way they did. One was that McMahon and company were afraid that Bret, who was reportedly poised to defect to the WCW, was planning on taking the belt to WCW and "dissing" it on *Nitro* by tossing it in the garbage — something former WWF women's champion Madusa Miceli (a.k.a. Alundra Blayze) had done a few years before. Frankly, I find it hard to believe that Bret would have ever even contemplated something as lame and disrespectful as that — especially when you consider that when Madusa did it, it had virtually no effect on anything anyway. Lest anyone think otherwise, it didn't hurt the WWF at all and, within a matter of weeks, no one seemed to remember, or even care. As I recall, the only person who suffered from it was Madusa, herself, as her once promising career seemed to go straight into the toilet after that. If Bret had done the same, I don't think it would have done much to enhance his marketability or his image, nor would it have affected the WWF anywhere near as much as some have made out.

As well, if Eric Bischoff and his WCW cohorts had, in their infinite wisdom, chosen to actually flog the WWF belt on their own show, I think it would have only served to make WCW fans perceive it as more prestigious than the WCW title.

I also read some irrational reasoning in Vince Russo's illuminating book *Forgiven*, which put forth the notion that the WWF had no choice but to screw Bret, because he had it written into his contract that he had creative control over everything he did in the ring, including finishes. I'm honestly not sure if Russo was misinformed, or simply full of shit, but if that was actually the case, something is seriously out of whack. Correct me if I'm wrong, but isn't that about like Carl Weathers (who played Apollo Creed) or Mr. T being given complete autonomy over what their characters can do in the *Rocky* movies and then, after sizing up the script, informing Sly Stallone, in no uncertain terms, that their character can't lose to Rocky Balboa? As Ric Flair exclaimed in his book, when assessing Bret's rationale for refusing to oblige the office: "Gimme a break!"

If there's one iota of truth to Russo's curious contention that Bret did, in fact, have complete creative autonomy over his finishes, the WWF should be embarrassed to even admit publicly that they were so naive or clueless they would actually submit themselves to something so ludicrous and they have no business even running a wrestling promotion.

Talk about the tail wagging the dog, the inmates running the asylum or whatever other clichés might apply! Taking things one step further, if the WWF was giving stars like Bret creative control, it stands to reason that they probably would have had to grant other equally exalted superstars, like Austin, 'Taker, Foley and others, the same type of creative autonomy. By that token, if the WWF happened to book two such superstars, with the same veto powers, against each other and neither was inclined to do the job for the other, how the hell would they resolve things? Rock, paper, scissors?

In case my esteemed colleagues — McMahon, Russo and whoever else — think otherwise, I'd like to point out that by no means was Bret the first champion in the history of the business who wasn't exactly thrilled about dropping a strap. In fact, in all my years in wrestling, I can't honestly recall anyone who, when they were asked to drop a belt, jumped for joy, gave a high five, did cartwheels or celebrated. Being asked to lose a belt is a blow to one's ego and can easily be construed as a form of rejection — like your girlfriend telling you she's dumping you for someone else, or a football coach benching some once vaunted veteran quarterback, like Brett Favre, for some hotshot new gunslinger, like Aaron Rodgers.

When I was booking our promotion for my dad, there were countless occasions when I had to break it to some recalcitrant, egocentric champion, such as David Schultz, "Rotten" Ron Starr or, for that matter, Bret himself, that the office needed them to drop their title. It was never, as I recall, met with unbridled joy, but I was usually able to get them to oblige and I never had to resort to any of the sleazy, cloak and dagger–type treachery that I saw in Montreal. As a rule, "ushering the skunk out of the parlor" — as my dad used to refer to getting reluctant prima donna to lose his title — is, frankly, nowhere near as difficult or complicated as McMahon and Russo tend to make it out to be. A bit of diplomacy goes a long way — such as thanking the outgoing champion for having done an awesome job with the strap (even if he didn't) and keeping the door open for down the road opportunities. I've also found that honesty, as they say, is the best policy. It's advisable to be forthright and to the point if you want a guy to lose a belt. Don't mince words, beat around the bush or evade the issue. Tell them straight up what you have in mind and why.

As I said before, while very few of them are thrilled to be informed you want them to do the job, most professionals understand it's all just part of the job description — like your boss asking you to perform some arduous task at work. Rarely will anyone who was worthy of being champion in the first place give you any grief over such a request. If, for some reason, a champion is still adamant in his refusal to oblige your request — which sometimes does happen — at that point you need to come up with an alternative course of action.

There are all kinds of quick fix options that will work in a pinch. For example, you can concoct some supposed story about how the champion was made to forfeit his title — because he wouldn't honor some purported contractual obligation; or, you can announce that the champion was stripped of his title for having violated some ostensible sanction. I've never been a big fan of taking that type of dubious escape route, but if all else fails, it's still a hell of a lot better than the type of embarrassing and messy bullcrap the WWF inflicted on the fans in Montreal.

As for my brother Bret's part in the whole shoddy affair, it pains me to say that he has nothing to be proud of either for the way he handled things. In any other sport, if a star player had refused to do what his coach/manager/boss had requested, then hawked a loogie in his face (in front of millions of fans on television) and then violently assaulted him afterwards in the dressing room, you can bet your ass that the player would have been universally condemned, fined and likely expelled permanently. Can you imagine the public outcry, for example, if A-Rod hawked a big wet one in Joe Torre's face in the dugout during the World Series; or if Roger Clemens punched out George Steinbrenner in the locker room; or if Terrell Owens had put the boots to Bill Parcells on the sidelines, during their tumultuous tenure together with the Cowboys? Hell, I remember a few years back when Latrell Sprewell accosted his Golden State Warriors' coach, P.J. Carlesimo (nowhere near as seriously, I might add, as Bret's assault on Vince). Sprewell, who at the time was considered one of the NBA's most charismatic and dynamic young stars, was suspended for a year, fined hundreds of thousands of dollars and his image never recovered.

I'm sure that if something similar had transpired in our promotion and some hotheaded superstar — like, say, "Bad News" Allen — was made to lose a title against his wishes and had subsequently put the boots to my father as a result, that Bret would have been among the first and most vehement to denounce him. It should be noted that within the wrestling fraternity there is a code of ethics, as far as titles or championships go. For example, when the promotion (be it the WWF or whoever else) puts a belt on a guy, it's implicitly understood from the get-go that whenever the promotion wants that guy to drop the belt — to whomever, whenever and wherever — that wrestler will endeavor to oblige them, to the best of his ability, without any hassles, qualms or reservations. It was that way when Ric Flair dropped the strap to Bret in Saskatoon; when Hulk Hogan put over Ultimate Warrior; when the great Buddy Rogers put over the then virtual unknown Bruno Sammartino and so on and so forth.

It should also be pointed out that when a champion does drop a belt to his successor, whoever that might be, that he shouldn't merely be "losing" to the other guy or letting the other guy beat him, but he should be striving to do his utmost to make the other guy look like a veritable world beater — the old "do unto others as you would have them do unto you" credo. All things considered, it's better for everyone — the new champion, the outgoing one and, most importantly, for the business.

As I said before, I found it hard to believe that Bret was giving the WWF all these supposedly extenuating reasons why he wouldn't or couldn't drop the strap to Shawn — including the fact that he hated Shawn's guts, or that Shawn wasn't worthy of wearing the belt or that he didn't like the idea of having to lose in his native Canada, among other excuses. If there's any truth to any of that scuttlebutt, it doesn't say much for Bret's sense of professional ethics. Sure, it would be great, I agree, if you only had to do jobs for guys you admired or respected and if you only had to lose in some out of the way locale — like Antarctica, with no television coverage — but that's unfortunately not how it works. If the office wants a guy to drop a strap to whomever, whenever and wherever, that's entirely their call — not the wrestler's. Anything else would be uncivilized!

Not to be facetious, but I've often wondered if Bret's being put up on a proverbial pedestal, as "the best there is, the best there was and the best there ever will be," may have perverted his perceptions. However, as one who happened to grow up in the wrestling business, he, of all people, should have been able to implicitly understand that dropping a belt is just part of the damn job description — nothing more, nothing less. I'm puzzled and, frankly, amazed that he could have ever gotten to the point where he would be so out of touch with the basic tenets of the employee/employer working relationship that he felt he could call the shots like that. In a lot of ways, the whole convoluted charade is akin to Dr. Frankenstein (Vinnie Mac) creating this increasingly uncontrollable monster (Bret), who, ultimately, turns on his master and wreaks havoc.

Not to digress, but not long after the Montreal maelstrom, I was talking with this renowned mountain climber named Laurie Skreslet, who happens to be the first Canadian to have scaled the summit of Mount Everest. In sharing perspectives with him, he related that while he was hailed as a conquering hero afterward and received all kinds of newspaper, television, magazine recognition, movie offers and whatnot, he would never have even been able to come close to reaching the summit or basking in the glory afterwards without the selfless contributions of everyone else on the expedition — the sherpas, the guides, the technical support staff, the base camp minions and the people who financed the whole operation. Skreslet, to his credit, was gracious enough to emphasize that though he, personally, had received the lion's share of fame and acclaim, his epic achievement was, indeed, a team effort all the way.

That got me to thinking about our sport — where the highest mountain one can climb is to win the WWF title. Just as my friend Skreslet would never have come close to reaching the "top of the world" without the selfless sacrifice of all the others, the same holds true for Bret's ascending to the top of the wrestling world. By that token, if it hadn't been for former champions — like Hogan, Flair, Sammartino and Backlund — all of whom had expended their blood, sweat and tears to make the belt so revered — and promoters and visionaries like Toots Mondt and the McMahons, who had conceived of the belt in the first place; not to mention the countless others who had contributed along the way, including people like my father, fellow workers (be they superstars or lowly jobbers), bookers, referees, television commentators, trainers, friends, supporters, wives and whoever else (most of whom have never received any credit — nor, for that matter, ever sought any either), my beloved bro would never have even come close to scaling wrestling's hallowed summit.

In choosing to conduct himself in the self-serving and narrow-minded manner in which he did — by punching out the guy who had placed his faith and trust in him by putting the belt around his waist in the first place (regardless of whether he was a saint or not), and then proceeding to subsequently drag the whole business through the mud afterwards — Bret wasn't merely hurting McMahon, the WWF or Shawn Michaels, he was showing disrespect and disregard for the entire industry. By that token, he was letting all of his aforementioned "teammates" down as well. In the quaint vernacular of my kids, "that ain't cool, bro!"

During one of his pre-game sermons, the legendary football coach Vince Lombardi once pointed out to his world champion Green Bay Packers that there is no "I" in the word "team." After all the time Bret spent being schooled in my dad's Dungeon, that's one spelling lesson my brother should never have been needed to be taught, if you catch my drift.

A few days after the Montreal travesty, I was at my dad's Dungeon, readying to conduct a training session and my father, as he often did, descended the basement stairs to observe the workout. While we were waiting for the trainees to arrive, I was curious as to how he felt about the Montreal screwjob and sought his opinion. Stu, who had dedicated over seventy years of his life to the wrestling business and whose roots traced all the way back to its founder, Farmer Burns, frowned somewhat pensively and ruefully remarked that it was a shame that neither Bret nor Vince had been willing to put aside their own self-serving agendas and do what was best for the business — which, he duly noted, had made both of them rich and famous. He then pointed solemnly to a sign above the doorway to the storied Dungeon, where a virtual who's who of wrestling legends had broken into the sport and shook his head. I glanced at the tattered and faded handwritten sign. Paraphrasing President John F. Kennedy, it read, "Ask not what wrestling can do for you but, instead, ask what you can do for wrestling."

My dad paused — perhaps for me to reflect on what I'd read — and then remarked, in his own inimitable style, that if more people, including Bret and Vince, had upheld that simple credo, the wrestling business would be in a hell of a lot better shape than it is today.

Well put, Dad. I couldn't agree more.

59
PMS (POST MONTREAL SYNDROME)

When the smoke had cleared after Montreal, Bret appeared to have come out of it in pretty good shape, or so one would think. When he went to wcw, he had a contract that paid him considerably more than he'd been making in the wwf and the whole thing had made him a martyr, which served to enhance his marketability. Unfortunately though, Bret couldn't seem to get over the whole thing and, as a result, the Montreal screwjob would come to exact a heavy toll — not just on him but on so many others as well.

Bret's fellow Hart Foundation teammates Davey Boy, Anvil and Owen were the first to be dragged into the mess. Even though Davey and Jim were under contract with the wwf and had been happy with how they'd been treated there, they both quit out of protest for the way Bret had been treated. I was told later that they'd also been promised, by Bret, that Eric Bischoff would pay them more than what they'd been making in the wwf. They should have gotten it all in writing though, as, upon their arrival in the wcw, Bischoff — realizing that they'd burned their bridges with the wwf — suddenly claimed he knew nothing about the figures Bret had told them. Instead he offered them only a fraction of what they'd been expecting.

Davey Boy and Anvil then asked Bret if he'd go to bat on their behalf, but he pretty much turned his back on them — telling them that they should have gotten it in writing beforehand and that he couldn't do much for them. They didn't have much choice except to accept Bischoff's bargain basement offer, but were furious about the whole thing.

That seemed to be the catalyst for Davey Boy, who had been having an on-and-off battle with drug addiction, to revert back to drugs, which would cost him not only his career but ultimately his life. Jim "The Anvil" Neidhart would similarly see his career and life turned upside down as well.

Owen, who remained in the wwf, didn't take the financial hit that Davey and Jim did, but was quite decimated with the strife that ensued. In *Forgiven* by Vince Russo, the wwf booker at the time, Russo said that Owen called him shortly after the Montreal screwjob "on the verge of tears" and pleaded with him, "Vince, you've got to help me . . . Bret is telling me that if I continue to work for Vince [McMahon] he is going to disown me as a brother."

Unfortunately, that's pretty much what happened. Bret was steamed at Owen for choosing to remain in the wwf and I'm not sure if they ever resolved things before Owen's death a year and a half later — which is extremely unfortunate and, I'm sure, must have weighed heavy on Bret's mind after the accident.

As for Vince McMahon, the jury remains out as to how he came out of the whole fiasco. A while back I was talking to my old friend Mick Foley and he told me that, in his humble opinion, Montreal was the best thing that had ever happened to Vince or the wwf, because it exposed him as a double-dealing shyster — which was the impetus for the highly successful "Mr. McMahon" heel persona. That, in turn, led to the wwf's decision to abandon its family-oriented format and opt for the adult-oriented, politically incorrect, more violent, hard-core style that, at least for the short term, resulted in a jump at the gates.

While I can see Foley's point, I'm not sure if I agree with the claim that the Montreal screwjob was the best thing that ever happened to the wwf. It's like suggesting that the Monica Lewinsky charade was the high water mark of Bill Clinton's political career.

As for the other main player in that fiasco, Shawn Michaels, one would be hard pressed to say that his image didn't suffer as a result. Even though he was one of the best workers of our generation and a surefire Hall of Famer, the whole unseemly affair still tends to tarnish his legacy — kind of like the anabolic allegations against Mark McGwire. I'm sure the Heartbreak Kid regrets ever having been a part of it.

As far as I'm concerned, the biggest casualty of the infamous Montreal screwjob has been the wrestling business itself — which was needlessly dragged through the coals and incurred a lot of derision and ridicule as a result. I'm not sure that it's ever really recovered from it.

60
REVIVING THE FRANCHISE

While the WWF's celebrated Canadian Stampede pay-per-view earlier in the year had been a source of frustration and disappointment for me on a personal level, it had nonetheless been acclaimed as a huge success, which resulted in a great deal of interest in reviving Stampede Wrestling once again.

My dad, my brother Ross and I — who owned the Stampede Wrestling trademark — had been approached many times since we had shut down back in 1989 about starting up the legendary promotion again; however, most of the interested parties didn't have two cents to rub together. After the Canadian Stampede though, some serious players came around, including former world middleweight boxing champion Donny Lalonde, world and Olympic curling champion Ed Lukowich and movers and shakers on the Calgary sports and business scene that included Ron Folstad, Trevor Countryman, Joe Paulowicz, Bill Bell and Wendell Wilkes.

I was flattered, but told the prospective investors that one of the main reasons we'd been forced to shut down before was that the WWF was always raiding our talent and that if this was going to work, we needed to establish some kind of working agreement — kind of like the type of relationship a triple-A baseball team might have with a major league team, so that if the WWF was taking our stars, they had to subsidize us and also augment our cards with established stars and that type of thing.

I spoke to my brother Owen, who was still working for the WWF, and asked him to extend some feelers on our behalf. He called me back and said that the WWF had no desire to be giving handouts to anyone just wanting to start up a wrestling promotion, but that if we were able to show we were legit by getting the promotion up and running first, they might be interested in coming onboard.

That wasn't exactly the news I'd been hoping to hear, but I could see where they were coming from and took that back to the investors, who decided to proceed.

Ross and I spent the fall and winter of 1998 preparing for the re-launch of the new Stampede Wrestling, lining up television, lining up towns and training new recruits down in the Dungeon. We had our pilot television show on the new A-Channel in February and the reviews were generally favorable — so much so that the network gave us the thumbs-up for a weekly television slot on Saturday afternoons, commencing in May. It was precisely the news we'd been hoping for.

When we opened up the promotion full time in May 1999, our gates that first week were good. Our young talent — in particular, my nephew Harry Smith (son of Davey Boy, now wrestling in the WWE as David Hart Smith), my niece Natalya Neidhart, T.J. Wilson (now Tyson Kidd in the WWE), Robbie Dicks, "Quick Kick" Kirk Melnyk, "Principal" Dick Pound and the Calgary Stampeders captain Marvin Pope — all elicited rave reviews, which was quite encouraging.

On Sunday morning, May 23 — the day after our first week of shows — my brother Owen called me, long distance from Kansas City, to see how the shows had gone. When I related that the shows had all gone extremely well, Owen said he was pleased and was now quite confident he could pitch the WWF to come onboard. He told me that he'd be talking to Vince McMahon later that night — after the pay-per-views they were having. He would run it by him and get back to me when he was in Calgary later that week.

61
OWEN

The big item on the agenda for most people in our family on May 23, 1999 was the final of the Memorial Cup tournament for national junior hockey supremacy between the Ottawa 67s and the Calgary Hitmen — of which my brother Bret was part owner. The game was a thriller even before the Hitmen lost in overtime. It was a downer, but couldn't even compare to what transpired later that day.

After the hockey game, we headed up to my parents' place for Sunday dinner — a weekly ritual among most in the family. The meal that evening was my mother's spaghetti, which was a family favorite. After our usual meet and greet we were sitting down to eat in the dining room when the phone rang. Someone — I think it was my sister Alison — went back into the kitchen to answer it. A few seconds later, I heard this ear-piercing shriek and she staggered back into the dining room, ashen-faced, and gasped, "Owen's dead!"

When we pressed her for details, she said she didn't have any, other than he'd been injured from a fall and had been pronounced dead in the ring at the show in Kansas City. As you can imagine, the scene at the dinner table was suddenly completely insane, with everyone trying to wrap their heads around what had happened. I was sitting beside my mother at the far end of the table and she was weeping inconsolably, while, at the other end of the table, my dad was just staring ahead impassively. For some reason — perhaps it was wishful thinking — I kept telling myself that it must be a work: some kind of contrived fake death scene, which the WWF has, on occasion, pulled. As I surveyed everyone at the table crying though, I was half-pissed that they hadn't at least chosen to let us know beforehand.

The first time it began to dawn on me that it might not be a work and that he actually was dead was when Tammi Christopher — the sports reporter from CFCN television and a family friend — showed up at the house, teary-eyed, and confirmed that it was no work. My initial reaction was of sadness and disbelief, but after I'd been appraised of how he'd been killed — on some silly entrance stunt from the ceiling of the arena — I was livid.

At my dad's behest, we all headed over to Owen's house — which was only about five minutes away — to offer our condolences and to do what we could to comfort his wife, Martha. As you can imagine, she was beside herself with sorrow, but when we endeavored to extend our sympathy, she was extremely cold. She made a point of telling my parents how much she'd always hated the wrestling business and that Owen had never really wanted to be in it either, but had been pushed into it, and that he had been looking forward to getting out of it. I didn't think that was called for.

Everyone has their own way of grieving, I suppose, but I didn't hear Dale Earnhardt's widow condemning NASCAR after his fatal accident at Daytona, because she knew he had died doing something he loved doing. Having been the one who brought Owen into wrestling, I can attest that he genuinely loved the wrestling business. In fact, there's no way he could have been as good as he was without having had a lot of passion. Any conjecture to the contrary is horseshit, as far as I'm concerned.

I didn't care for the way Martha treated my parents — almost as if she'd been the only one who'd suffered any loss — but we all kept our mouths shut and left shortly thereafter.

When we got back to my dad's, the phone rang and I answered it — it was Carl De Marco, the supposed president of the WWF. He launched into this scripted-sounding spiel that almost sounded like he was reading it. "This is

Carl De Marco, the president of the World Wrestling Federation; on behalf of the World Wrestling Federation, I'd like to extend our sincerest condolences to the Hart family on the untimely passing of their son, the Blue Blazer, Owen Hart . . ."

I angrily cut him off and snarled, "Vince McMahon should have the fucking stones to call himself and not have some fucking figurehead flunky call to cut a fucking promo." After I hung up, I felt kind of bad — the old don't-shoot-the-messenger credo — but I had meant what I said.

Later that evening, at about two in the morning, the phone rang again. Since my parents had finally gone to bed after a long, devastating day, I didn't want them awakened, so I answered it downstairs. It was Vince McMahon himself. In the past, whenever I'd spoken to him, he'd usually been pretty aloof and imperious, but this time around, he was quite understated — almost subdued — which isn't surprising, given the circumstances. I've been told that Vince doesn't drink, but he sounded like he may have had a few stiff ones before he made the call. I know that I probably would have.

He mumbled, in a half whisper, that he was sorry about what had happened to Owen. I was in the process of telling him that Owen should never have been made to be doing some silly, non-wrestling stunt like that in the first place and that wrestlers should be allowed to be wrestlers and not have to be stuntmen, trapeze artists or circus clowns.

Vince, quite honestly, sounded as if he was in a trance, and just kept repeating how sorry he was, when, all of a sudden, I heard this click on the phone. At first I figured my dad might have picked up the extension upstairs, but I immediately heard this female voice, which I recognized as my sister Alison's, launch into this vitriolic rant, berating Vince for having killed Owen. I thought her tirade was uncalled for and I damn well knew how bad I would have felt if the tables were turned and, say, Shane McMahon had been killed in an accident while wrestling for Stampede Wrestling. I found myself in the unlikely position of having to act as a peacekeeper. I kept trying to tone things down.

Thankfully, Alison ran out of steam and finally just hung up, after which I endeavored to offer apologies for her outburst. Vince was pretty understanding about the whole thing though and we hung up at that point.

The next morning, my dad's house resembled Graceland after Elvis died, with media from all over the world descending. I was tremendously impressed with the quiet dignity my parents showed over the next few days. Although both of them were distraught over the loss of their youngest son, they went out of their way to make sure everyone — be it media types, friends, wrestlers or wrestling fans just dropping by to offer their condolences — was made to feel welcome. They patiently lent themselves to interviews, photographers and whatever else. In its own perverse way, I suspect that having to deal with the media and all the other responsibilities may have helped take their minds off the enormity of the tragedy.

Two guys who really made an enormous impression on me and my parents that week were Chris Benoit and Chris Jericho. At that time Benoit and Jericho were still in the WCW, but upon hearing of Owen's death, they booked themselves off for the rest of the week, just to be there. Every day they were up at my dad's, bright and early, making coffee, cleaning, greeting guests, babysitting or anything else they could do to be of help — all of which was incredibly thoughtful and gives you some impression of what kind of guys they were.

On Thursday evening that week, my brother Bret — whom I hadn't spoken to since he'd pulled the rug out from under me at *Monday Night RAW* in Edmonton, nearly two years before — called me at home.

I assumed he might want to commiserate about Owen, since he knew how close we'd been, but after briefly touching on that, he quickly cut to the chase. He informed me that after having consulted with police, crime scene investigators, riggers and whatnot, he had arrived at the conclusion that Owen's death hadn't been an accident but had been deliberately orchestrated by Vince McMahon, as a means of getting back at Bret for what had happened in Montreal. Bret then said that in order for the lawyers to build their case, it was important that everyone in the family sign a document attesting that we were of the opinion that Vince had killed Owen.

Frankly, I was completely stunned at the whole charade and asked Bret why the hell Vince would kill Owen — who'd remained loyal to the WWF and with whom he had no ostensible issues with. I told Bret that if Vince was, indeed, as sick and twisted as he was suggesting, then why the hell hadn't he just hired a "hitman to kill the Hitman."

Bret seemed pissed that I'd even have the audacity to question him and snarled that killing Owen was Vince's way of getting back at him for what had happened in Montreal. I shook my head, in exasperation, that the fucking Montreal affair was still rearing its ugly head, and finally told Bret that while he was entitled to his own opinion, I couldn't see Vince doing something like that.

The day before Owen's funeral, my mom asked if I could deliver a eulogy on behalf of our family, since Owen and I had been quite close all our lives. I told her I'd be honored to oblige her and spent the rest of the day endeavoring to do justice to Owen's memory.

When we assembled at the chapel for Owen's funeral, I spotted Martha and Bret already seated in the pews at the front. I approached them and respectfully inquired as to when she wanted me to speak. Before she had a chance to reply, Bret, sitting beside her, interceded and snarled, "You're not speaking — fuck off!"

I was pissed, of course. I'd been as close as anyone in our family to Owen, having been the best man at his wedding as he was at mine. But now I was being denied because Bret wanted to grind his ax with Vince over Montreal. I'd not only put my heart and soul into my speech, but also was intending to address some of the things that really needed to be addressed, such as how wrestlers weren't disposable commodities but human beings — fathers, brothers and sons — and that the WWF should never be putting their lives in jeopardy simply to propagate some frivolous story line. At the same time though, I wanted to make it clear that, having been promoters ourselves, we were empathetic to the WWF's pain. They, too, had lost a family member, and it was time for healing, not fanning the flames of acrimony — a sentiment I'm sure Owen would have been in agreement with.

After the service, we piled back into our limousines and the funeral procession, which must have been half a mile long, made its way to the cemetery on the other side of town. After the interment, I was escorting my dad, in his wheelchair, back to our limousine, when one of the WWF attachés came up and asked my dad if he'd like to ride back with Vince McMahon in his limo. My dad said that he welcomed the opportunity to discuss things, man to man, so I helped him into Vince's nearby limo and off they went.

Later on, back at the house, I saw Vince's limo pull up and helped my dad disembark. When I inquired as to how his conversation with Vince had gone, he said that he was pleased that Vince had taken full responsibility for Owen's death and had said that while nothing could bring Owen back, he'd like to give my dad and Martha a substantial out-of-court settlement — so there would at least be some closure for everyone. I asked what kind of figure Vince was talking about, and my dad said that Vince had thrown out the figure $90 million — roughly divided to sixty for Martha and thirty for him and my mom. I was interested in hearing my dad's response. He told me that no amount of money could change what had happened but that, all things considered, he'd be inclined to take the settlement and that would hopefully allow everyone to have some closure and get on with their lives. At the same time he said that he first had to confer with my mom and Martha and see what they thought and go from there.

62
BATTLE LINES DRAWN

I was pleased to hear that things might be resolved quickly, as I don't think anyone had any appetite for a big legal battle at that point. Shortly thereafter though, as my dad was visiting with some of his wrestling cronies whom he hadn't seen in years, such as Terry and Dory Funk, Bret and the lawyers dragged him inside and sequestered my mom and him behind closed doors for several hours. The next morning in the newspaper I was distressed to see headlines announcing that the Hart family had declared war on the WWF and were suing for $500 million, alleging that Owen's death may have been premeditated.

I was kind of shocked and spoke to my dad later on that day to ask what had happened to make him change his mind. He heaved a heavy sigh and told me that neither he nor my mom had any desire to embark on a long, drawn-out legal battle that he was sure wouldn't resolve anything and, he feared, would tear the family apart. He said that Bret was bound and determined to get back at Vince for Montreal and after he'd convinced Martha to proceed with the lawsuit, he and my mom had no choice but to go along with them, as they would have been perceived as insensitive traitors if they hadn't.

It didn't take long for my dad's fears about the family being ripped apart to be realized. The day after Owen's funeral, on June 1, 1999, Davey Boy started back with the WWF. Everyone in our family, including Bret, knew that he'd been given that starting date back in March and that it had been Owen who'd gotten him booked in the WWF. Bret, however, chose to ignore that and wrote a scathing putdown of Davey in his weekly newspaper column (the one that I used to ghostwrite for him). Bret likened Davey's return to the WWF to a dog rolling in excrement. As a result, a lot of fans at the house shows — who'd been big supporters of both Owen and Bret — began carrying signs and chanting "dog in shit, dog in shit" at the house shows. Davey Boy, who was pretty fragile to begin with, let it get to him and he soon was back on drugs — which would prove to have disastrous consequences.

Bret next targeted my older brother Smith, who, like me, had also refused to sign the affadavit. Smith had been one of Bret's biggest supporters from way back and, in fact, had been the one who'd started Bret's career when he took him to Puerto Rico in 1977. Not long after the court proceedings had started, Smith's common-law wife, Zoe, died and Smith was seeking custody of their son, Chad. Since Smith was the biological father, the case originally appeared to be a mere formality but, out of the blue, Bret showed up at the custody hearing and testified before the judge that, in his opinion, Smith was an unfit father. Because Bret's opinion carried a lot of weight, Smith was denied custody — which was heartbreaking for him.

Things would get even worse once the court case began. In one of his first appearances in court, my dad described Vince McMahon as an old friend and testified that he believed Owen's death had been an accident. He was censured afterward for not having condemned Vince as the monster they wanted him to be perceived as, and the lawyers then sought to have his remarks disregarded, on the grounds that he was "mentally incompetent," claiming he suffered from advanced dementia.

My mother was the next to incur the wrath of the lawyers. After one particularly stressful courtroom session, there was a recess and outside the courtroom, she bumped into Linda McMahon, whom she hadn't seen since the funeral. Linda is one of the classiest and nicest people I've met in wrestling. She and my mom exchanged a tearful embrace and Linda expressed her regrets that things had become so strained and acrimonious. At that juncture, one of the lawyers ran up and snatched my mother by the arm and scolded her so harshly that she burst into tears.

As I mentioned before, one of the early casualties of the bitter battle with the WWF had been Davey Boy. Bret's unwarranted dog-in-shit column had resulted in Davey getting back on drugs and by the spring of 2000, his life and career were in a such a shambles that the WWF finally ordered him to go into rehab down in Atlanta. While he was in rehab, he got wind that my sister Diana (his wife) — who was pretty fragile herself at that time — had left him for some other guy. Furious, he checked himself out of rehab and headed back to Calgary, where he encountered Diana and her new beau up at my dad's house. A violent altercation ensued and my dad, in the process of trying to break it up, was shoved backwards down the stairs by Davey Boy. It was a bad fall and Dad had to be ambulanced to the hospital, suffering from cardiac arrest. Dad would recover and be released a few weeks later, but it was a sign of things to come.

63
BREAKING UP IS HARD TO DO

When the WWF got wind of Davey Boy having pulled himself out of rehab and all the rest, they suspended him — which pretty much marked the end of his once celebrated wrestling career.

Just after his release from the WWF, Davey Boy was hospitalized with a serious staph infection — brought on, I'm told, by years of steroid abuse, which had ravaged his immune system. I felt sorry for him, as he'd been unjustly maligned by Bret, had seen his marriage crumble and was incurring some serious health issues. I went up to visit him and to offer him some moral support.

After my visit, I was talking to my wife, Andrea — who is an expert on natural healing and homeopathic remedies and that sort of thing — and told her of Davey Boy's health problems. Andrea said she had some holistic remedies that might help him and decided to visit him to see if she could be of some help. Little did I realize what a can of worms that would soon open up.

I should perhaps give you a brief bit of background on the stormy relationship that had existed for years between my wife and my sister Diana. Since I first had been going out with my wife, way back in 1982, she and Diana had never gotten along. Most of the time, their antagonism took the form of cattiness, but after Davey had made it big in the WWF, Diana tended to flaunt her wealth and look down her nose at my wife, which only added fuel to the fire.

When my wife went up to the hospital to see Davey, her intentions, I believe, were good. She was primarily concerned with trying to help Davey get off drugs and get his health back, through homeopathy and changing his diet. When my sister heard that her archenemy Andrea had been visiting Davey at the hospital, she flew into a jealous rage, accusing him of having an affair.

Davey Boy quickly deduced that he could perhaps use my wife as a ploy to get Diana back and soon began giving her money and letting her drive his big BMW and enjoy the trappings of wealth, which she'd seen Diana enjoy all these years. Under normal circumstances, I'm sure my wife would never have gotten involved, but because of her abiding contempt for Diana and perhaps because she felt like she'd been deprived all these years, she couldn't resist the temptation. Perhaps it was to piss off Diana and, perhaps, to enjoy the good life that she'd seen all the other wrestling wives enjoying.

One thing led to another and in the fall of 2000, my wife told me that she and the kids were moving in with Davey. Having my marriage on the rocks was pretty discouraging, because my wife and kids had been, by far, the most important thing in my life. A few weeks after my wife moved in with Davey, she returned Rhett to me.

While I was glad to have him back, it was exceedingly tough as he was heartbroken that his mom, whom he was extremely close to, had abandoned him. He couldn't figure out what he'd done to deserve this — I couldn't either.

At about the same time as my marriage was hitting the rocks, the acrimonious lawsuit was dragging on, with no end in sight, and everyone's nerves were frayed. In October 2000, I was talking to my parents just after they'd returned from another frustrating courtroom session down in Kansas City and they told me how discouraged they'd become and how they feared it could go on for years. The next day, I happened to receive a phone call from Jerry McDevitt, one of the WWF's lawyers. He was calling about some aspect of the case and, during our conversation, I related how discouraged my parents had become with the whole ordeal and that they both just wished it could somehow be resolved.

McDevitt — whom I'd always found to be a pretty decent guy, unlike most lawyers — said that he'd mention that to Vince and see if something might be worked out, as they had no desire to have it drag on any further themselves.

I'm not sure if my conversation with McDevitt had anything to do with it, but a few weeks later, it was suddenly announced that the lawsuit had been settled out of court, which was a relief. We hoped that we could move on and, perhaps, get our lives — which had all been put on hold — back on track. Those hopes, however, didn't materialize, as the family, especially Bret and Martha, remained quite bitter and acrimonious afterward at those who hadn't signed the document. As such, there is still quite a bit of bitterness and division within the family.

64
THE DISORDER OF THE ORDER OF CANADA

On February 14, 2001, after what had been a long siege, there was finally a bit of good news, when my dad was informed by the Governor-General of Canada that he'd been inducted into the Order of Canada, which is Canada's highest honor — kind of like being knighted in the United Kingdom or being given the Congressional Medal of Honor in the States. My parents were thrilled and humbled at the honor and they excitedly made plans to attend the gala induction ceremony, which was scheduled to take place at the end of May. As a goodwill gesture, my parents invited Bret and Martha to join them on the cross-country train trip down to Ottawa for the big occasion.

About six weeks before the Order of Canada ceremony was to take place, I received a call from Chris Benoit, who at that time was the WWF champion. He said he was pleased to hear my dad was being awarded the Order of Canada and, as a means of expressing gratitude for all my dad had done for him, he and fellow Dungeon graduate Chris Jericho wanted to pay tribute to my dad in the ring on *Monday Night RAW*, which was scheduled to take place in May — only a few days before the award ceremony.

I ran the idea by my dad, who told me that since the lawsuit with the wwf had been settled and he'd made peace, he didn't see anything wrong with it. I called Benoit back and was pleased to give him thumbs-up for the tribute.

If I might, I'd like to interject something about Chris, here and now. I'm sure you've all heard about his unfortunate murder/suicide in 2006. After that extremely tragic scenario, I had all kinds of media types calling me, seeking my perspectives on what could have driven such a seemingly nice family man to do something so heinous. I told them that I didn't profess to be a psychologist, but that since it was pretty well-known — at least in wrestling circles — that Benoit had used steroids, it was certainly possible that steroids, which have been know to make people aggressive and violent ('roid rage, as it's called), might have been a contributing factor.

I also related that the Benoit I'd known had always been a nice kid and that for him to have committed such an abhorrent crime, he must have been delusional — which, I'm sure, most others wouldn't have argued with. In any case, the next day in the newspaper, there was this big headline "Hart Calls Benoit a Delusional Juice Freak" — which wasn't really what I meant. I felt bad afterward, because it looked like I was dumping on him as well — which wasn't really the case and certainly didn't reflect the high regard I'd always had for him.

While I'm not trying to understate the atrocity of his crime, nor am I trying to justify anything, nonetheless, I think it's a shame that he's remembered primarily for having committed that crime, rather than for having been one of the greatest workers of his generation or for having been one of the nicest guys in the business.

On *Monday Night RAW*, Benoit and Jericho — who were two of the hottest faces in the wwf at the time — delivered a really touching tribute to my dad, which had many in the crowd of 20,000 in tears. I was pleased my dad was able to enjoy it and had seen nothing, whatsoever, wrong with it. Unfortunately though, when my brother Bret caught it on television, he went ballistic and went over to my dad's place — where my mom had this kind of shrine on the wall, dedicated to Bret and Owen. Bret tore down all the pictures and memorabilia and then proceeded to tear a strip off my mom for having allowed my dad to appear on *RAW*.

Subsequent to that, my sister-in-law Martha called, furious that my dad had been on *RAW*. She announced that she and Bret wouldn't be accompanying my parents on the trip to Ottawa and angrily vowed that my parents would never see Owen's kids, Oje and Athena, whom they were quite attached to, again. My poor mom was devastated.

Speaking of overreacting, the next morning Bret even went so far as to call the Governor-General's office and demanded that they rescind the Order of Canada honor to my dad — a request which, of course, was refused. Dave Meltzer, the publisher of the *Wrestling Observer Newsletter* and a big supporter of Bret's, subsequently slammed my dad for having appeared on *RAW* and suggested that the only reason my dad had even received the Order of Canada in the first place was because he was Bret's father and not for any of his own accomplishments.

While I've always had a lot of regard for Meltzer, both as a friend and as a journalist, I thought that was unwarranted. If he'd done a bit of research, he'd have found that my dad had a huge body of work in wrestling long before Bret ever set foot in the ring, not to mention having been a tireless pillar of the community for decades, and that Stu Hart was a more than worthy recipient of the honor.

65
A HOUSE DIVIDED

The day after my parents returned from the Order of Canada ceremony in Ottawa, I went up to the house to see them and was anxious to hear all about the details of their big celebration. Instead of regaling me with all the happy details, my mom, near tears, was despondent and told me that Bret and Martha's overreaction had ruined the whole thing. She asked why they had to be so cruel and insensitive.

I had no answers but was dismayed that a once in a lifetime, crowning moment like that had been ruined, simply because, once again, Bret was being a mark for himself and couldn't seem to let go of the Montreal fiasco — which was ridiculous.

Sadly, the Order of Canada honor proved to be the last hurrah for my mom, as a few months later, in September, she suffered a serious seizure, which landed her in the hospital, in a coma, fighting for her life.

The week after my mom entered the hospital, this ill-conceived book entitled *Under the Mat*, which had been written by my sister Diana, hit the bookstores. I'm not sure what possessed Diana to write it — whether it was vindictiveness, or if she may have been quite unstable at the time. In any case, the book slandered damn near everybody in the family: my parents, myself and my wife and, most of all, Bret and Martha — both of whom she crucified. When the book came out, the first reaction by everyone in the family was concern for how my poor mom would react to it after she emerged from her coma.

Near the end of October, she rallied and briefly emerged from her coma, which gave us hope that she might recover, but she then suffered another even more serious seizure and we were summoned to the hospital to pay our last respects.

On the night my mother died, about an hour before she passed away, Bret showed up. Seething over what Diana had written about him in her book, he immediately made a beeline for her and grabbed her by the throat, over my mom's body. He began screaming at her for what she'd said about him in the book. With Diana screaming hysterically, hospital security was summoned and they had to physically remove Bret. All of this turmoil was hard as hell on my poor dad — having to deal with that while his wife, who was the love of his life, was on her deathbed.

Later that week, the day before my mother's funeral, I was driving home from school and turned on the radio to this talk radio station. I heard a familiar voice. It was my sister Diana, talking about her book, and the radio announcer said that they'd now be taking calls. I hadn't heard what Diana had said before but heard another familiar voice as the first caller, my brother Bret. Bret's first words, to my horror, were "You're a fucking liar!" I thought the station had bleep delay, but apparently not. In any case, hearing my brother and sister engaging in this sleazy *Jerry Springer*–type conflict on a national radio broadcast was just another in a series of embarrassing and almost surrealistic scenarios that took place that fateful week.

The next day, prior to my mom's funeral service, family members and friends were gathered in the waiting room, outside the main chapel. At some point, Ed Whalen — who'd also been denounced in the book — came up and was expressing his displeasure to Diana over something she'd said about him, when Davey Boy, who was still with my wife, but apparently trying to make an impression on Diana, interceded and threatened to punch Whalen out. That brought Bret into the fray and he immediately got in Davey Boy's face. It looked like they might reprise their celebrated SummerSlam brawl of a few years back.

In a matter of seconds, all hell appeared to be breaking loose, with everyone pushing, shoving and swearing while my poor dad — who was sitting in a wheelchair — was pleading for everyone to stop. Finally, things simmered down, but the whole scene was gut-wrenching and heartbreaking.

My dad had asked me beforehand if I could speak at the service and, given what had transpired, I felt compelled to address the discord within our family:

> If there are any regrets, it's been that the last few years, a time my mom should have been able to enjoy life, indulging in her grandchildren and reflecting on a life full of notable triumphs and accomplishments, were marred by stress, dissension and strife within our family — all of which, sad to say, probably contributed to her untimely passing.
>
> Abraham Lincoln once said that "a house divided is a house in ruins" and I implore members of our family to keep that in mind. I realize that everyone, of course, has different opinions and perspectives, but brothers and sisters should be able to resolve their differences without incurring such acrimony and duress.
>
> If I may, to reinforce my point, I'd like to allude to the horrific terrorist attacks that took place a few weeks back, on September 11, in New York City. Out of the ruins of that decimating tragedy, people of different races, creeds and socioeconomic backgrounds — many of which have been in conflict as well — have now come together, with a renewed sense of brotherhood. I'm hopeful that members of our family can do the same, because, in my humble opinion, keeping our family bond intact is the greatest honor we can bestow upon my mom's legacy. United we stand and divided we fall — the choice is yours.

The message seemed to get through to most, as that Christmas, for the first time since before the Montreal screwjob of 1997, there was "peace on earth" and most of the family attended — with the exception of Martha, who had never attended before, anyway, and Davey Boy and my wife, for obvious reasons.

Even though it was subdued without my mother, everyone seemed to be in good spirits — which was a nice respite for everyone, especially my dad.

66
THE TRIPLE THREAT DOGFIGHT
WITH NO WINNERS

Like some Middle East peace treaty, the calm didn't last long. Early in the new year Davey Boy was in the news again. Since he'd been released by the WWF and taken up with my wife, his life had been in a downward spiral. As he'd blown most of his money — reportedly on drugs — he had seen his house foreclosed, had his car repossessed and was now down and out, living in the basement of my mother-in-law's cramped condo.

Things went from bad to worse for him in the spring, when he was caught on a surveillance camera breaking into Diana's townhouse, where he stole her wedding ring — which he subsequently pawned for a few hundred dollars, allegedly to buy drugs.

He was subsequently arraigned on charges of breaking and entering and theft and was looking at some serious jail time.

Diana, however, decided to drop the charges and that seemed to rekindle some sparks between them, as a few weeks later, he showed up for Sunday dinner at my dad's with Diana. Before dinner, he asked if he could have everyone's attention and then stood up, and apologized for all the embarrassment and pain that he'd caused; he then announced that he and Diana were getting back together — which drew a loud applause from everyone, because, in spite of everything, he'd been a respected and much loved member of the family.

Beaming proudly, Diana then interjected that Davey and their son Harry were forming a new tag team, called the New British Bulldogs. She said that the next weekend they were heading to Manitoba to make their debut on a couple of indie shows out there.

Davey boasted that he and Harry would be even better than he and Dynamite had been — which was saying a lot because many considered them to have been the best tag team in WWF history. Davey then kind of broke down, tears streaming down his cheeks, and whispered, "I just want my life back."

Even though it was nice to see him trying to make a comeback, I still found the whole scene quite sad, because only a few years back, Davey had been at the very top of the mountain in wrestling and now he was getting his hopes up at the opportunity to drive 1,500 or more miles for a $200 payoff.

After dinner, Davey asked if he could have a word with me. He and I went down to the Dungeon and he said that he wanted to apologize for having "fucked up" (as he put it) my family. He stammered that he'd only been intending to "use" Andrea to make Diana jealous, but that things had kind of gotten out of hand and he couldn't admit, to either Andrea or Diana, that it had been a work. In any case, he said he felt quite bad that so many people had been hurt in the process. We ended up shaking hands and left on good terms.

As he got up to leave, I found myself thinking what a twisted fairytale this had been: first, Cinderella (Andrea) hooks up with the handsome prince (Davey Boy) and they drive off to his castle in his chariot (BMW 740), but the castle and the chariot both get repossessed. Bummed out, he then sticks a needle in his arm and turns back into a destitute frog, but decides to dump Cinderella anyway and then runs off with the wicked witch (Diana); and everyone lives unhappily ever after. Whoopee! It kind of sounds like one of those twisted story lines from the creators of Chuck and Billy's fairytale wedding.

The week after Davey and Harry got back from Manitoba, my wife Andrea — whom I hadn't spoken to in a long time — called me up and asked if she could meet me for coffee. I wasn't sure if she knew of Davey's surprise appearance at my dad's a few weeks back or of his announcement that he was getting back with Diana, so I didn't mention it and arranged to get together with her.

The past few times I'd seen her, she'd been kind of smug, but this time around, she was pretty humble. After a bit of awkward small talk, she related that she and Davey were breaking up and that she wanted to move out of her mother's place but was broke — which, of course, was why she wanted to see me. I probably could have gloated, but didn't say anything. Instead I cut her a check for $3,000 — which I could ill afford. She smiled, although it was a decidedly sad smile, and then got up and walked away, in silent humiliation. As I watched her drive away, something my old Freebird crony Michael Hayes used to say came to mind, "Be careful of what you wish for — because you just might get it." For years, she'd wished for Diana's life and she'd finally gotten it. Had she ever.

Two days later, my brother Ross and I had a Stampede Wrestling show and our main event that night was a grudge match between our top heel, Elvis da Silva, and Harry. Harry and Elvis were supposed to go into the ring around 9:30, but by 9:15, Harry, who was usually quite reliable, hadn't showed and we were starting to think we might have to substitute somebody else for him.

He finally arrived just before the match. As he was hastily getting dressed for his match, I asked him why he was so late. He seemed quite frazzled and divulged that there had been a huge altercation at home between Diana and Davey. It seems that Diana had found out that Davey was going out to Fairmont, a tourist town west of Calgary, with Andrea. Harry said Davey had claimed the only reason he was going out there was to officially break things off with Andrea, which was kind of strange because everyone had been given to believe they'd already broken up. Adding insult to injury, Harry said that Diana was furious because she'd asked my dad to loan Davey $5,000 — supposedly to help him get back on his feet. Diana was now accusing him of using the money to go on a drug binge with Andrea. When I heard that, I was also pissed, because I was wondering if the $3,000 I'd given my wife was being used for the same purpose.

I also felt sorry for poor Harry, because he and his sister, Georgia, had been through a lot the past few years — as had my kids — and just when it looked like things were beginning to stabilize, the games were being played again.

The next afternoon, I had just returned from a grocery shopping outing with Rhett, when my sister Ellie suddenly burst through the front door and, ashen-faced, told me that Davey Boy had just been found, dead, out in Fairmont — of an apparent heart attack. I was saddened to hear the news, as it was just one more in what had seemed like an epidemic of unfortunate events, including my nephew Matt, Brian Pillman, Owen, my mom . . . and now, this. Even though he'd caused me a lot of stress, I still considered Davey to be more of a victim than a perpetrator.

Even after Davey's death, the game of one-upmanship continued, with Diana having a big funeral service for him (attended by Vince McMahon, Hulk Hogan and most of the wwf stars), while my wife also tried to have a funeral for him — with each endeavoring to make out as if they'd been the one who'd won the battle. As I was reflecting on the whole sad scenario, I found that, in many ways, it was like the Montreal charade between Bret, Shawn and Vince, in that you had three individuals, none of whom wanted to be the one to do the job. As it turned out, Davey did the ultimate job, but, just like in Montreal, there were no winners, only losers and, again like Montreal, there had been a hell of a lot of subsequent casualties.

67
BRET'S STROKE

The weekend after Davey Boy had been laid to rest, I was up at my dad's place, just winding up our Saturday Dungeon workout, when my brother Bret wheeled into the yard in his hot new Lexus convertible and invited me to come for a spin. It had been quite a while since I'd had any kind of conversation with Bret, but we'd been on good terms since my mom's funeral and we got around to catching up on things as he drove.

He mentioned, among other things, that he felt bad about Davey Boy's demise and was reflecting on their awesome match at SummerSlam back in 1992, as well as the great run they had in 1997 when the Hart Foundation was at its peak. Somewhat uncharacteristically, he said that he felt bad about having written the infamous "dog in shit" article about Davey — something that many felt had played a role in Davey reverting back to drugs, which had been the beginning of his long, sad, downward spiral.

I told Bret that it was hard to tell whether that had been the sole cause for Davey's downfall, as he had a long history of drug abuse before that, but before I could even make my point, Bret was soon angrily laying the blame on Vince and Shawn — claiming that if they hadn't perpetrated the fuck job in Montreal, Davey would never have had to leave the WWF in the first place and he'd likely still be here today. Bret continued down the same road, claiming that if not for Montreal, Owen would also still be here today, because if he'd been in the WWF at the time, he would never have allowed him to have gone up on the catwalk in Kansas City in the first place. Once again, I told him that it was all speculation and that he shouldn't be beating himself up about what could have or should have happened.

He seemed almost oblivious to what I was saying though and continued on this vehement tirade, cursing Vince and Shawn for having fucked up his life and the lives of so many others, and on, and on, and on. . . . As he continued, I found myself thinking, "Here's a guy who seemingly has the world by the tail — a multimillion dollar gig with the WCW, a brand new sports car, a nice family, house and everything else, while I've been through a hell of a lot more than him the past few years, yet I'm still relatively happy, while he's acting like he's carrying the weight of the world on his back. Why the hell doesn't he just let go of it?"

A couple of days later, my dad called me up and said that Bret had suffered a stroke and was in the Calgary Foothills Hospital. It was pretty sobering to see him lying in the bed in that state, half-paralyzed, unable to even mumble, unable to feed himself and looking helpless. As I saw him lying there in that condition, I thought to myself, I'll take health over money, anytime.

Later on, I heard conjecture that a potato (stiff shot) from Bill Goldberg was being blamed for having caused the stroke, but in talking to neurologists at the Children's Hospital, whom I'd come to know through my son Rhett, I found they were dubious about a blow to the head causing a stroke. If such was the case, boxers, football players and whatnot would be having strokes all the time. They told me that, for a relatively young guy, in seemingly good shape, stress was a more likely cause. When I thought back to Bret's tirade a few days before, about Shawn, Vince and the Montreal screwjob, it occurred to me that carrying all that baggage had probably contributed to his near fatal stroke. I said to myself, if that's the case, that it was just one more misfortune in an epidemic of tragedies and catastrophes due to that Montreal nonsense. The fallout is almost mind-boggling. It's not the least bit funny, but it's laughable that a comedy of errors like that could ever have been allowed to result in so much tragedy. Doesn't anybody realize that it's a work?

I'm pleased to report though that, after several months of difficult rehabilitation, Bret made a near complete recovery and in so doing, showed more fortitude and courage than in any match of his storied career. I'm also pleased to relate that he now seems to have discarded most of the emotional baggage that was burdening him (and many others), and appears to be far more tolerant and less judgmental.

POST MORTEMS
(OR PARTING SHOTS)

68
THE WORLD ACCORDING TO STU

Even though my dad was one of the strongest, most resilient people I've ever known and seemed to never let anything get to him, all the accumulated tragedy and infighting of the past few years had begun to take their toll. In his typical stoic manner, though, he usually kept it to himself — which probably made things even worse.

In September 2003, he was hospitalized because of pneumonia and exhaustion and while he didn't appear to be in any imminent danger, doctors said he needed some rest and that they'd monitor his condition.

On the morning of October 14, I happened to be teaching near the Rockyview Hospital and found I had a spare in the last period of the morning, so I decided to drop in to see him. I'd been up to visit a few times since he was admitted but on previous occasions, he'd been occupied with nurses, doctors or other visitors, so I hadn't really had much of a chance to talk with him. This time around though, he was all by himself, having just finished his breakfast. When I arrived, he was sitting in a chair, gazing out the window on a glorious autumn day, with the sun illuminating the Elbow River Valley and the majestic Rocky Mountains in the horizon. My dad seemed pleased to see me and beckoned me to pull up a chair. He then passed me a copy of *Sports Illustrated* that he'd been reading and asked me to check out this article on pro wrestling.

The article, which was entitled "In Need of a Fix," with a sub-heading suggesting that "Vince McMahon's once mighty wrestling empire is on the ropes." To support that contention, the article cited that annual revenue was down $31 million; that WWE stock had dropped sixty-three percent in the last three years, while ratings for *RAW* and *SmackDown!* had been falling just as fast. In summary, it declared that "wrestling has rarely been this sickly" and then posed the sobering rhetorical question, "Is this how it ends — not with a twenty-first century heir to Gorgeous George, but with a fake gay wedding ceremony and two women wrestlers kissing in mid-ring while an announcer gushes about hot lesbian action?"

By no means was this the first time I'd seen a major magazine or newspaper take potshots at wrestling. In fact, during the boom era of Hulkamania, it was fairly common to see magazines like *Time* or *Sports Illustrated* take swipes at the wrestling business — for being rigged or politically incorrect or for pushing the boundaries of good taste. What I found most disconcerting about this article was that *Sports Illustrated* was almost feeling sorry for the poor, pathetic wrestling business — almost in anticipation of its imminent demise, kind of like when some famous person who is terminally ill and on his last legs (John Wayne and Henry Fonda during their farewell appearances at the Academy Awards come to mind) is being paraded and put over for the last time.

I mentioned that to my dad and he said he felt exactly the same. In those last years — perhaps because he was getting on in age and was increasingly hard of hearing — a lot of people tended to think my dad was becoming a bit senile or beginning to slip, but that morning, he was lucid and clear-thinking as he began his dissertation on the wrestling business.

Gazing out the window to collect his thoughts, he told me that when he first broke into the wrestling business back in New York in the 1940s, wrestlers were accorded the same respect as other athletes of renown and recalled having rubbed shoulders with icons from the New York sports scene, including Jack Dempsey, Joe DiMaggio, Babe Ruth and Jesse Owens, as well as heavyweights

from the entertainment spectrum, such as Frank Sinatra and Humphrey Bogart
— all of whom, he said, treated the wrestlers as equals.

Since a lot of people had attributed wrestling's downward slide to Vince
McMahon's ill-conceived decision to expose the business (divulging that it was
a work), I queried whether my dad felt that had been part of the problem. I
was somewhat surprised when he replied that while he hadn't approved of it,
nonetheless, he didn't really think that had been that big of a factor. He pointed
out that there had been cynicism about wrestling being on the level as far back
as Frank Gotch and George Hackenschmidt's big tilt back in 1911 and that,
over the years, wrestling had been exposed several times before Vince did it in
the '80s.

He said that as far as he was concerned, wrestling, no matter which way you
sliced it, was either sport or it was entertainment, if not a combination of the
two. By that token, since both athletes and entertainers were revered, admired
and placed on lofty pedestals by the media and the public, then so, too, should
wrestlers.

When it was put in that context, I had to agree with him and was about to
grant him that . . . but before I could, he stopped me and said that wrestling
— specifically the WWE — had no one but itself to blame for the way it had
come to be perceived. He said that he couldn't blame the media or the fans for
knocking it — given the gay weddings, hot lesbian action and assorted other
bullshit that had been inflicted on the fans in the past decade. Perhaps the
biggest indication, in his estimation, that traditional wrestling fans had turned
their back on the WWE was the recent meteoric rise in popularity of UFC, Pride
and mixed martial arts in general, which, he said, wasn't much different than
what pro wrestling had resembled back in the day — minus the Octagon.

He then pointed out that if a person didn't have any respect for themselves
— which seemed to be the case with the WWE — then how the hell could they
expect anyone else to respect them either?

He speculated that one of the likely reasons wrestlers seemed to have so little
respect for the business was that, unlike in the old days, so few of them had
been made to pay their dues the way they had in the Dungeon and other hard-
scrabble environments, where their mettle was severely tested before they were

deemed worthy of being welcomed into the wrestling fraternity. The mission of men like Billy Riley, Lou Thesz, Dory Funk Sr., Verne Gagne, Gene LeBell, Karl Gotch and Hiro Matsuda was never to abuse or to infict pain, but to instill respect. He said that these days, all too often, the guys coming into the business hadn't paid their dues and had been pushed simply because they had impressive physiques or whatever else, and, as such, not only didn't they have much respect for it, but they didn't have much passion for it either. Without passion, he said, it was damn near impossible to attain any level of greatness at anything.

He also said that another significant reason for wrestling's present sorry state had been the erosion of the sport at the grassroots level — specifically, the disappearance of the smaller promotions, or territories as they used to be called. The territories had not only been where all the great workers had been broken in and, by trial and error, painstakingly honed their craft, but the territories were also where generations of wrestling fans had come to develop their passion for the sport. My father shook his head somewhat ruefully and said he'd never quite been able to figure out why Vince McMahon Jr. had gone out of his way to systematically wipe out the territories — as they were never any threat to him and were a reliable means of supplying him with talent, testing marketing concepts and renewing his fan base.

If anything, he figured that Vince should have thrown the territories a bone, rather than snuffing them out, and pondered where the NHL would be now if it had chosen to do away with minor and youth hockey leagues — or what the state of the NFL or the NBA would be today if they'd destroyed football and basketball at the grassroots levels.

He also suggested that with the elimination of the territories and the significant drop-off in the number of great workers, it was no coincidence that the WWE now had to resort to excessive gimmickry — sex, sleaze, slapstick and other crap — as cheap compensation for wrestling. It wasn't the way to go because, as he put it, "There are no shortcuts to any place that's really worth going to."

It wasn't the first time wrestling had faced this dilemma, he argued. As far back as the 1940s, after Gorgeous George had become the rage, there was a proliferation of gimmickry — "freaks, geeks and misfits," he called it. And almost overnight, the business hit the skids. At that time, a number of the more conventional promoters, himself included, got together and made a conscientious effort to bring wrestling back to the middle of the road, to restore wrestling's image and make fans feel they were a part of the equation. It created a stability that would last for almost forty years — until the wwf's rise.

He believed it was key for the wwf to stop bullshitting itself — and everyone else — that there were no problems and everything was fine. Until it looked itself in the mirror and took the proverbial bull by the horns, he didn't see things getting much better.

At that point, one of my dad's nurses interrupted us and said that she needed to take my dad in for some tests. He extended his big left paw and gave me one of his patented bone-crushing handshakes and smiled — as if he was glad to have gotten all of that off his chest, and I bid him farewell.

Two days later, I was driving home from school when I heard on the radio that my dad had passed away that morning. I was amazed at the reaction — it received front-page coverage in newspapers, not just in Calgary, but across the country. His passing was news on radio and television, locally, nationally and internationally. It was as if a head of state, a Churchill or a Reagan, or an iconic movie star or athlete, a Paul Newman or Rocket Richard, had died. All of it would have pleased my dad, but it probably would have humbled him as well because, as Dory Funk Sr. had put it, he'd never become a mark for himself.

69
PASSING THE TORCH

For a long time after my dad's death, I found myself reflecting on his impassioned take on the wrestling business and wondered about passing it on to Vince Almighty. Given the ongoing acrimony between the Harts — specifically Bret, who still refused to bury the hatchet — and the WWE, I never bothered. I figured it would only fall on deaf ears.

In January 2010, as a new decade was dawning, like many of you I was surprised to learn that hell *had* frozen over. My beloved brother Bret, nearly thirteen years after the big blowoff in Montreal, resurfaced on *Monday Night RAW*. From there, he shot an angle that would lead to his big showdown with Vinnie Mac at WrestleMania XXVI in Phoenix.

As part of the story line and to show their good intentions, the WWE flew me, my brothers, sisters and assorted nieces and nephews in as well. Then, to cap my surprise, they invited me to participate in the match — as the guest referee.

On the morning of WrestleMania, the WWE had us assemble at the stadium and we were given the script for the match. We were told it was going to be a no-disqualification bout, and the rest of the Hart clan would be stationed around the ring to act as "lumberjacks," just in case Vinnie Mac had anything up his sleeve.

The match would consist of Bret kicking the shit out of Vince from start to finish — battering and bashing him with a claw bar and a steel chair and occasionally throwing him out to the lumberjacks (who would also beat the crap out of him) — while I, as ref, would aid and abet the Hitman as well. For the finish, of course, Bret was to apply the sharpshooter. Vince would then submit, and the Harts would come into the ring and abuse him a bit more, just for good measure.

When they ran it by me, I began to shake my head. To my way of thinking, it was far too one-sided. What was the point of having Bret and his entire family gang up to beat the living crap out of a defenseless sixty-year-old non-wrestler? Worse, I worried it might even transform poor Vince into a sympathetic figure — which, as far as I knew, wasn't the desired effect.

Beyond that, Bret and Vince's big showdown had been nearly thirteen years in the making, and it seemed to me that they were denying themselves a sequel or two: rematches that could generate huge revenue.

Taking it all into consideration, I told Vince, Michael Hayes and Vince's son-in-law Triple H that, while I certainly wasn't going to tell them how to run their business, as someone who'd booked a few finishes and been involved in a few matches, the whole charade seemed pointless. I mentioned that when I used to book I would regularly invite input from the boys and, quite often, someone would come up with an alternate finish that might better suit the situation. I pointed out that since Bret and Shawn Michaels had just buried their own hatchet on live TV a few weeks earlier, and because Shawn had been the one who had eliminated Hunter (Triple H) at the recent Royal Rumble, the pieces were nicely in place for what I was about to suggest. Instead of having Vince get the shit beat out of him, I said, they could get more mileage by having McMahon, an obvious heel, get some heat on Bret using whatever dastardly tactics he wanted. It would have been easy, seeing as this was Bret's first match after his stroke, not to mention that Bret was supposedly nursing injuries from a story line "car crash."

I even advocated for Vince generating more heat by getting some color on Bret, drawing his blood, and having Bret sell his ass off — in order, of course, to set up the big, hot comeback. After a long, calamitous sell, Bret would finally mount a stirring, balls to the wall comeback, culminating in him getting Vince, at long last, in his signature finish. With Vince writhing in agony in the sharp-shooter, but bound and determined not to incur the humiliation of having to tap out to his longtime nemesis, I suggested that he could signal his daughter Stephanie — who would be seated at ringside with her hubby, Hunter — to take me, the referee, out of the equation. Hunter would then hit the ring and nail Bret from behind, and then prepare to give him his own signature finish, the Pedigree. The fans, at that point, would have been screaming in protest; I advocated for the unlikeliest candidate to come to Bret's rescue. The Heartbreak Kid, Shawn Michaels, would hit the ring and give Hunter his "sweet chin music." At that point, I told Vince and company, they could have Bret cover McMahon for the finish or have a double disqualification. All the pieces would be in place for an awesome tag match nobody would have ever expected: Bret and Shawn taking on Vince and Triple H, perhaps at SummerSlam.

I think Vince and Hunter were actually intrigued by the idea. They were considering the obvious possibilities. Neither of them rejected it, nor did Michael Hayes. To my surprise, the guy who did give it the thumbs down was . . . my brother Bret — the person, to my way of thinking, who had the most to gain from the idea.

Bret felt it might compromise his insurance policy with Lloyd's of London and he stressed that while he was allowed to get in the ring with Vince, he wasn't allowed to engage in any kind of actual fight or to take any bumps or shots to the head. This made me wonder, out loud, why he was even getting in the ring in the first place. Bret continued emphatically: this was a one-time-only affair. After it was over he'd be retiring and riding off into the sunset. There wasn't much point in pursuing my angle, after that news.

So you can imagine, I was intrigued and somewhat puzzled when only a few weeks after WrestleMania, Bret returned to the ring. He appeared in a contrived and convoluted story line that had him become the general manager of *RAW*. Later, as you likely know, he was stripped of the position and attacked by a faction of rookies called Nexus. Ultimately, this led to him returning to the ring, again, to wrestle with John Cena and friends against Nexus at . . . SummerSlam. So much for his adamant assertion that he was only allowed to have one match.

Not to cast aspersions on the creativity of the WWE or my brother Bret, but in my humble opinion, if the Heartbreak Kid and the Hitman had teamed up against Vince and Hunter, it would have captured the public's imagination far more than the Nexus angle. Especially since Bret, contrary to what some would have you think, was just a spare part in that SummerSlam charade.

Anyway, WrestleMania went on as planned and it was one of the most bizarre — almost surreal — things I've ever been a part of, with Bret relentlessly bashing Vince, while over 70,000 fans roared in approval.

At some point, I leaned in and exhorted Bret to ease up on Vince. Bret nodded but continued his onslaught. I might add that he didn't appear to be holding back or pulling any of his shots.

The onslaught continued for close to fifteen minutes, with Vinnie absorbing hellacious punishment. I noticed a smile on Bret's face and realized that his pain — which had been festering for more than a decade — was being eased.

Strangely enough, I found my own pain also abating. As I looked toward ringside, I could see the smiling faces of many of my brothers and sisters and nieces and nephews and sensed that their pain, too, was being eased. It then occurred to me that somewhere up yonder perhaps, the pain of my dad, my mom, my brother Owen and even that of my beleaguered brother-in-law Davey Boy was also subsiding.

It was almost as if a dark cloud, which had been hovering over us for years, was finally moving on. It was definitely cathartic. For that, my estimation of Vince McMahon grew exponentially. I felt a debt of gratitude toward him for allowing us to finally have some closure. He didn't have to submit himself to that kind of humiliation and beat down but, I think, in his own perverse but sincere way, he was doing his best to atone for the past. For Stampede, for Montreal, for Owen. If such was the case, good on you, Vinnie.

I never did get a chance to hook up with Vince after the match — it was complete chaos afterward. But after I got back from Arizona, I was reflecting, once again, on my last visit with my dad and his impassioned message about the wrestling business. I got to thinking that since the hatchet had finally been buried and the lines of communication have been reopened, I might be able to offer Vince a different perspective on wrestling — straight from the Hart, so to speak.

Now, I can't see why not. So, here goes nothing . . .

Yo, cousin Vinnie, thanks for your time. I'd like to begin by thanking you, on behalf of my brothers and sisters and others in the family, for the gig in Arizona. Everything, from the Hall of Fame Ceremony for my dad to the accommodations, was first class and very much appreciated. Contrary to what many people on the periphery of the business might think, I don't consider you to be anywhere near the monster or unadulterated asshole you've often been made out to be.

While I obviously haven't been in agreement with many of the things you've done, you have authored some monumental triumphs and have also made a lot of wrestlers — including several from my family — rich and famous. For that they should all be quite grateful.

Still, on behalf of the old-school types, including my dad, there are a few things I'd like to bring to your attention. I'm not happy with the state of the wrestling business and I'm concerned about where it's headed.

Wrestling, at its finest, is an art form — especially when performed by artists like Dory and Terry Funk, Harley Race, Lou Thesz, Jack Brisco, the Dynamite Kid, Shawn Michaels, Ric Flair and my brothers, Bret and Owen, all of whom could take little more than a finish and would then render, on canvas, master-pieces that for wrestling fans were every bit as timeless and compelling as the work of van Gogh, da Vinci or Picasso — and a far cry, I might add, from the sterile, scripted "paint by number" offerings that so many of today's so-called workers consider classics.

Keep it simple, plausible and logical, Vince; don't constantly insult people's intelligence or bullshit yourself and the fans that overkill and sleaze are sub-stitutes for wrestling. As well, refrain from making the product so contrived, complicated or sleazy that it's not suitable for kids — who still comprise the largest, most enthusiastic segment of your fan base.

Some of your most outspoken critics will argue that one of the reasons for wrestling's decline is that there just aren't many great workers around today. And while there may not be as many as there were, say, back in the '80s, from what I can see, there's still some phenomenal young talent — guys like Randy Orton, Rey Mysterio, C.M. Punk, Edge, John Cena, Ted di Biase Jr. and my nephew David Hart Smith. But since wrestling itself has become so compromised with all the bullshit I've been alluding to, it's pretty hard for the workers to rise above it.

All sports, I'll grant you, have evolved to some degree — we now have artificial turf, three-point baskets, designated hitters, big-busted cheerleaders and state-of-the-art scoreboards but, for all intents and purposes, football is still football, baseball is still baseball, and basketball is still basketball. Wrestling should still be wrestling, Vince, not the misbegotten mutation that it's become.

To use a gridiron analogy, I'd recommend that you use the run (wrestling) to set up the pass (the high spots and histrionics). You'd be surprised at how well the fans will respond when you re-establish the basics.

I'm not advocating a return to wool trunks, black boots, black-and-white television and two pot-bellied old farts rolling around for an hour. Having been the creative impetus behind Stampede Wrestling in the 1980s — when it was as cutting-edge as it gets — I'm not at all adverse to new concepts and innovations. But they should have a discernible purpose and they should make sense — unlike most of the implausible crap I see on *RAW* and *SmackDown*. Too much of it seems like it's being concocted on the fly.

When I was a kid, Vince, there were thirty or more thriving, vibrant territories, with hundreds of great workers giving fans all over the continent their weekly fix of pro wrestling. They became the fan base for your promotion later on. Not only did this system create a huge and loyal following for the WWE, it also provided an awesome (and free) farm system. I'm sure you don't need to be reminded where guys like Curt Hennig, Hawk and Animal, Roddy Piper, Hulk Hogan, Randy Savage, Junkyard Dog, Jake Roberts, the British Bulldogs, my brothers Bret and Owen and so many others got their start.

For some reason, though, back in the '80s, you needlessly and indiscriminately chose to destroy the farm system — the promotions in Calgary, Texas, Minneapolis and other wrestling hotbeds that were supplying you, free of charge, with your talent. That's like the NFL or NBA, for some stupid reason, going out of their way to wipe out college football and basketball.

The wrestling business has been good to you and your family (and mine). It's made you rich and famous and has given you power and glory. Please, Vince, clean up your act. Make a concerted effort to restore wrestling to its rightful place at the forefront of the sports/entertainment spectrum. To paraphrase a line from one of my all-time favorite movies: if you rebuild it, Vince, people will come!

There's a very distinct possibility, Vince, I'll admit, that upon reading or being apprised of my unsolicited critiquing of the wrestling business, you may well respond, "Bruce Hart can kiss my ass. It's none of his damn business what the hell I do with my wrestling business, because I own it and can do whatever I want with it."

That may well be the case. However, I'd like to point out that your equally imperious but recently departed fellow New Yorker, Gorgeous George Steinbrenner, owner of the Yankees for close to forty years, might have perceived of himself as the Godfather of baseball. But he did not own the memories or legacies left behind by the likes of Babe Ruth, Joe DiMaggio, Mickey Mantle, Yogi Berra, Billy Martin, Thurman Munson, Reggie Jackson or Derek Jeter. Steinbrenner is merely bearing the torch — to be passed on to the next generation.

The same, I'd venture to say, is the case for you, cousin Vinnie. You are the bearer of wrestling's torch — the one that was once so proudly borne by my father, your father, your grandfather, Toots Mondt, Sam Muchnick, Frank Tunney, Aileen LeBell, Dory Funk Sr. and all the others who have paved the way.

I don't want to pontificate, Vince, but as far as I'm concerned, the greatest honor we can bestow upon them and others, such as my brother Owen, who dedicated their hearts and souls to wrestling is to preserve and perpetuate the business that they made so great. Thanks for your time, Vince.

While I'm at it, I'd also like to offer thanks to you, wrestling fans, because without you, there wouldn't be any wrestling business. I sincerely hope you've enjoyed the read as much as I've enjoyed the ride.